Connections and Commitments

Reflecting Latino Values in Early Childhood Programs

Costanza Eggers-Piérola
of
Education Development Center, Inc.

EDC
Newton, MA

HEINEMANN
Portsmouth, NH

Heinemann

A division of Reed Elsevier Inc.

361 Hanover Street

Portsmouth, NH 03801–3912

www.heinemann.com

Offices and agents throughout the world

Library of Congress Cataloging-in-Publication Data

Eggers-Piérola, Costanza.

    Connections and commitments : reflecting Latino values in early childhood programs / Costanza Eggers-Piérola.

       p. cm.

    Includes bibliographical references and index.

    ISBN 0-325-00740-3 (alk. paper)

1. Latin Americans—Education (Early childhood)—United States.

2. Education, Bilingual—United States. I. Title.

LC2670.E44 2005

372.1829'68073—dc22   2004021495

Editor: Danny Miller

Production coordinator: Elizabeth Valway

Production service: nSight, Inc.

Cover design: Cat and Mouse

Cover photography (girls): Karl Grobl © KarlGrobl.com

Cover photography (mural): Roberto Chao

Composition: nSight, Inc.

Interior design: nSight, Inc.

Manufacturing: Steve Bernier

Printed in the United States of America on acid-free paper

09 08 07 06 05 VP 1 2 3 4 5

This book is dedicated with love and admiration to my daughter Alea and my son Jacob, through whose eyes I saw the wonder of learning in a shining new light, and who, with their bright and generous souls, teach me every day.

I also dedicate this book to the memory of Liliana Aragón, a committed and loved teacher, who generously shared her thoughts and wisdom with a stranger.

The author and publisher wish to thank those who have generously given permission to reprint borrowed material:

Adapted excerpt from Alma Flor Ada and F. Isabel Compoy, *Authors in the Classroom: A Transformative Education Process,* 1/e. Published by Allyn and Bacon, Boston, MA. Copyright © 2003 by Pearson Education. Reprinted/adapted by permission of the publisher.

Activities from *Entérese, Prepárese, Actúe: Talleres par las Familias de Estudiantes Latinos* by Costanza Eggers-Piérola and Stella Acelas. Copyright © 2000 by Costanza Eggers-Piérola and Stella Acelas. Published by the Latino Parents Association, Boston, MA. Used by permission of the authors.

"Documenting Growth Tool" from *Understanding by Design* by Grant Wiggins and Jay McTighe. Copyright © 2001 by Grant Wiggins and Jay McTighe. Reprinted by permission of Pearson Education, Inc., Upper Saddle River, NJ.

"My Tongue Is Like a Map" by Rane Arroyo. Copyright © 2001 by Rane Arroyo. Poem is from the collection entitled *Love to Mama.* Copyright © 2001 by Lee and Low Books, Inc. Permission arranged with Lee and Low Books, Inc., New York, NY 10016.

Excerpt from "Clouds Come from New Hampshire: Confronting the Challenge of Philosophical Change in Early Childhood Programs" by Ellen P. Dodge, Barbara N. Dulik, and Jon A. Kulhanek. Copyright © 2002 by Ellen P. Dodge, Barbara N. Dulik, and Jon A. Kulhanek.

Figure 6–2, "Family Intervention Model for Hard to Reach Families," conceptualized by Dr. Gloria G. Rodriguez, Founder, President, and CEO of AVANCE, Inc. Copyright © AVANCE, Inc., 118 North Medina, San Antonio, TX 70207.

Graphic Gameplan Model. Copyright © The Grove Consultants, International. Used by permission of Grove Consultants, International.

"Mi Mama Cubana" by Mimi Chapra. Copyright © 2001 by Mimi Chapra. Poem is from the collection entitled *Love to Mama.* Copyright © 2001 by Lee and Low Books, Inc. Permission arranged with Lee and Low Books, Inc., New York, NY 10016.

Contents

Foreword

The attention given to the early development of a child could never be overemphasized. The concepts, values, skills, and attitudes towards reality achieved in early childhood will have significant consequences throughout the life of an individual. When children grow up in a bilingual environment, where the home language and worldview are not the same of the dominant sectors of society, the responsibilities of the adults influencing their development are increased.

How will the language and culture, the deep-rooted worldview of the parents, be treated in relationship to the language and culture of an early childhood program? The options can be seen along a continuum ranging from a perfect match between the early childhood program and the home, with both developing the same language and cultural perceptions; to various degrees of respect and celebration for the home language and culture and provision for its maintenance and development alongside the dominant language and culture; to lip service paid to the values of bilinguism and biculturality; to a complete ignorance of the home language and culture and even to the point of denigration.

Most economically privileged children participate in early childhood programs that reinforce the language and values of the home and the dominant society. While in this case, most of them will not benefit from the advantages of learning a second language at an early age, they will see a continuous reinforcement of their development process and a validation of their family and of themselves as members of that family.

A few economically and pedagogically privileged children have the enriching situation of participating in an early childhood program that provides the opportunity of learning a second language and being exposed to another culture while reinforcing the language and culture of the home and dominant society. These children have all the advantages of the previous group plus the added value of learning a second language at the time in which children are best equipped for language acquisition. All children should have this privilege.

Most children whose home language is other than English face the risk of attending early childhood programs, where the emphasis is placed in the acquisition of the dominant language, and where no or little attention is given to the child's continuous development of the home language, and where little understanding of the values of their home culture occur.

These children are being subjected to an early alienation from their parents and families. At a very tender age, when they have had no opportunity to develop a mastery of the home language or a serious foundation in their culture's values, their development process is interrupted. Instead of added knowledge, they are being encouraged, either overtly or by default, to subtract from their previous knowledge, to substitute one language with another, one set of cultural understandings with others.

It can be claimed that this usually does not happen as a result of any malicious intent, but simply due to a lack of awareness. But the consequences of these actions can be equally detrimental.

While our society professes to believe in the importance of the family, it often supports early education programs where very young children learn to ignore or even reject the language of their parents.

In most cases, parents whose home language is other than English depend on that language for the expression of their deepest feelings and for the transmission of traditional folklore, in the form of legends, folktales, proverbs, and fables. These family members can only discuss important issues with ease in their home language, and they also need that language to pass on family traditions, to share life examples of themselves and others.

When young children stop speaking the home language and either forget how to speak it or see their use of the language reduced to a few expressions, deep communication at home ceases to be possible. And the role of the parents as educators is eroded and diminished. The consequences of this erosion are severe. Many children lose respect for their parents, judging them on the basis of their inability to express themselves fluently in English or without a marked accent, and, as a consequence, discount their guidance in vital areas.

In most instances, these will be the children that will not remain in school, forfeiting in this way their parents' highest dreams and the reason for their struggle and sacrifices. They may be the children who seek an authority figure outside of the home, in the streets, in the gangs.

The issues we are discussing are not superficial—they cut deep into the possibilities for the future of a large number of children and for the future of an entire society.

A strong family requires a common language for dialogue, for sharing, for joint reflection. Parents who speak a language other than English deserve to have their worldview respected in order that their children, products of a bilingual reality, may be able to learn from both sides of their heritage and create their own composite and richer understanding of the world.

Because of the significance of these issues, this book is very important.

Costanza Eggers-Piérola understands intimately the world of bilingual children, from her own experience, from that of her own children, and from her solid scholarly background and her long experience in the field.

She has been able to present with utmost clarity a schema that will demystify what are the fundamental values that support this complex and varied culture of Spanish-speaking people. With her remarkable pedagogical abilities, she makes the content of this clear and engaging book practical and applicable.

This book is a necessary read for anyone involved at any level—policy making, organizational leadership, community activism, or educational practice—with early education or in truth with education, in general, of Spanish-speaking children. All readers, regardless of their previous familiarity with the field, will find this text invaluable.

I can only thank Costanza Eggers-Piérola for having written it.

— Dr. Alma Flor Ada

Acknowledgments

Education Development Center, Inc. (EDC) and I recognize that the work involved in this book and the project that informed its creation could not have been possible without the goodwill and thoughtful participation of many dedicated people.

First, on behalf of EDC and myself, I extend heartfelt thanks to the A. L. Mailman Family Foundation—especially Luba Lynch and Betty Bardige—for contributing their support and encouragement from the inception of the project that led to the *Connections and Commitments Framework* and to the development of the book.

I have the deepest appreciation of EDC and my very knowledgeable and collaborative colleagues at EDC's Center for Children & Families, especially Director Joanne Brady, a visionary leader who always believed in this work. I also deeply thank the two dedicated and skillful editors who helped me through this process, developmental editor Kimberly Elliott at EDC and Danny Miller at Heinemann. I also thank Su Theriault for her wonderful photos.

Many friends and colleagues have given me strength, inspiration, and feedback during the development of this book, including Magdalena Rosales-Alban, Janet Gonzalez-Mena, Alma Flor Ada, Isabel Campoy, Cristina Igoa, and Yvette Rodriguez.

Mi familia y mi gente—my extended family and my people—Mamina, los Chao, the Thompson-Elliotts, *mi hermana* Beatriz Teleki, and friends Kori B. and Aileen Lynch all contributed to this book in some way or another.

I also thank the Improving Access and Opportunity for Latinos in Early Education consortium member organizations and their representatives, who worked with us to identify key issues, enthusiastically supported our efforts, and extended their guidance and ideas through their representatives. This includes the Latino Caucus of the National Association for the Education of Young Children, represented by Luis Hernández; the National Association of Child Care Resource and Referral Agencies, represented by Marta Rosa; the National Council of La Raza, represented by Angélica Santacruz; the National Latino Children's Institute, represented by Bibi Lobo; and the Wheelock College Institute for Leadership and Career Initiatives, represented by Cecelia Alvarado. And my appreciation to Julio Saldana and all the many generous and thoughtful *compañeros* from the Americas who shared their views and wisdom on *familia, pertenencia, educación,* and *compromiso.*

Finally, with permission, I end my acknowledgments with a personal story.

Twenty-five years ago, as a storyteller and teacher in a program called *Books from My Head,* I began to tell the story of my name. At first, as a newcomer to this country, I did not want to stand out. In many ways I could pass, but my name always gave me away. My five-part name, with hyphenation and accents, led to problems in the filing systems of schools, immigration agencies, and doctors' offices. It caused frowns and frustration in people trying to hear and say my name. It was rarely remembered. It was always mispronounced, even by my own *compatriotas.* You see, my father had consciously left out one letter from the familiar version of my name—Constanza—because he wanted to honor a favorite composer's opera heroine. Finally, after hearing a hundred times, "That's so hard. Do you have a nickname?" I surrendered, and gave myself an American nickname… until that time twenty-five years ago when a friend told me, "It's a beautiful name. Help others learn it. Make others learn it!" I wish that freedom for each and every child with a cherished name and identity.

Gracias, Papito, for naming me.

CHAPTER 1

Connections and Commitments

A Framework for Understanding

Focusing on Connections and Commitments

The First Day of a Newcomer

My father held my hand tight on that first day at my new school in my new country. I was five. Papito would repeat this ritual many other times at many other schools. I remember, probably like every single child there on their first day, the butterflies in my stomach. Papito took me to the principal's office, where I heard him say my name, Asunción, its Spanish cadence ringing in his tender, proud, deep bass voice, and say some words in English as I timidly began reaching my arm out to shake the principal's hand. But she nodded her head and picked up a piece of paper instead, and talked with my father. Then Papito shook the principal's hand, gave me a kiss on the forehead, and left me as the principal led the way to my classroom.

This time, like almost all the other times, I appeared in the classroom for the very first time when everyone already knew each other, knew what the teacher expected, knew the "drill." I remember the fear of looking at all these unfamiliar faces, the confusion of hearing a language and expression so foreign that I could not even guess if my teacher was glad or mad at having me enter her class in the middle of the year.

The teacher looked at the index card the principal had given her, filed it in a box, and pointed to the back, where there was an empty desk, announcing to the class, "This is María." My heart sank. Why did she call me this? Didn't the principal tell the teacher my given name, the name Papito used to introduce me? The teacher couldn't guess that my name means "rising" and stands for one of the most joyful feasts in my hometown. I felt every eye on me as I slowly walked down the aisle to the back of the room, my head and eyes down, tears already welling inside me. I never dared to correct the teacher. I sat silently at the back of the classroom all year long. I wanted to learn all about this new country and my classmates, and so I watched and listened, since it was not my place to ask. No one asked me any questions, no one was interested in where I came from or who I was, and later the following year, I left the school and the town, and still no one knew me or my real name.[1]

This vignette illustrates some conflicts commonly faced by newcomers from different cultures when they enter American institutions. Above, the importance given to greetings and introductions, the teacher's reluctance to make the effort to utter and learn an unfamiliar name, the deference to authority, and the new social rules and expectations are all potential sources of misunderstandings and clashing between the culturally-different child and teacher. Although small and subtle, these unspoken conflicts contribute to a strained relationship between schools and families of different cultures and values and to a sense of isolation and marginalization on the part of those who are not fluent in American ways.

"Newcomer" is a term used to describe the recent immigrant, but, in a sense, all children are newcomers in our classrooms as they move from the home environment to a school environment. Each child, as he begins the year, feels overwhelmed by the strangeness, misses the intimacy, safety—we hope—and familiarity of his home, his family, and his daily routines.[2] But then, little by little, as he recognizes certain utterances, expressions, and songs, he bonds with others and begins to unravel the ways of doing things in the new place. Then the child is ready to discover and participate without apprehension. On the other hand, imagine how a truly "newcomer" child must feel, with little to hang on to in a place where perhaps no one speaks her language, where there are few references to her home and what she knows, and where what she brings and is used to may not fit with how things are done in the classroom. Whether a newcomer or in this country for generations, Latinos bring particular values and beliefs that are often not represented in our educational institutions and may, in fact, be in direct conflict with what and how we teach. As the number of Latinos in our classrooms increases, so does the need to understand the cultural and linguistic issues that impact teaching and learning.

Much has changed in the past forty years; since then Latino and other ethnically and linguistically diverse populations have been escalating at a rapid pace. Now many more immigrants from many countries are in our classrooms, bilingual programs have been instituted in many schools, and teachers may make an effort to know and pronounce the given names of each and every child. More and more, the importance of the family, what it brings, and what it knows is being viewed as essential to a quality education for all children. Classrooms now may look different from what "Asunción" saw when she entered kindergarten. There may not be any "back of the room" desks in our preschool and kindergarten classrooms, just activity centers and individual cubbies. Many elementary classrooms have also moved away from individual rows towards group seating. Yet children can still be invisible and isolated when they don't feel understood or when they don't feel a sense of belonging.

As we guide the development of children, how can we best prepare ourselves to help each child succeed when faced with this rich and complex reality? What do we need to understand? How do we bring in the best of what each child brings, including the richness and diversity in language, style, and culture? How can we ensure that all children can attain the knowledge and skills they need to thrive, contribute, invent, and dream? What do we need to change in order to reach and support everyone?

But more importantly, who can support us? No one can do this alone. With the increasing demands and multiple roles of teachers in diverse classrooms, helping every child develop, regardless of race, language, gender, or ethnicity, can be a daunting task, like exploring new territory. This book is written to serve as a companion in that journey of exploration.

Connections and Commitments is not just about teaching young Latino children, it's about building relationships that foster their joyful development. The book provides a framework for bringing together the adults who touch children's lives—teachers, trainers, other service and care providers, and extended families—around their common commitments to children. It helps non-Latino educators in both preschool and early primary settings to understand and embrace values central to Latino culture and to look beyond children's individual skills and achievements as they work in concert with others to build nurturing communities and provide enriching experiences. I hope that this book will provide teachers of children from infant to age eight a frame of reference to see the enrichment possibilities of working with diverse children, families, and staff. To this end, *Connections and Commitments* focuses on making connections that bridge cultural differences and on nurturing a sense of belonging and commitment that allows each child to "learn to be":

> Learning to be: The aim of development is the complete fulfillment of man, in all the richness of his personality, the complexity of his forms of expression and his various commitments—as individual, member of a family and of a community, citizen and producer, inventor of techniques and creative dreamer.[3]

Latino Communities in the United States

Our immigrant children, especially Latinos, many of whom come as the children of migrant workers who keep close ties to their native towns, can appear in classrooms midyear, may have extended absences, and may leave before the end of the year. Integrating and supporting these "outsiders" to the classroom culture is a constant challenge for educational systems as well as for teachers.

The Numbers

Getting the big picture of Latinos in the United States today will give us a context for understanding the challenges and possibilities we face teaching and learning with Latinos. More than thirty-seven and a half million Latinos live in our fifty states and territories, representing all Latin American countries and a broad range of backgrounds, needs, and expectations.[4] One third of this population is children. By 2010, the Latino population is projected to reach forty-two million—more than the total population of Canada right now. Latinos represent forty-three percent of the total future growth in population. By 2020, one in four children will be of Latino background. With increasing numbers of young Latino children entering our early education system, it is critical that teachers be prepared to work with this group.

The Challenges

More than half of the current population of Latinos is foreign born. Compounding the challenges of becoming bilingual and bicultural, Latinos face a number of obstacles that affect their access to resources that address basic needs and their growth and development. Latino families are least likely to have health coverage, and their children are underrepresented in licensed childcare centers.[5] Latino youth have the lowest high school completion rate when compared to other ethnic groups—approximately half the rate for African Americans and one quarter the rate for non-Latino Whites' high school completion. Latinos are less likely than other groups to be employed, and they receive the lowest pay. The unfortunate reality is that many Latino families live in poverty, a reality that will have repercussions throughout American society and economy if not addressed. The reasons behind this poverty are complex and varied, including living outside the legal system as migrants, having truncated educational experiences in war-torn homelands, and being excluded from decision-making and leadership positions because of differences in language, views, and interests. However, across the board, newcomers from Latino backgrounds come to work hard and are eager to be part of American society. On the other hand, our schools and institutions face challenges in evolving to reflect and integrate this growing and diverse population.

The Contributions

Notwithstanding the hurdles, Latinos come with hope, great capacity, and motivation, succeeding and becoming invested in American life. Latino home ownership, media, products, and Latino-owned businesses are steadily increasing. Once the doors are opened, Latinos have the potential to contribute in every sphere of American life. They bring bilingual and bicultural knowledge that enriches the texture of this country. In addition, the importance of providing education, materials, products, and services that reflect the needs and preferences of Latinos is constantly reiterated in various fields, especially in the early education field, where the most growth is expected. What happens in the early years is critical to providing a stepping-stone towards this potential.

Granted, children from any culture, race, and gender need the same close attention. *Connections and Commitments* can serve as a model for an approach focused on including and representing any difference, be that of color, of language, of ability, of learning style, or of values.

Good Beginnings

To truly see the benefits of a good early childhood education, we must look beyond the gains for individual children. Policymakers and advocates have to grasp not only the long-term benefits of a quality early childhood education for individuals, but also the benefits to society as a whole. Early childhood education is a cost-effective and needed solution as well as a means to equalize access and opportunity.

The early years are pivotal years in development, we now know. Recent research on brain development and the lifelong benefits of high-quality early education underscores the vital role that preschool teachers play in ensuring young children's later success in school.[6] In fact, we know that every dollar spent in early childhood education saves seven dollars in later education costs. Achievement scores and high school graduation rates go up, and grade retention and special needs placements go down.[7] In the long run, the schooling cost per child is reduced for those who have been in preschool programs, as is the incidence of crime and welfare participation, thereby reducing the criminal justice and social services that are subsidized by our taxes.[8]

In the recent past, the education field has made important strides in examining its own professional standards. Diversity clauses and bilingual specialization competencies have been added to some accreditation and certification standards, and efforts have been made in various sectors of the early childhood field to support cultural tolerance and integrate antibias, humanistic, or democratic practices.

Notwithstanding this progress, the issue of diversity must be revisited. Definitions of quality are intrinsically value based, and values are shaped by culture. Before we can truly take into account diverse beliefs and practices in our early childhood policy and programs, we must first understand and tease apart some of the differences and recognize that each cultural group has distinct beliefs and practices that are valued over others.

Core Values of Latino Cultures: The Framework

Connection and Commitments was developed to provide guidance to early childhood educators, including center and family child care teachers, primary school teachers and administrators, family service providers, as well as trainers and training institutions interested in building their capacity to respond to the Latino population. The framework shaping this book is based on cultural values, principles, and best practices identified in successful programs and training materials, standards documents, a broad review of research and position papers, and the input of families, practitioners, and experts in the early childhood care and education field.

The cultural and linguistic values[9] and practices outlined here are also aligned with the principles of lifelong learning that ensure the development of individuals within a social context and as members of a global community that cooperates in order for all to advance and prosper. Education, according to the principles of lifelong learning, is not simply a means of human development, but more pragmatically for the future of our children, a means to grow to be a critical thinker, a problem solver, a collaborator who understands the world and who can envision its future. This quote from a Latina mother embodies this concept of education:

> I want them to be aware of all the things that are around them. I want them to be active. Well, you know how some people just live in a place and they don't care about everyone else and the betterment of their surroundings? They say, "Okay, I'm just going to be here. I'm going to take care of my little corner, but I won't care whatever happens to anyone else." I want them to be aware of everyone else's feelings. [Here in the U.S.] we're not raising kids to be...upstanding...some kind of citizen, but that's what I want. I want them to be out there taking care of the children, of their surroundings, of the schools.[10]

The Latino-based framework this book is based on identifies those values, principles, and practices that—if understood and infused throughout practice—can increase the capacity of early childhood programs and training institutions to be responsive to the many people of Latino background in the United States and to help prepare these future citizens by integrating the multiple strengths and understandings they bring.

The four major values we highlight in this book—*familia* (family), *pertenencia* (belonging), *educación* (moral, social, and academic education), and *compromiso* (commitment)—are intertwined. They also incorporate other values that are well defined and practiced among Latinos, such as respect, courtesy, trust, responsibility to others, duty to family, loyalty to friends, and respect for hierarchy and authority. Some of these values and practices are echoed throughout many world cultures, and so, understanding these four values will help educators understand another world view that stands in contrast to a culture focused primarily on the individual. Duty to family, group identity—discussed in *pertenencia*—the practice of peer learning as opposed to individual achievement—discussed in *educación*—and the expectation that each individual contributes to the betterment of others are important values in most cultures around the developing world, where many of our newcomers and ethnically diverse American citizens originate.[11]

However, at times our field loses sight that education comes with its corresponding values, and that some values favor individual achievement and skill building that is remote from the lives of most children. The emphasis of current educational thrusts such as Leave No Child Behind is fundamentally about developing literacy skills—as if these skills were the aim, not the tool for development. As teachers and as parents, we know that literacy develops in context, in relationships, in the environments and daily lives of children. Language first develops in infants as a means to express need and as a way to recognize who cares for them and protects them. Infants become familiar with their first language by learning to understand nonverbal cues, words, tones and nuances, and rhythms that indicate the speakers' interest, state of mind, and agreeableness to fill the infant's needs. To truly scaffold the literacy of all children, caregivers and educators need to understand how to build from these contexts, be it a family's eating rules or the place and respect elders hold in the education of the children. And our educational settings need to put in place processes for teaching and accountability that respond to the true nature of learning as a social tool, not simply as a means to build individual capacity.

Each of the four values in the framework reflects a relationship: a teacher's relationship with families, with a child, with the classroom, with colleagues, and with the community. The chapters of this book are organized according to these values.

Familia/Family: With the Family, for the Children (Chapter 2)

The most essential component that brings families and teachers together in an authentic way involves reversing the traditional expectations teachers have about parent involvement and redefining it as teacher involvement with the extended family. Teachers who open their hearts and respond to the whole community surrounding the child create lasting and mutually supportive relationships. For

Latinos, the extended family and its circle of friends and communities are key to the child's upbringing. Families will respond to a committed teacher who reaches out to their communities. A culturally and linguistically responsive teacher therefore understands that to know and serve a child, she must know and include the child's extended family, and she extends her work to reach the child's community. She goes into the homes, into the neighborhoods, and into the churches in order to get a full picture of the child's life. She also welcomes members of the child's community as co-teachers, co-planners, and initiators of activities. This value, discussed in more detail in Chapter 2, is also a thread across all the chapters.

Pertenencia/*Belonging: Welcoming All Children (Chapter 3)*

Pertenencia is about building an early childhood environment that echoes the positive relationships and bonds within families, where children form identity, feel part of something greater than themselves, and feel supported. In a place where children feel *pertenencia*, they also feel ownership and responsibility to the group. To belong, children must feel accepted as they are, so shaping an identity as an individual and as a group member goes hand in hand with feeling a sense of belonging. The center that reflects a sense of family and caring begins by welcoming the children and the differences they bring, as well as reflecting the solidarity and commitment of a family. Relationships and the skills and joys of living together are the grounds for building a sense of belonging.

Educación/*Education: A Holistic and*
Relational Approach to Teaching and Learning (Chapter 4)

Educación and success are tied together in Latino cultures. The teacher who builds caring relationships understands that a child's development goes beyond acquiring and constructing knowledge. The teacher knows that the child's voice, mind, body, and heart all must be engaged for the child to want to learn. The whole child learns through communication, relationships, and everyday experiences. Literacy is a skill that enables communication and learning; it is not an end unto itself. From the first, a child hears and imitates sounds a mother makes in order to establish a bond. The first exposures to language outside of the womb are the means the infant has to understand and relate to its surroundings.

The concepts involved in *educación* generate life-long skills that go beyond building knowledge to building the capacity to act and solve problems collectively as well as to become a valued member of a community.

Compromiso/*Commitment:*
Shared Commitment to Professional Growth (Chapter 5)

Compromiso means to be bound in a promise to others, as in an engagement to be married. It is a mutual act. *Compromiso* is a solid agreement between partners to achieve a goal, to each act in order to reach a tangible gain for all parties or for a cause. This chapter focuses on the shared responsibility among educators to participate actively in defining their own development and to grow in their understanding of differences.

Actúe/*Take Action: Supporting and Sustaining Change (Chapter 6)*

This chapter is about extending beyond the usual boundaries of a job description, becoming active in promoting change and improvement in the program, in the field, and in the community in order to serve the comprehensive needs of her students and families. Therefore, the culturally responsive teacher is envisioned here as a leader, an advocate, a resource, an advisor, and a model for the child's community.

Using This Book

Unfortunately, pre-K–grade twelve teachers, family service providers, curriculum developers, and other professionals lack resources to assure the school success of Latino children. While many early education teachers are anxious to advance Latino children's school readiness, they have an acute need for materials and training that will enable them to foster children's learning and work effectively with families. Throughout the book, I have placed some running features in select places that key the reader to particular perspectives or actions. These features include *Building on Strengths, Keeping a Balance, What Would You Do?, Bringing Ideas to Life, Programs That Inspire, Challenges for Teachers,* and *Turning Obstacles into Opportunities.* In addition, I have included relevant resources and discussion questions to support you in your work.

Key Ideas

The purpose of this book is to stimulate a dialogue about how to improve the cultural competence of your program, your practice, and your services and to provide suggestions of resources that you can draw on to enhance your program's work with diverse families. Cultural competence is the ability and willingness to respect, understand, and integrate into practice differences in knowledge, belief, practice, and experience. In other words, this book will serve as a basis to understand, communicate and negotiate with, and accommodate children and families from Latino cultures. Each chapter will open the door to understanding a particular aspect of Latino culture in relation to a daily concern of the early childhood educator, from partnering with families to creating a welcoming environment and from teaching and learning practices to the program's relationships with the community and beyond.

The book can be used as a reference and stepping-stone to begin discussions, plan activities, and assess progress in supporting the development of Latinos within your program. Perhaps you will find that the guidelines, tips, and recommended strategies may benefit others as well, since they are based on best practices that are aligned with and even exceed the standards now required for early childhood certification.

In the next five chapters, I guide you through a more detailed and specific approach to building intercultural understanding and responsiveness in five aspects of early childhood education and family programs:

- Family partnerships
- Program climate and physical environment
- Teaching and learning strategies
- Professional development
- Program change and advocacy for early childhood

Beginning Your Journey

The most important message in this book, however, which is supported by many of the tools provided within each chapter, is that as educators in an increasingly multicultural society who are aware of the importance of including prior knowledge and approaches that allow all children and families to participate fully, we must expand our role to that of ethnographer, continuously observing and inquiring into children's and our own thinking and ways. This is the base for building intercultural understanding with diverse children and families.

As teachers, we cannot rely simply on a degree, on a checklist of standards, or on "cookbooks" of best practices. To teach, especially to teach these days, means teaching from the heart, engaging our minds in ways we had not thought of and transforming the way we do things.

The underlying theme throughout this book is solidarity, another word for unity around a cause—in this case, the children. This means people coming together to build unity among programs and children's families and communities as well as between children and adults around social and learning goals. It means the commitment of practitioners and programs to go beyond the boundaries that often limit their capacity to advocate for the families they serve. Solidarity stands for both connections and commitments—connecting with others and committing to a unified cause or goal—and is not only harmonious with many Latinos' cultural and historical heritage, but also a major goal of global reforms to combat inequities and exclusion.

Keep in mind, as you read this book, that Latino culture—like any other—is varied and rich, continuing to evolve in disparate directions in response to circumstances, personalities, and choices. Furthermore, many Latinos, both life-long U.S.

residents and newcomers, face changes in their family structures, economic supports, and other factors that impact their ability to practice the values they espouse. Therefore, we cannot assume that the values and principles here are representative of all Latino cultures. Rather, my goal is to provide a platform for a dialogue on values and practices shared across many Latino cultures and to stimulate a thoughtful review of the ways early childhood education programs and practices can be shaped to reflect Latino cultures and language in a meaningful way and to welcome *any* child to participate in learning. In the end, teachers can never have all the information on cultures needed to understand each child's needs. What I propose in this book is to provide a foundation that, along with inquiry, discourse, and reflection, will enable more intercultural understanding and mutual accommodation.

This book presents what I wished my teachers had known when I first began kindergarten in the United States. Ideally, I would like this book to be an exploration, a voyage. The ideas in this book are intended to inspire, to be customized, to be used as a starting point, and not to prescribe a menu of strategies and activities. As teachers and advocates for children, our journey is one of inquiry into ourselves, into our students' lives and thinking, and into our profession. No menu of strategies and guidelines can offer any of us a clear direction that we can apply to teaching all our children.

Summing Up: Walking in Two Worlds

"Walking in two worlds"—or "becoming" a hyphenated American—is challenging and conflictive, at times forcing bicultural people to make life-limiting choices.[12] What some may consider traditional roles or cultural customs in Latino societies may not, in fact, be desirable or a preferred choice for Latino children today. For instance, unquestioning obedience is being replaced by measured trust and freedom. This book does not intend to criticize all that is Anglo-American, Eurocentric, or individualistic, nor to portray all that is group-centered or Latino as better. Living in two worlds should not mean giving up the values, knowledge, and identities that shaped the early years and that draw on connections with family and history from other places. It should mean having the choice to take the best of both worlds, as indicated by a Latina mother:[13]

> Learning another culture teaches one a lot. You have two cultures, you have to maintain the other one, but in certain aspects, not all aspects. Because when you have two cultures, you can take the best from each and leave behind the worst. Even if it's traditional. There are things that don't go. There's many people who can't adapt. They think that they can survive with only our [Latin] culture here. The truth is that you can't. You have to grab something from here also. If not, you're lost.[13]

Endnotes

1 This story, inspired by Alma Flor Ada's work and stories about names, is invented from my memory. The stories, vignettes, model programs, and quotes throughout this book that are not referenced are composites of my experiences, research, and memories of what others have generously shared with me.

2 For the sake of simplicity, I will alternate use of male and female gender where appropriate, instead of writing "he or she."

3 UNESCO. *<www.unesco.org/delors/ltobe.htm>*

4 Ramirez, R. R., and G. P. de la Cruz. 2003. *The Hispanic Population in the U.S.: March 2002. Current Population Reports,* 20–545. Washington, D.C.: U.S. Census Bureau.

5 National Council of La Raza. 2000. "U.S. Latino Children: A Status Report." Washington, D.C.: National Council of La Raza. Fuller, B., C. Eggers-Piérola, S. D. Holloway, X. Liang, and M. F. Rambaud. 1996. "Rich Culture, Poor Markets: Why Do Latino Parents Forgo Preschooling?" *Teachers College Record* 97 (3): 400–418.

6 Barnett, W. S., and J. T. Hustedt. 2003. " Preschool: The Most Important Grade" *Educational Leadership* 60 (7): 54–57. Shonkoff, J. P., and D. A. Phillips. 2000. *From Neurons to Neighborhoods: The Science of Early Childhood Development.* Washington, D.C.: National Academy Press.

7 Barnett, W. S., and G. Camilli. 2002. "Compensatory Preschool Education, Cognitive Development, and 'Race.'" In *Race and Intelligence: Separating Science from Myth,* edited by J. M. Fish, 369–406. Mahwah, NJ: Erlbaum.

8 Barnett, W. S. 1996. "Lives in the Balance: Benefit–Cost Analysis of the Perry Preschool Program through Age 27." *Monographs of the High/Scope Educational Research Foundation.* Michigan: High/Scope Press. Masse, L. N., and S. Barnett. 2002. Benefit Cost Analysis of the Abecedarian Early Childhood Intervention. National Institute for Early Education Research. NJ: Rutgers University. Reynolds, A. J., J. A. Temple, D. L. Robertson, and E. A. Mann. 2002. "Age 21 Cost–Benefit of the Title I Chicago Child-Parent Centers." *Educational Evaluation and Policy Analysis* 24 (4): 267–303.

9 As referred to here, *values* are the cultural beliefs that underlie action and behavior.

10 Holloway, S. D., B. Fuller, M. F. Rambaud, and C. Eggers-Piérola. 2001. *Through My Own Eyes: Single Mothers and the Cultures of Poverty,* 106. Cambridge, MA: Harvard University Press.

11 Greenfield, P. M., and R. R. Cocking, editors. 1994. *Cross-Cultural Roots of Minority Child Development.* Hillsdale, NJ: Lawrence Erlbaum Associates. Greenfield, P. M., C. Raeff, and B. Quiroz. 1996. "Cultural Values in Learning and Education." In *Closing the Achievement Gap: A Vision for Changing Beliefs and Practice,* edited by B. Williams, 37–55. Alexandria, VA: Association for Supervision and Curriculum Development.

12 Henze, R. C., and L. Vanett. 1993. "To Walk in Two Worlds — or More? Challenging a Common Metaphor of Native Education." *Anthropology and Education Quarterly* 24 (2): 116–134.

13 Holloway et al., *Through My Own Eyes,* 112.

CHAPTER
2

La Familia/Family

With the family, for the children

Focusing on *La Familia*

More than ever, there is a growing consciousness among educators that supporting children's development involves family-centered and not just child-centered approaches. Young children come to early childhood settings not as blank slates, but rather with extensive imprints of knowledge, predispositions, and behaviors that teachers must understand in order to build on their experiences.[1] Children's families, cultures, degree of poverty, and immigration and migration experiences are some of the major factors that influence their development.

Establishing a trusting, open relationship with the whole family circle can help us understand children's strengths, needs, and habits as well as the social and cultural foundation that impacts them both inside and outside the home.

Latino presence in preschools is currently a key issue that concerns parents and teachers of both preschoolers and kindergarteners through third graders. Although research shows that a quality preschool contributes to school readiness, Latino children are underrepresented in licensed centers (see Figure 2–1). And, we know that Latino parents of young children use relative or in-home care more than any other care option.

This tendency involves various cultural and linguistic influences, such as language barriers, personal connection between caregiver and parent, and shared values about socialization and education. While parents may not expect preschools to match all of their cultural beliefs and practices, they still prefer a family-like environment where their young children can continue to be exposed to some essential values that may not be understood or emphasized at child care centers, such as more authoritative discipline and respect for elders.[2]

National data clearly shows that family involvement is a constant in quality programs at all educational levels.[3] Family involvement is especially critical when the children's cultural background and home language differ from the program's main culture and language.[4] While I focus on the importance of the Latino family network in this chapter, people of other cultures may find their own beliefs about family reflected. Data shows that the support of kith and kin holds a great importance in many group-centered cultures, increases the ability of mothers to engage with children, and positively impacts the child's success in school.[5] Thus, the strategies you use to connect with extended Latino family networks can benefit children of other cultures as well.

In the pages that follow, I provide an introduction to some of the values and practices that many Latinos share about the family and its role in educating children. However, since this book is not meant to one-dimensionally characterize all Latinos, I encourage you and your staff to investigate further, consulting with the families you work with and the resources included in this book, to reach a better understanding of each child's background.

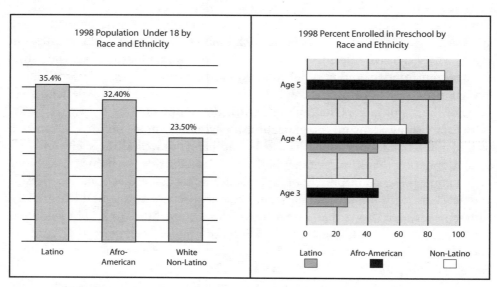

Figure 2–1 *Population of Children and Preschool Enrollment (Source: U.S. Census Bureau, Census 2000 Summary File)*

A growing concern regarding the healthy growth of our world centers on the debate about individual and group values. Some believe a focus on individualism or individual development poses a serious threat to a group's survival and believe the values associated with group-centered (called *collectivist*) cultures can better benefit individuals' achievement, families' stability, and the economic development of the larger society.[6] Certain characteristics of individualistic cultures, including competitiveness, aggressiveness, ignoring consequences on others, lack of attention to pro-social motivation (a sense of responsibility towards others), and the lack of collaborative decision-making have dire effects on the stability of neighborhoods, work places, and opportunities for the future. However, for many people of different cultures in America, both individual-oriented and group-centered values coexist. Wouldn't you say a majority of people might put family first, for instance? However, that does not mean letting go of individual identity. And doesn't everyone like to win? But winning as a team player is valued in both individualistic and collectivist cultures. So this evolution game in America need not be *Us versus Them*, but rather a blending of the best of both cultures, or all cultures with which we come in contact.

Latino Views on the Family

For many Latinos, life revolves around the tightly knit, loving bonds of *la familia*. By tradition and by design, grandparents, aunts and uncles, cousins, and friends of all ages are a constant presence in the family nucleus and assume responsibility for one another's well-being. Typical in Latino cultures in the U.S. and in Spanish-speaking countries, the value placed on *la familia* as the heart and soul of life ensures that each member is nurtured and supported by a strong network of kin related by blood and by affection.

Growing up doesn't entail the separation from family that is typical of many American families. Instead of going off to live on their own or at college, grown children may remain in the family home and contribute to the household until they form their own family units. To this day, both in Latin America and in Spain—a source for many traditions and practices—many adult children routinely live with their parents, even beyond age thirty, and departing without good justification may cause friction both within and outside the home. As a thirty-year-old Latino male told me, "I've been gone for more than two years, and my mother hasn't yet told her neighbors and friends, she is so ashamed. Both my parents keep asking, 'What did we do wrong?'"

In most Latino communities, loyalties and responsibilities extend beyond the family circle to the surrounding community, from friends and coworkers to church cohorts, shopkeepers, and neighbors, all of whom may have a say in how the children are brought up. In the neighborhood and the family network, other adults are counted on to share responsibilities and be there for the children, both in "formal" arrangements such as *comadre* and *padrino*,[7] as paid care givers, and through informal, unspoken expectations, as in the case of *vecinos* (neighbors) watching out for the children playing in the street or monitoring when the schoolchildren arrive home. In this way, an extensive, informal network of support—a circle of care—is created that early childhood professionals can tap into and strengthen through inclusive family outreach and involvement.[8]

For the majority of Latinos, the family and its networks are key in helping them to prosper because they provide resources and information that help them get citizenship, jobs, child care, services, and other necessities of everyday life. In addition, the family circle is a source of inspiration, as family and community members serve as mentors and models for future endeavors. Garnering forces, wisdom, *pautas* (rules), and even dreams from trusted sources, children who are being reared within a large group can interact with a wide variety of role models who take a part in raising them and loving them. Being part of *la familia* can provide strength and opportunity, but it can also be a burden and a source of stress at times. The child growing up within an extended family circle may be accountable to the expectations of various adults, and the parents may have to bear the child-raising advice of others. The social nature of *la familia* means that interactional skills are key to survival, but also that there are many voices interposing, interrupting, and perhaps even interfering with each individual's life. The priority placed on family may also create tensions for early care and education practitioners,[9] who may misjudge parents whose children do not attend the center or school consistently because of family duties, migrant work, trips back to the homeland, or even due to family celebrations.

In an extended family network, all have a stake *and* an obligation in the well-being of each child. Because childrearing is viewed as a shared responsibility—or rather a *compromiso* (commitment)—a child's accomplishments or downfalls reflect on the whole community. Because parents are the children's first and lifelong teachers, and because the Latino family circle can exercise such a vital influence on parenting practices and children's upbringing, collaboration with and inclusion of the extended family network is vital in serving Latinos. The ultimate goal—children's well-being—is served by forming alliances with all of the adults who touch the lives of the children.

Figure 2–2 *Grandmother and Baby at the Fair* (Photo by Su Theriault)

Evident in the daily life of families, the structure of the community—even in the architecture of their ancestral cities—the group-centered, social nature of Latinos calls for intergenerational gathering places. Traditionally, *la plaza*—town square—served this purpose. The plaza was the center of life both in villages and in the big cities where all generations and classes of people met. *Mi Plaza* offers a metaphor, a slice of Latino culture that will enable you to experience the themes of this chapter: creating intergenerational engagement in the program and becoming involved in the child's community. The child care center or school, after all, is a public space, where children gather, play, form bonds, and grow. But, the adults who come in and out of this public space—as in the metaphor below—also shape the interactions and the activities within.

My Town Square

Me acuerdo de mi plaza—I remember my town square—the vendor with ears of corn—*maíz*—all dipped in dried cheese and cream… he saved the broken ones for us little ones, the last ones who played outside until our mothers would come late from la *fábrica*[10] to fix our suppers. The balloon man, he knew all us kids' names, and he always let us pump the air in one or two of his balloons, on Sundays, with our *Mami* and *Papi* and *Abuelita*—

Granma—watching proudly and cautioning, "Now, stop, that's enough Lucecita, you're going to burst his balloon!" I remember hearing the quick, sharp clicks of the dominoes when *un abuelito*—Granpa—jumped up from his game to pull out Miguelito, who had fallen into the fountain when he was fishing for his little paper boat. The whirring sounds of the pinwheels of another vendor still delighted me when I grew older, and he made a huge circle of poles, topped with the brightly striped pinwheels, when I had my *quinceañera*—fifteenth birthday party—right there, in the plaza, with Chinese lanterns and cut paper *manteles*—tablecloths—on long tables full of food that everyone had brought. I remember giggling with my friends after school, watching *el cortejo*—the courtship: young men, in pairs or small groups, circling the outside of the plaza, where young women, chatting animatedly, were seated on the benches, pretending not to look, until someone caught someone's eye. Elders sitting nearby interjected every now and then, with either humor or caution, *"Ay no, mijita, ese no!"* ("Oh, no, my dearie, not that one!") Now I see some of the same boys and girls, now middle-aged couples, strolling arm in arm after supper, stopping here and there to chat with friends and neighbors…*¡mi plaza!*

Bridge this snapshot to your own experience:

- What are your memories of a public space where you felt safe, comfortable, and connected as a child?

- What moments had the most impact on you in that space? What made you feel comfortable?

- Think about the people in that space. Did you see the same people over and over again? Who were the strangers? How did people interact?

- Can you imagine a space for your program, inside or outside, that could provide elements and experiences that make each child comfortable?

- In plazas, sounds, textures, objects, movement, seating, fountains, vendors, rhythms, and landscaping are a backdrop for the social life. Consider what could form the backdrop for your "public space" within the program.

A New Vision for "*La Plaza*" in Early Childhood Programs

Although the story of *Mi Plaza* may seem like a sidetrack to our work with young children, in this chapter I draw on the image of *la plaza* to evoke an approach, and not simply a space, that we can create within our early childhood center or schools and communities. As a family service provider, Head Start manager, supervisor, program director, or teacher, you join a child's extended family and play a key role in providing culturally and linguistically responsive education for young children.

You are in a position to help "rebuild *la plaza*" in your program by:

- Getting to know and understanding the family and its values and practices
- Establishing respectful, enduring, and productive relationships with families
- Serving as a link between the family and the child care community
- Helping children's transitions by incorporating elements from their home lives

By extending your partnerships with parents to involve the whole community surrounding the child, you can recapture the welcoming, supportive spirit of *la plaza* within your program. Your program may be the first educational institution in this country that some families—Latino and other newcomers, migrants, and displaced families—encounter. By working to assure strong connections and positive interactions with families and their communities, you will help counteract the isolation and multiple barriers these families face and build on the strengths of all families.

Did You Know?
La Familia's Influence on Day-to-Day Life

1. Celebrations and rituals are intergenerational. Instead of a party with classmates, a child's birthday is celebrated by gatherings that include the presence and contributions of grandparents, aunts and uncles, cousins, *comadres*, and *compadres.*

2. Family, including older siblings, and friends are very frequently the caregivers of very young children, to the extent that Latino children are underrepresented in centers and Head Start.

3. Socialization is the major focus of parenting, teaching the child to be *bien educado,* or polite and respectful—essentially, well brought up—since many adults are watching and intervening in how the child behaves in public.

4. Teaching "book learning" can be viewed as the job of teachers and schools, not the parents.

Find out more about how the culture of the family may influence critical moments as well as daily life, such as when a child is born, when a child is sick, when a family is going through a hard time, or when a relative dies. Some helpful resources are:

- Rodriguez, G., 1999. *Raising Nuestros Niños: Bringing Up Latino Children in a Bicultural World.* New York: Fireside.
- Dilworth-Anderson, P., L. Burton, and W. Turner. 1993. "The Importance of Values in the Study of Culturally Diverse Families." *Family Relations* 42: 238–242.

In the next few sections of this chapter, I identify potential obstacles to forming partnerships with *la familia* and provide information, strategies, and tools to help you:

1. Connect with family networks
2. Bring families and their communities into your program
3. Visit families and their communities

Vignettes, activity ideas, and descriptions of model programs that have been successful in welcoming diverse families will help you assess your program's current practices and envision how to recapture *la plaza* in your program. Replicable tools in this chapter include a bilingual home activity sheet, a sample family interview or home visiting guide, and planning logs that track the progress of a center's or school program's involvement with family networks. Although I offer some guidelines and activities, I encourage you to be an active learner and generate your own questions and adaptations to the activities that suit your particular needs.

Turning Potential Obstacles into Opportunities

To recapture the spirit of *la plaza*, you must understand that some parents' situations or beliefs—especially those of newcomers—may affect their participation in your program as well as their own parenting practices. As you prepare to deepen your work with families and their networks and to experiment with some of the strategies that I describe, you must be aware of the changing family structure, language issues, parents' perceptions of their role and the teacher's role, and teachers' perceptions and practices. As you reflect on these potential obstacles, think about ways the challenges families face give you a chance to reshape your programs to respond to and build on the changing needs and possibilities of the Latino family.

1. **CHANGING FAMILY STRUCTURE:** Newcomer parents may have lost the support of the extended family they left behind, and they may lack social networks of friends they can count on as *comadres* and *compadres* to share the responsibili-

ties and joys of child rearing. Perhaps those who are most affected by the loss of the safety nets of extended families are the youth. Many parents of young Latino children are very young themselves and lack guidance and knowledge that were previously passed down from the extended family and community. In many cases, young parents may give up care of their children completely to others. As of 1998, 5.4 million young children were living in the homes of grandparents or other kin; 2.1 million of these children did not have parents present in the household.[11]

- How can you turn these challenges into strengths? Grandparents in Latino culture are viewed as holders of knowledge and are the ones that pass down family stories and morals. At times, they may be more traditional and strict than the younger generation, but they are zealously dedicated to young children, even those outside their own families. Teenage parents and sibling caregivers are also an enriching addition to an early childhood setting, bringing in fresh views and possibilities. In order to bring out these potential contributions, focus on reaching out to grandparents and younger caregivers, as well as on representing these complex and committed relationships in the activities and materials at your center.

2. **LANGUAGE ISSUES:** Language plays an especially important role in educating the more than 12.5 million young Latino children in the United States because the greatest growth of this population is of immigrant children with limited English skills. Research in this area indicates that disconnection between the home and the educational setting's language and culture can adversely affect Latino children's progress through school as well as their relationships with their families.[12]

- Being bilingual is actually an advantage, not a disadvantage, because it engages the brain in making critical connections and discerning patterns in the structure of language and discourse that those mastering only one language lack. The culture and language gap, one of the three critical issues identified at Northwest Regional Education Laboratory's conference on *Improving Student Success through School, Family, and Community Partnerships*, need not be seen as a great divide, but as a chance to "travel" standing still.[13] Children and families who bring diverse languages, cultures, and experiences can enrich your own culture and thinking, help you go beyond one perspective, and inspire you to celebrate and use multiple languages daily in your programs. For example, in programs that use a dual language approach, the power of being bilingual is shared, and the stigma associated with learning a new language is erased, because all are discovering new and unfamiliar words and ways of communicating.

3. **PARENTS' PERCEPTIONS OF THEIR ROLE AND THE ROLE OF THE TEACHER:** Key to involving families is understanding the role, status, and authority held by teachers in Latino societies. In many Latino families, there is delineation between "socializing" and "educating" children. In Latin America, as well as in the United States, families may perceive their role as preparing the child to be educated, to be part of a group, to succeed as both an individual and a contributor to their society, as well as providing for the basic needs of the family. Latino parents may feel it is the teacher's job and expertise to make decisions about their child's education within school.[14] In Latino cultures, teachers are respected as experts in their field, that is, in educating children. Reading, writing, math, and other "school" skills are not explicitly part of the parenting role, and institutions may be expected to take on sole responsibility. Out of respect, parents entrust their children to teachers and may not feel comfortable questioning their authority.[15] Further, many Latino parents may not have the education, sense of entitlement, or amenities other families enjoy, because there is a higher incidence of poverty for Latino two-parent families than for their White non-Latino or Black counterparts.[16]

- The respect Latino families have for teachers can provide you with fertile ground to build a trusting, working family-teacher relationship. Once parents understand that your early childhood program is not just a care-giving facility, but an educational setting, and once you cultivate this respect by communicating to families that they are also experts, you will form a strong, equal partnership that will strengthen your program.

4. **TEACHERS' PERCEPTIONS AND PRACTICES:** As early childhood educators, we all have our own preconceived notions of how a child should develop and grow. Our own beliefs and practices can present a challenge to working with families of different cultures when our practices conflict with their home practices.[17] We may tacitly judge certain behaviors or beliefs less appropriate or adaptive to Anglocentric culture, be it asking for help to put on a coat, sitting on the teacher's lap, or being unable to pour milk in a glass. In addition, the place and value we assign, as educators, to teaching certain skills, such as "giving," in contrast to teaching "literacy," should be part of our ongoing discussion. Valuing academic and social skills unequally may present a dilemma to children transitioning from home to center to school. If, for instance, dinner talk is valued at home, but teacher-guided questions are valued at school, children may participate less in school or expand less on their vocabulary. If we acknowledge that the child grows and develops in the home as well as under our care, these inconsistencies have to be addressed. Chapter 5 delves more deeply into how to prepare to work with families with different views on what is appropriate in raising a child.

- Balancing multiple perspectives always has the potential to help you go further than your own thinking and experience can take you. Your ongoing development as an early education teacher depends on reflecting on differences and adapting practice to include them. Let's not always take the easy answer and persuade families to take on our views and practices or simply adapt to an existing, rigid program. Consider that a quality program is flexible and ever changing to accommodate its diverse population.

Guidelines and Strategies for Involving *La Familia*

Connecting with families and their networks, bringing families and their communities into programs, and going to the communities are three key principles for putting into practice the values associated with *la familia*. Building on what you learn about *la familia*, you can establish ongoing ties with the child's community, from family and friends to neighborhood leaders, and invite them to participate actively in the school environment. You and your colleagues can reach out to the child's community, going into homes and neighborhood places to get a full picture of the child's life within the community. You can welcome members of the child's community as co-teachers, co-planners, and initiators of activities. Enlisting elders and older siblings in the extended family as valuable partners in the education of young Latino children strengthens her program. Building a relationship with families creates opportunities for them to serve as a resource to the program, as they can provide their expertise and support in efforts to include the culture and language of the children, recruit caregivers and families, and identify needs and priorities in their communities.

To truly support the transition of children into early childhood environments, programs and schools also should be aware of the needs of the whole family as circumstances that affect the child's well-being in the classroom may be hard to identify in families with cultural and language difficulties.

Connecting with the Family Circle

Consider the following guidelines and strategies to expand your knowledge of families' dreams and desires for their children, the values and practices of families and their communities, and families' needs and resources (see Figure 2–3).

Honor the Family's Dreams and Expectations for the Child

When you enter a family's home, or engage in conversation about the education of children, your first priority is to know what the family wants for its children. Every program has its own methods and tools for gathering needed information about

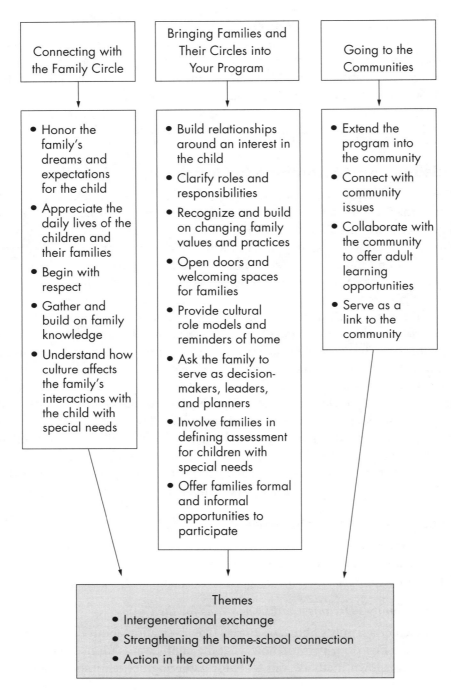

Figure 2–3 *Concept Map of Guidelines and Strategies for Involving* La Familia

the children and families when they enroll. However, establishing a relationship with Latino families can also be done in informal or fun ways, such as the *Family Dream Puzzle Blocks* activity that follows. Parents and extended family members will be more likely to participate and feel comfortable in situations that are familiar to them, that is, more consistent with their daily interactions or that take a multi-layered approach, than if they simply fill out a form or answer a series of closed-ended questions.

BRINGING IDEAS TO LIFE
Family Dream Puzzle Blocks

This activity, which can be done as a home activity, or in a parent/child workshop facilitated by program staff, is a wonderful way to include families and their dreams for their children in the everyday play materials that are accessible to all the children. Family day care providers as well as centers and elementary schools can take advantage of this activity.

Materials:
- Commercial block puzzle pieces without a raised texture
- Nontoxic glue
- Old magazines
- Scissors
- Photocopies of family photos that include the child
- Polyreuthane and paint (for use by teachers only)

Steps:
1. Tell the families that you would like them to contribute by making a set of block puzzles for the classroom that will represent all the families of the children in the program.
2. Ask families if they could lend you a photo of their family that includes the child.
3. Photocopy and enlarge each photo to fit on six large puzzle blocks.
4. Have each family member place their six blocks together, and glue their family photo on top.
5. Once the glue is set, cut the photo along the edges of each of the 6 blocks.
6. Whether the activity is carried out in the classroom or as a home activity, ask the families to choose some images from the magazines that represent some

of their dreams for their children, for instance, what they wish for their futures, what they would like the children's surroundings to be, what they would like their children to be doing, whom do they see surrounding them, and so on.

7. Ask the parents to cut the images to fit each block and glue to the reverse side of the blocks with their family photo.

8. Once dry, paint several layers of polyurethane on the blocks to protect them from wear.

9. Display the blocks prominently so all the children can use them. Share them with children at circle time, when each child can talk about her family and what she wishes for them, and use the blocks to stimulate conversations with parents about long-term aspirations for their children and how to achieve them.

Appreciate the Daily Lives of Children and Their Families

There are many ways to learn about the values and practices of a family and its community. In model projects throughout the developing world, a key component of early childhood initiatives is the active collaboration of teachers and families. For instance, a global effort extending into rural communities in the developing world involves educators in "mapping" the community. The teachers' task is to know the assets and realities of the community where children live. One activity enlists parents in creating cards with names and symbols that represent their families and what they hold as important to their well-being. Families and teachers then sort through the cards, comparing differences and similarities and creating a blueprint for schooling based on the community's values and symbols. In another participatory learning and action program, families visually represent their own conceptions of a life span and the markers that define important life transitions. In some cultures, the life span is not seen as linear, but rather as a circle, where development— what people can do and be—comes back to a kind of beginning, implying children and elders may have some parallel needs for support and possibilities. From these representations of life cycles, teachers ask parents to define what children need to know at each point, who teaches them, and how.[18]

A great way to get to know the families and their communities is through their own eyes. The next activity, *Nuestro Barrio/Nuestra Gente*—Our Neighborhood/ Our People—provides an opportunity for all members of the family to share their lives with both adults and children in the program. By providing tools and a focus that they can approach however they wish, you are showing the family that you are interested in every aspect of their child's life and demonstrating that learning can build upon everyday occurrences.

BRINGING IDEAS TO LIFE
Nuestro Barrio/Nuestra Gente
Our Neighborhood/Our People

This activity will help you and the families in your program get to know each other and will build your knowledge and understanding of the community that surrounds the child. Moreover, you will be acknowledging the value of the daily activities in which the family involves the child, from doing chores to running errands, and that they are all occasions for language development.

Materials:
- Instant camera and film for at least twenty photos
- Tape recorder and tape
- Poster board
- Photo corners
- Labels
- Glue stick

Steps:
1. Through bilingual letters sent and, preferably, also face-to-face, such as when parents or caregivers come to pick up the child one day, ask all families to participate in a classroom activity on the family.

2. Give families the instant camera and film or the tape recorder and tape. Ask them to let every member of the family take at least one photo depicting what they do and where they go in the neighborhood with the child.

3. Suggest that they can also use the tape recorder to capture sounds in their daily activities with the child. For instance, a teenage sister might take the kindergarten student to the park and take a photo and recording of a group jumping double dutch; a grandmother might take a photo of a trip to the market, or a food preparation, recording the dialogue between her grandchild, shopkeepers, and herself. Even a regular meal offers opportunities to see and hear how the child is socialized and learns vocabulary in a daily, routine context.

4. As a classroom activity for families, ask each family to bring their photos and, together with children, create a multi-media poster exhibit that can be displayed in a "family corner" or in a family/teacher resource room. As an alternative, you can give the families the poster board, labels, photo corners, and glue sticks so they can make the exhibit at home.

5. Provide a digital camera to families so they can take photos at home, if needed, and use the cameras to record the activity.

6. Engage families in follow-up activities that build on this project, such as developing an ABC book with the pictures of fruit, vegetables, and other food that are familiar to the children.

As an example of a possible follow-up activity, the *Our Storytellers Mural and Intergenerational Story Project* engaged an intergenerational group of neighbors from four to sixty-four years old in capturing the likeness of the people around them who told stories.

Figure 2–4 *Participants Painting the Storytellers Mural, Cambridge, Massachusetts* (Photo by Costanza Eggers)

Begin with Respect

Home visits give you an opportunity to build an equal relationship with families and to gather essential information about the family's needs and resources, both of which will contribute to the quality and effectiveness of your program.[19] The Funds of Knowledge Project in California is an example of a successful program that involved elementary teachers in visits to Spanish-speaking homes. However, it's important to bear in mind that people from many cultures are wary of people coming into their homes or asking pointed questions about their lives and experiences. There are many good reasons for this, from the way bureaucracy works in Latin America to the repression and control exercised in many countries. Providing personal information or giving answers to someone who is writing down what that information can be looked at askance by immigrants without a legal status and others who have suffered discrimination and barriers in this country or in their own countries.

Always keeping the child and respect at the center of conversations with Latino families will go a long way toward combating some of these apprehensions and establishing trusting relationships. It's also a good idea to involve families in structuring visits. Engage them in planning during the initial phone call or personal contact by asking the mother, father, grandparent, or other primary caregiver to decide where to meet, whom to include in the visit, and how to collaborate on use of the information shared.[20]

 Building on Strengths
Drawing on a Family's Strengths

Tomás, a lively, bright-eyed, four-year-old Puerto Rican boy, had become increasingly quiet and less cooperative in group activities. During a home visit, Ms. Rodriguez, the director of the program, asked the mother if there had been any recent changes in his life. The mother shared that she had recently separated from her husband and that the father had been less active in Tomás' life since the separation. Ms. Rodriguez approached the father the next time he came to pick up Tomás and discussed ways in which he could become involved in the center. She found out that the father was a chef at a local restaurant, and together they worked out a lesson that he could plan for all the children in Tomás' classroom. Ms. Rodriguez created recipe cards and labels in Spanish and English to reinforce the vocabulary of the cooking lesson and provided the ingredients the father needed. She invited the father to take center stage by leading the cooking class and sharing his expertise with the whole center. Ms. Rodriguez recalls, "The teachers got so inspired, they carried out parallel projects in their own rooms, reaching out to families, and making a whole multicultural food fest as well as follow-up activities that brought families into the center to lead activities that engaged children and showed what they do in their work. "The children were so proud of their parents!" This example shows us how Ms. Rodriguez—director of Escuelita Boriken in Boston—responded to a critical point in a child's life by learning more about his home life, drawing on the "funds of knowledge" the family holds, and helping to fill a void the child was feeling.

What could you do routinely to be better in touch with the child and family's strengths and needs? What supports and services inside and outside of your program can you coordinate with to create a team approach with adults whom the family trusts? Can you think of ways to reach out to extended family members when the child's behavior is fluctuating?

Gather and Build on Family Knowledge

A process or tool for finding out about the child's home life and preferences should capture more than the individual child's skills, personality, and behavior. It should also give you an idea of the whole family's interactions with the child, as well as shared responsibilities for the child, in order to get a picture of how the household is organized to accomplish day-to-day living and to contribute to the child's well-being. Where are the gaps? What are the challenges? Does an older sibling in charge of caring for the child in the afternoon have a hard time completing homework? Is the care of the child pieced together each day with various caregivers and places? Does a grandmother serve as advisor for the young mother?

You can use the information gathered from an interview or home visit to map a child's progress in the use of "playground vocabulary," sharing skills, interest in science, and the curriculum you have designed to aid in this development. If, for instance, you and the parents set a goal for the child to establish bonds and respectful behavior with adults in the center, you may want to begin by making a diagram of all the adults now interacting significantly with the child and chart the child's contacts in this way. Visual representations such as this may help you communicate with families from diverse backgrounds and show them how your work with the children links with their goals and their child's experiences at home.

The following *Family Interview Guide* could be useful for home visits or center or kindergarten registration, ensuring that activities and assessments reflect children's strengths and preferences. When you make home visits or ask caregivers to provide information, keep in mind that birth parents may not always be the most influential players in bringing up a child. Tailor your inquiries accordingly, and place a special emphasis on including the perspectives of elders and siblings.

BRINGING IDEAS TO LIFE
Family Interview Guide

Many states require that parents fill out forms when they enroll their children in preschool and school programs. Routinely, these forms gather information on health, personality, and habit, and perhaps a description of a typical day for the child. The information is typically used to individualize curriculum and to support social and emotional development. To be culturally responsive, home visitors or teachers interviewing the family also need to understand the interactions between adults and children in the family, as this will give a window into the ways the child is being socialized into the home culture and the context for child-rearing in the home. As you complete a home visit protocol, or even a registration interview, include ways in which to capture child-rearing cultural differences that you should know about:

1. What behaviors and skills are explicitly taught at home, and how? Is the child encouraged to sit and talk with adults at mealtimes? Is the child discouraged from looking at an adult's eyes when they are being disciplined?

2. What words are repeated to children daily (e.g., gracias, mamá)?

3. When and where does the child smile, laugh, play, rest, watch T.V., eat?

4. What is the child interested in?

5. What does the child dislike?

6. How do various members of the extended family respond when the child cries? Behaves inappropriately? Masters a word or a skill? Asks for food, an object, or help?

7. Where do family members go for advice?

8. Who are the adults and children who regularly interact with the child outside of the home? Do they speak Spanish or English in front of the child?

9. What are the out-of-home experiences that give the children pleasure and give them an opportunity to learn what you think is important?

10. What are the out-of-home experiences that challenge the child?

11. What are the family's goals for the child?

With your co-teachers, with each individual family, or in a team of parents and teachers, decide how you will use the information that you gather with this form. Any kind of assessment or intervention that concerns a child's development should be focused on the strengths that already exist within the child and within the family and its context. Building on this foundation, you can examine needs and obstacles most effectively.[21]

Understand How Culture Affects the Family's Interactions with the Child with Special Needs

Latino children have a high presence in special needs programs throughout the United States, in many cases due to cultural and linguistic differences or due to the cultural inappropriateness of assessments. Special needs encompass an array of physical, behavioral, and psychological disabilities or challenges that are not easily diagnosed in children from different cultures. Later on I discuss the problem with special needs assessments. Cultural beliefs can impact how parents deal with their children, from their perception about disabilities to their expectations for their children. Finding a respectful way of broaching these delicate perceptions is essential to teaching the child with disabilities.

If parents believe:	You can try:
They need to constantly hold their older infant, overprotect their child, or limit the child's physical experiences in order to ensure safety.	• Talking about how their child enjoys climbing on the ladder, reaching for the ball, etc. • Explaining how you support the child by being at the child's side when she or he attempts a new task. Emphasize that the child is safe and share a vignette of a particular accomplishment, as well as the steps you or a peer took to guide the child in succeeding. • Sharing information about how limiting physical experiences may further impact the cognitive development of their children. • Suggesting that the parents go on a visit to a children's museum with the classroom, where the child can have many sensory experiences alongside friends and family. • Showing parents of an older infant how placing her on her stomach encourages her to use her developing muscles.
They show their love and protection by doing things for their children and believe	• Telling them about a "buddy" system, where each special-needs child has a peer for playing, reading, eating, etc.

If parents believe:	You can try:
dependence on and help from older siblings is essential to the child.	• Talking about all the occasions for group learning and support that have helped the child reach milestones.
Their child with special needs should not stand out in the school system, that they should refuse special education support, and that their child is to learn only English.	• Informing families of the various arguments for and against a child learning two languages simultaneously. Some special needs educators believe a child with a cognitive delay should learn only one language and leave their maternal language aside. Some believe that fully developing their first language is key to the cognitive development of young children with special needs. • Encouraging parents to provide a language-rich environment, as advised by researchers and specialists, that includes talking, listening, and nonverbal communication. These elements are accessible to any family, even if they do usually read and write at home. Using music, rhythmic sounds, language, and rich modulations in tone assist the language development of children with special needs. • Conveying the important idea that a language-rich environment, in whichever language they feel most comfortable, is what will benefit their children the most. • Being sensitive that not all parents may have mastered reading and writing, even in their own language, and making sure to use multiple visual and oral communication strategies with families.

Families may believe their child's disability is a punishment for a sin, a god-given burden, or as their destiny, over which they have no control.[22] Extended families may indulge a child with snacks and sweets or may use folk medicine to remedy an illness. A strong home–school connection depends on an approach that takes under consideration the wishes and beliefs of the parents, using these as a means to open the dialogue about how to provide multiple ways for the child with disabilities to grow and thrive.

Bringing Families and Their Communities into Programs

To welcome families and their communities into your program and develop equal and respectful partnerships, you can draw on these guidelines:

- Build relationships around an interest in children and their lives.
- Clarify roles, expectations, and responsibilities.
- Recognize and build on changing family values and practices.
- Open doors and create welcoming spaces for families.
- Provide cultural role models and reminders of home.
- Ask extended families to serve as decision makers, leaders, and planners.
- Involve families in defining assessments for children with special needs, and offer families formal and informal opportunities to participate.

 Did You Know?
Communication Is Key

Many teachers may not be able to speak the home language of their students, but they should understand how to access and use interpreters, coordinate with bilingual service providers, and reach out to family service workers and community leaders who can act as liaisons. In this way, teachers can communicate in the manner most comfortable to and respectful of the family network. Make sure that all the communication you send out, even if translated, is written in simple Spanish and includes the phone number of a Latino staff member the family can contact with questions.

Build Relationships Around an Interest in the Child

There is no better way to engage Latino families in the life of your program than to show a sincere interest in their children, both inside and outside of the center, school, and home. Remember, children are their hope and their measure of success as a human being. Communicating informally with parents on a daily basis offers a chance for you to show how much you care about their children. You can share a shining moment of the child's day with the family caregiver, inquire about the child's experiences and habits, show the child's work, and so on. Realistically, however, most teachers, especially in the primary school, will not have this opportunity. In that case, consider maintaining a portfolio of each child that you can review with parents, including photos of the child enjoying his or her favorite activity, sample art work the child has created, observation notes, and descriptions of the child's interactions with classroom buddies. One school I visited had a "visual" report in the form of a postcard that they handed to each parent when the child was picked up at the end of the day. The postcard had a happy face, a sad face, and an exclamation point, with a few words next to each, for example "jumped high today" or "lost her apple." The teachers all seem to like this convention: "We just got into the routine of doing it, and we photocopy these forms, so it takes no time. And the children see us doing it and giving it to their parents, and they always ask us what we're writing about them. 'What are you putting? Put that I'm happy about the rabbit.' I found that it even helps their behavior, because the paper is a conversation starter for parents and child."

First and foremost, someone on staff who shares the family's language and culture and who understands how to approach the family in a personal, respectful way can be your best ally in overcoming the distance between teachers and parents. Among people of similar cultures, personal connection is evident in tacit ways, from mannerisms, tone, rhythm, and verbal and nonverbal communication. A history of cultural knowledge affects how we greet people, knock on a door, and what liberties we take when beginning a relationship. However, what transpires naturally through the course of an interaction is hard for those from different cultures to understand or duplicate, so no guidebook of rules and practices will truly aid educators, especially as the Latino population is so diverse, complex, and ever changing. An authentic interest in understanding and acting on the family's wishes and a sense of respect will indicate to the families that you truly value their child and their opinions.

Clarify Roles and Responsibilities

Explicitly acknowledge the role of parents and extended family members as experts and shapers in their children's lives. Encourage parents to contribute as experts, not simply as helpers and passive participants. Families should be quite clear about where they do have input and see that it is taken seriously. They should also know the bottom line for which you, as a teacher, are accountable; for instance, what regulations prohibit, what program or school policies and practices entail, and what recourses and rights families have when obstacles present themselves.

Your expectations of how families should be involved will play a role in establishing the boundaries of your relationship with them and your role as either an authority or an equal partner in educating their children. If parents are expected to simply drop off their children, receive mostly written information and reports on their children, and have little conversational contact with the staff, their involvement can be hampered by these formal limits. Whenever the situation makes it possible, whether at the center or at the door of the classroom, a warm greeting and a good word about the child is a welcome exchange for parents. In primary schools, where the children are bused or where a monitor takes the children outside to be picked up, this may not be possible.

Recognize and Build on Changing Family Values and Practices

Families from different cultures, especially newcomers, are likely making conscious choices as to what to keep from their home culture and what to acquire from the host culture. Most parents want their children to survive in both worlds, that is, become bicultural. As a result, they may be open to examining some of the practices that you offer as alternatives to some of their own, both out of respect and because they are actively creating a "third culture" that bridges what they experienced in their childhoods with what may work here.[23] However, it is important to avoid disregarding families' home cultures and practices all together—doing so creates a tension between the children and their extended family. Therefore, the more that you attempt to bring in meaningful threads of connection between the home and the center, the better the children's transition and development will be. They will see and hear familiar cues to shape their behaviors and understanding, they will feel less disconnection, and supportive relationships with their families will be strengthened.[24] When children see that the adults around them are united on their behalf and that home practices are reinforced at the same time that they learn new cues and language, they find it easier to adapt to new surroundings.

If you use the strategies described in the previous section to learn more about families' desires, values, and needs, and if you adjust your interactions to reflect this understanding, you can help build bridges between children's homes and your program. For instance, to acknowledge the respect for elders and hierarchy that is vitally important to most Latinos, make an effort to address grandmothers always by their last name, no matter how intimately you know the family. In Spanish, the formal noun for "you," "usted," is still used in many countries to address one's mother and definitely to address new acquaintances and those of higher status. Calling an elder by their first name could well be seen as inappropriate and demeaning and could undermine your attempts to build respectful relationships. Nurturing equitable, collaborative relationships does not necessarily entail forgoing polite, formal ways of address.

You can also enhance your center's or school's environment based on what you learn from activities such as the home visit described in the previous section. Your center may already have a variety of materials that represent foods, music, stories, festivities, and people from various cultures. However, more subtle differences such as preferences, behaviors, interactions, and sense of beauty may be harder to integrate. Home visits provide a wonderful opportunity to see some of these more invisible aspects of culture and gain a deeper understanding of differences without falling into stereotypical interpretations of Latino culture. Once you discern the aspects that unite many Latinos, including language and the group-centered framework that shapes values and practices, you can use the following activities to explore the differences in how each individual family and child grows from these roots and contributes to their own cultural script.

BRINGING IDEAS TO LIFE
Exploring Differences Among Latinos

Working with colleagues or on your own, create a chart using the information that you have learned from your family interviews, informal interactions with parents, and from observing the child and the family. Add your own categories to gather differences in approaches, behaviors, religion, valued objects, celebrations, and immigration experiences. A sample chart follows.

	Yolanda & her family	Tomás & his family	Luis & his family	Martita & her family
Family's cultural background				
Who lives in the home				
How long the family has been in the U.S.				
What the family does together				
Some family customs				
Some family values				
How the values translate to practice				

	Yolanda & her family	Tomás & his family	Luis & his family	Martita & her family
How the family shows caring				
Mealtime routines				
Story of the child's name				
How the parents' child raising differs from their own parents'				
What they do the same as their own parents				

Open Doors and Create Welcoming Spaces for Families

Encouraging family members not only to enter but to explore and move freely within the center or school and to feel at home is a sure way to establish trusting and enduring relationships with families. Admittedly, in some cases many adults coming in and out of an early childhood classroom may be a cause for concern. But, a quality program—with stable staff—may have the capacity to develop different ways to deal with situations. One of the most successful international models for involving and training adults in early childhood education was the "red door" program—community sites, each distinguishable by a red door, where unstructured activities and many materials, as well as modeling, were available to kith and kin and all caregivers who entered with children.

What makes a space welcoming for families? One of the most effective ways to welcome families is to have an informal "open door" policy, where the environment and the interactions suggest to the whole family that their presence is valued and a natural part of their children's entry into the program. This can be achieved in daily interactions, in the visual displays, and in more formal communications between staff and families. Your school no doubt has various "official" events throughout the year for parents to attend. However, a trusting and productive relationship with families is best built through frequent and varied contact. One school, for instance, set up a web page for each teacher to post news, schedules, photos, and questions to parents. A collaborating library program helped parents access the bilingual page and email teachers with their own news, questions, and responses. Many and varied paths to involvement allow families who cannot be present in schools a way to connect. During drop-off time, as children arrive and families head off to start their days, you may be able to connect briefly with families, chat, or inform them about upcoming events. Pick-up time, however, generally allows you more time to have personal, one-on-one discussions about the child's day or provides opportunities for friendly interactions between families. These informal opportunities are a gateway to building a trusting and comfortable relationship with families, as many families, unfamiliar with the way things work in American institutions, look for your lead when establishing relationships.

Allowing relationships to build slowly provides families with a chance to observe the program, other children, and how adults in the setting interact among themselves and with children. These interactions provide clues to parents about the culture of the school and how best to act within this setting and can perhaps also open up avenues for dialogue based on concrete activities and interactions, such as "Why do you think your child chose to change centers right then?"

BRINGING IDEAS TO LIFE
Family Resource Room

Dedicate a space to a family and staff resource room where families, including kith and kin who care for children outside the *center*, can gather and access resources. This "drop-in" space can be operated by a parent coordinator or teacher who may set up different activities, display different materials and toys, and informally model how to use these with a visiting child, sibling, or a pair of children from the center. Perhaps the teachers' lunchroom could have a parent corner, and teachers can extend their lunch schedule to be present at assigned open hours. The room can also serve as a place for teachers to access on-line teaching ideas, prepare activities, and research individually or in small groups, thus creating an atmosphere for adult learning through modeling and interactions.

Materials:

- Collect a wide variety of materials, such as toys, books, and games from different countries; multi-language videos on parenting; program activities, and so on. Neighborhood merchants may be willing to donate some materials, or your school may have a corporate partner willing to fund such purchases.

- Comfortable furniture, pillows, and chairs.

- Computer with Internet access.

- Science and math manipulatives and exhibits with which families can interact.
- Snacks and refreshments.

Steps:

1. Find a teacher's room in your program that can serve as a resource room and gathering place for families as well as staff. Enlist families to help you prepare and stock the room. Post photos of all the families, staff, and children on the walls.

2. Advertise widely about the availability of the space and resources. Be sure to personally invite home caregivers and family members to come. Welcome families to bring infants and older siblings along.

3. Post a lending schedule when a staff member or coordinator can be present and available (perhaps while preparing lessons or looking through materials) to guide family members to materials based on their needs and interests.

4. Expose families to the computer by exploring web pages from their home country, online newspapers from different Latin American countries, as well as Spanish-language media from various parts of the United States.

5. Have families contribute to a wish list of materials and development activities and use these ideas as a platform for planning sessions.

Provide Cultural Role Models and Reminders of Home

For children of all cultures, role models provide a sense of pride and possibility. For Latino children, role models who maintain their bilingual and bicultural roots acknowledge and affirm their rich heritage. Encourage the presence of diverse adults in the program, including teachers, family coordinators, guests from the Latino community, bicultural and bilingual workshop leaders, and authors.

Include family photos, objects from children's homes, parent/child art work, a *Nuestra Gente/Nuestro Barrio* poster or exhibit, and the *Family Dreams Puzzle Blocks* in the materials you use daily to engage children and make them feel both at home and interested in the lives of other children.

Ask Extended Family Members to Serve as Decision-Makers, Leaders, and Planners

If you truly value the families in your program and their opinions, seek their input in more than the traditional ways of coming to outings, training workshops, cele-

Figure 2–5 *Planning Together* (Photo by Su Theriault)

brations, and fundraising events. Invite families to activities that go beyond boards and bake sales. Parents have a vested interest in ensuring the quality of education for their children, and even in small ways they can be colleagues in planning and collaborators on assessment and promotion.

When a choice is possible, families make choices about centers or elementary schools based on their opinions about quality and convenience as well as availability and affordability. Their word of mouth serves as the best publicity but, more importantly, their perspectives on quality should be considered in the assessment of your program. Offering them opportunities—such as focus groups—to discuss criteria that are important to them is essential in the ongoing assessment of your program.

If you organize a focus/discussion group that could at times include sensitive subjects, have a family-friendly title—such as "family circles"—and make this an ongoing group, rather than a one-time workshop led by a professional. You can even have parents take turns facilitating the group and simply step aside and offer them the space to get together on a regular basis. Families can thus establish bonds with each other and with the teaching staff, and they will feel free to discuss amongst themselves some issues that they would perhaps be too polite or intimidated to bring up in a mixed group. If you have several families of the same ethnicity and language, organize times that they can meet on their own. Whether you decide to form an ongoing family discussion group or to convene a one-time family focus group led by a professional, make sure that families know that you encourage them to come up with ideas your program can act on. By doing so, you imply respect for parents' opinions and place them in leadership positions, engendering a mutual responsibility where both parties have a role in defining and carrying out a plan that benefits the children *and* reflects both parties' perspectives. Whether we agree with families' views or not, we must keep in mind this is a process of building trust and respect between the adults that affect the child's growth and happiness. Carefully clarifying what the family's and program's goals are for the children is essential, but it is not sufficient to arrive at agreed-upon goals. Educators should also be open to finding multiple ways to achieve the same goals.

 ## Challenges for Teachers
When You Don't Agree

As we know, even people in the same family disagree about critical childrearing practices, from how to dress children for the cold to whether to allow children to help themselves from the refrigerator. If your expectations and the families' expectations of the children differ, seek ways to both examine your assumptions and talk with families about the different viewpoints. In Chapter 5, I offer some ideas and refer you to some resources that may help you better approach differences in beliefs and practices. One very comprehensive compilation of activities is a two-volume set entitled, "Honouring Diversity Within Child Care and Early Education," by Gyda Chud and Ruth Fahlman.[25]

BRINGING IDEAS TO LIFE
Family Focus Group

Invite families to participate in a family focus group. Explain to the participants that you want to find out what is important to them and that you wish to include their views on quality in your evaluation plan. Make sure that families who participate know that you also want to know what does not work for them. Many Latino families may not feel comfortable openly criticizing your program because of the respect for authority and the traditional politeness and deference to authority that is so intrinsic to their culture.

Steps:

1. Ask family members to come into the classroom in pairs and observe what they see in the interactions, activities, and environment that reflect or go counter to their language, beliefs, and home practices.

2. When all focus group participants have had an opportunity to observe in your classroom, bring them together at a time that is convenient for them. Have a staff member present to engage children in activities, so their care-givers will be free to talk. Offer focus group participants refreshments.

3. You can ask the focus group some of the following questions to stimulate a discussion:

   - What do you do at home that is the same as or different from what you saw here?

   - What behaviors, activities, or practices do you question?

   - What behaviors, activities, or practices do you encourage at home that you would like your children to carry over to here?

   - Could you suggest some familiar books, stories, music, or objects that will help your children feel more at home?

   - What did you notice about the interactions among children? Between children and adults? Among adults?

   - Is there something new you noticed about your child?

   - What do you think is strong in our program? What do you think is missing?

At times, there may not be a middle ground between parental views and your program's or school's guidelines. A teacher alone cannot go against a system-wide rule. Make clear to families what you are accountable for, but be sure to explain explicitly what these guidelines are and why they were made, emphasizing the concern for the safety and well-being of their children.

Involve Families in Defining Assessments for Children with Special Needs

Child assessments may not help you distinguish between language and culture differences and language delays or special needs that are behavioral or disability-related. A young child not accustomed to being interviewed, for instance, may not be responsive. Known-answer kinds of questions may confuse some children used to more directive or open-ended questions. Many cultural factors can influence how a child tests, and it is difficult for even teachers trained in special needs to distinguish what these may be. A trusting relationship with families is essential to getting a full picture of the child's ability, as well as familiar cues and behaviors. The accompanying chart suggests some approaches to delving deeper into the causes of some behaviors that are often used to define milestones may include the following:

If assessments ask:	You can consider:
How the child expresses needs compared to other children.	1. How the family meets the child's needs at home. Many families "read" or anticipate a child's needs or nonverbal cues and may have various family members attending to the child. 2. How home practices, such as feeding only at mealtimes, toileting on a schedule, and sleeping routines may mean the child does not have to express his needs. 3. Investigate how the child and his siblings are encouraged to express their needs.
How well peers and others understand what the child says.	4. Finding out about differences in communication styles and practices. In many cultures, language is linked with doing. Adults model and introduce language through an apprenticeship model, that is, in the course of doing chores or in giving disciplinary cues to protect the children from harmful or inappropriate behavior. Storytelling, another common form of communication, may require only nonverbal or chorus interjections from young children. Watching, doing, and listening are the language skills that are deemed appropriate. 5. The effects of being immersed in two languages, in particular the patterns of English learning that may confuse and contradict the primary language knowledge the child has developed.
How the child has mastered turn-taking skills and how passive or active she is in interactions with peers.	6. Learning about home rules for sharing and talking. For example, does hierarchy play a role in discourse, and older siblings dominate dinnertime conversation?

Offer Families Formal and Informal Opportunities to Participate

Once you know the family and the child, you can find informal as well as formal ways to bring families in to actively participate in the life of your classroom. An often-used activity involves grandparents in reading to the young children or telling stories. Older siblings can be invited after school or on days off to join a "family-style" meal, do an activity with a child, or to be a paid helper. Facilities may have funds for volunteer stipends or for substitutes that could be used for paying youth. Some community agencies also have youth programs that train and pay youth to work in educational settings or to do community service. Look for ways families can contribute to activities in an authentic and fun way, for instance, depicting a family routine, such as a meal, or a celebration through the use of dolls or puppets, ensuring you can show children the way different families approach the same routine.

In Latino culture, gender roles may influence the kind of participation and the approach you use to engage parents. Mothers, sisters, and grandmothers may take a more active role in raising young children than fathers, brothers, and grandfathers. The following Programs That Inspire section describes a program that found ways to include fathers in significant and empowering ways, whether or not their custom and background traditionally encourage their involvement. Take inspiration from this model initiative.

 Programs That Inspire
Bringing in the Good Guys

In a city in the Northeast with a 56 percent population of Latinos, this center responds to the changing needs of its families, many of who were transitioning from their welfare-to-work training programs to new employment schedules. The center tailored its operation schedule to suit parents' needs, and made a special effort to include the extended family in all its activities and planning.

In turn, parents were asked to extend their own commitment to their children's center by taking personal and vacation days to become involved in the program activities. The administrator would encourage parents to invest in their children's futures, telling them "Even if you lose a day's wages, you have saved thousands in therapy and pain for the rest of the child's life. Your children will know they can always count on Mami and Papi." Fathers and other male caregivers—who in Latin America traditionally take a less active role in childrearing—were invited to participate in a Good Guys program where only fathers and their children spent time together in outings and activities, guided by two Spanish-speaking male family service providers. In an inspirational tone, fathers were invited to take charge of their children and to join them in an experience that the children would remember for the rest of their lives. At the end of each outing, tired and increasingly conscious of the hard work as well as the joy in parenting, the fathers became more understanding of the responsibilities mothers face when they are the main caregivers. The program is so successful that last year's ending activity involved nine hundred fathers. As a staff member recounted:

> For one family, our center's efforts had a dramatic impact, because a new avenue of communication opened between mother and absent father, and a new sense of family enriched the child. Robertito's parents had been divorced since he was 3 months old, and the father was never involved in his care. The mother was a strong and active caregiver, always insisting Robertito be involved in all center activities. When the Good Guys program began, I asked the mother to contact and invite Robertito's father, but the mother was reticent. Eventually, she came in and asked me to invite the father directly, as she didn't feel comfortable talking with him. Right there in her presence, I called and urged him to attend, saying, "We love Robertito, and we don't want him to miss out on this very important event." The father was reluctant, saying he didn't think the mother would allow him to take the child. The father and child went together to the activity, and to the following ones, including a session where the fathers and their children made a scrapbook with the photos they each took with a disposable camera provided by the center. Robertito's mother insisted on attending this session as a helper, since only fathers were invited, because she wanted to see how the father and son related. At first, the parents did not talk, but as the mother passed around materials, they began to talk about what to use, where to place each photo... At the end of the activity, the mother was crying and told me, "This is the first time in five years we have been able to do things together." At the end of Robertito's scrapbook, there is a photo taken at this session, with Robertito sitting proudly between his mother and father, smiling, with his arms around both of them.[26]

Going Out into the Community

Use the following guidelines to develop strategies and activities that link your program to the community, connect with community issues and opportunities, and help you know the communities you serve and become an active participant in the community through collaboration and resource sharing.

Extend the Program into the Community

In order to maximize chances for intergenerational relationships to form between your students and the community, involve children in activities that extend into their homes and neighborhood, such as weekly visits to a senior center or aiding neighbors in a community garden. Such program activities model a commitment to the children's communities. Model programs for serving Latinos of various ages in different areas have attested to the importance of interweaving services and activities across generations. The *Círculos* program, for instance, focused on providing culturally responsive family support by helping elders define their own strategies for linking their families with resources and keeping actively involved in the lives of young children.[27]

The *Nuestro Barrio/Nuestra Gente* project in the previous section can offer teachers and service providers a suitable background to begin to interact with the families' neighborhoods and communities.

The first step is to plan a visit to some of the sites the families frequent on a regular basis, whether it is a school, a clinic, a bank, or a playground. The *Nuestro Barrio/Nuestra Gente* project highlighted the places and daily activities where families include the young child. Pick one of those places that you think may be suitable for taking a group of children and their families. Outings with a group of young children and some family members are perfect opportunities to reinforce the social behaviors that are so valued by the family. The families that go will be proud when the children on the trip are *bien educados*—well behaved. Make sure you and the families talk about the rules that matter to them and to you and work together to uphold them.

To get the flavor of the life of the child, what can prepare teachers better than actually experiencing the places where the children and families spend time? Sit at the park where the child plays, observe how children share, bicker, and call for adult help. What are the obstacles and learning opportunities in this setting? How do the adults interact with the children in the markets where the family shops? In many cases, Latino families may live in enclaves, generating a call for products and food that are familiar to them, and frequenting the shops where they can relate to the personnel in Spanish. In other cases, Latinos may be more isolated, or a smaller part of the population, and therefore lack stores that reflect their tastes and needs. In such cases, they may be more inclined to go to large supermarkets or visit various stores to fill their grocery list. All of these offer different learning opportunities that you can draw on for your program.

As an introduction to a classroom trip to one of these markets, you can buy and take photos of some of the products with which you think the young children might be familiar. Bring back products with Spanish labels, as well as other ethnic foods, to incorporate in your play centers. Back in the classroom, during circle or meeting time, you can bring out these products and ask if any recognize them or know how their families use them. The following activity will give you ideas for your field trip to neighborhood sites.

BRINGING IDEAS TO LIFE
Visiting a Family's Favorite Place

As a follow-up to the *Nuestro Barrio/Nuestra Gente* project, organize an outing to one of the sites a family visits on a regular basis. Invite family members to join you.

This activity goes further than a community mapping, giving the whole class a more intimate experience of a place one of their peers frequents, as well as a chance for the children to be the "experts." The use of various media to make a multi-media representation of the place is especially helpful to second language learners and children with special needs.

Materials:
- Instant cameras and film
- Varied art materials
- Clipboards, paper, and pencils
- Audio or video recorders

Steps:
1. First, familiarize yourself with the site. Explain your plan and make sure you have permission and audio, video, and photo releases from the families and any people who are in charge of the sites you will visit.

2. Prepare a clipboard for the adults and older siblings, as well as the younger children. Divide the group into three smaller groups. Depending on whether you go to an indoor or outdoor site and how many adults join your outing, ask them each to pick an aspect of the place they would like to focus on: social environment, physical environment, or action. Brainstorm what they think they may find in each area.

3. Discuss ways in which you can gather information about the site. For example, children who frequent the place can talk about what they do there, who they come with, and what they like about the place. Clipboards for each aspect can have questions that you have brainstormed before leaving the classroom, such as:

Who is here?	What is here?	What is going on?
• People	• Buildings, trees, objects	• Games
• Greetings	• Art, animals, traffic signals	• Traffic
• Interactions	• Fountains, benches, play structures	• Movement
		• Reading

4. If you are at an indoor site, or a site that is supervised by an adult, make sure you introduce yourself and the group to the people in charge and have children greet these adults respectfully. Understand the rules.

5. Children and adults can watch and describe, draw, take photos, make an audio- or videotape, and participate in the goings-on.

6. For follow-up activities, you can engage the adults, siblings, and children in creating a book about the place using photos and drawings. For example, they can capture the games they saw children and adults play, include the conversations they heard between people as captions; or portray the action in postures, friezes, puppet plays, or a three-dimensional model of the place.

Connect with Community Issues

A Latino family's strongest asset is its interdependence with others. As Dr. Gloria Rodriguez, founder of AVANCE, points out, historically, *la comunidad* (the community of neighbors and friends) has been key to the survival and development of Latino children and families in the United States, from the *hermandades* (brotherhoods) formed to help the transition of compatriots immigrating to the United States to the *mutualistas* (mutual aid societies) that gathered community resources to support neighbors or members in need.[28]

As programs that serve young children benefit from strengthening their ties to the communities, the presence of program managers and teachers in community forums is vital for forging lasting relationships with families. First, early childhood educators can meet families on their own ground, where they are problem-solving the comprehensive needs of the family. Second, they can learn about the resources and assets that exist in the community, as well as the challenges. This will enable teachers to both hear and share educational priorities within the context in which people live, making sure the interests of the children are always considered in any plan or initiative, from neighborhood revitalization to housing and schools.

Remember that when people in these forums see you are interested, that you take your role as a teacher as a civic duty and reach beyond the classroom door, they will develop a sense of loyalty to your program, and may be delighted to respond to your requests and contribute to your program. Families will respond to a committed teacher who reaches out to their communities. Rely on Latino community liaisons, *comadres*—literally, one who shares mothering responsibility, mentors, advocates, translators, and religious leaders to co-teach, share information, recruit, and gather needs and priorities from their constituents.

 ### Programs That Inspire
A Migrant Program Reaches Out

In a rural, isolated area where the harvest season attracts a large population of Latino migrant workers, the Migrant Head Start program took the lead in responding to the needs of its growing community of migrant families—many of whom were increasingly settling more permanently in this beautiful, mountainous, and harsh area. While the federal migrant program funds no longer supported school-age migrant children during the summer, the Migrant Head Start program applied for USDA funds to provide these children meals and coordinated parent volunteers to prepare and deliver meals to the children in the migrant camps.

This program's responsiveness extended to building relationships outside of the center that blossomed into an organic helping community of families adopting families, supporting each other, just like the *hermandades* of the early Puerto Rican immigrants. This effort resulted in uniting diverse families to provide stability and a smooth transition into this rural area. Starting with a Christmas meal outreach, the Head Start program and the migrant families united with Mormon families—who had been established in the area for generations—in order to build ties and link with resources and local knowledge. In this way, a coalition was formed that integrated the newcomers into the life of the region through personal connections among families.

Once these community connections were forged, other connections followed. Now the center's monthly professional development for parents counts on the expertise of many community resources. For instance, representatives from the legal aid service offer workshops dealing with immigrant issues and legal status, and family therapists provide support and training on topics that include emotional concerns and abuse.

Understanding the significant housing challenges faced by migrant families, the early childhood program sought federal funds to design and build a welcoming space for families in their new child care center, a homelike place with computers and a sofa where parents could drop in and that incorporated resources for the whole family. In the same vein, to further serve the comprehensive needs of families, the program brought the food bank to the center, instead of families having to go to a food bank.

Collaborate with Other Institutions to Offer Adult Learning Opportunities in the Community

Empowerment of the family is beneficial to children, their families, and to the quality of the program. Empowerment to Latinos does not usually mean status or achievement, but rather having the respect of others, serving as mentors and models for the community, and advocating for their own and others' children.

Seeing the family in its place in the community, the program can facilitate this empowerment by providing development activities that build the skills of family members, beginning with their responsibilities as parents and role models for their children and expanding to their roles in the community, both a commitment and an obligation that is highly valued in many cultures. In order to support these developments, you can connect with local community learning centers that offer adult development classes to families of young children and combine efforts to include your students' families in the literacy and other professional development these centers and schools offer. You can build a learning wish list based on questions from the brainstorm list of the *Family Focus Group* activity in the previous section. Approach an appropriate agency that would have resources and expertise in some of the topics families have identified. Community learning centers may already offer computer classes and English as a Second Language classes; local factories may also offer workplace English language instruction; local clinics or hospitals often give workshops on disabilities, nutrition, prenatal care, socio-emotional issues, and much more. Negotiate a role your program—including staff and families—can play in designing, teaching, and participating in these learning opportunities.

Serve As a Link to Community Resources

Quality programs emphasize the value of building knowledge about community resources and, in fact, dedicate portions of their program assessment to document progress on this particular focus.[29] Preparing the teacher to join in mutually supportive partnerships with families calls for an inquiry approach, one that focuses on listening to and learning from the child's community. Where are the community's assets? How can your program work with community agencies towards common goals? The following Community Assets questionnaire and corresponding inventory form can serve as examples if you wish to pursue collaboration or if you simply wish to create a resource book for future planning and development.

Frequently, family members join groups where they take a leadership position or have ongoing responsibilities, such as a lay church group or a neighborhood action coalition. Recognizing and building on the expertise of families is part and parcel of being a respectful, committed, and equitable teacher. Families shouldn't always be viewed as "in need." They can provide you with support and connection with their communities. Once you gather information from the agencies with which you want to connect, you can use the *Community Assets Inventory* in the Appendix as a model to build a resource book that can be used and added on to as your relationship with surrounding communities deepens.

Another way to unite forces in the interest of the children is a visioning process such as the one carried out in a Beacon School in Brooklyn, NY. The whole community was gathered, including preschool teachers, families, and children, as well as the feeder schools that would receive them in the future, service agencies representatives, the pastor and congregation of a neighboring church, political figures, and other movers and shakers in this poor, crime-ridden section of Brooklyn. The retreat, which was videotaped and then distributed to families as well as other stakeholders and the media, involved everyone in imagining the future of their children, of their neighborhood, of their schools. The results of this process were used to plan the school's curriculum, create family-style clusters of teachers, and formulate current and future reforms. More importantly, the video was continuously played to maintain the spirit of the retreat and inspire the community's betterment.

A strategy that can be successful, perhaps as an outgrowth of family focus groups or a family workshop, is to engage families in defining their own action plans to carry out in their homes, in the preschool and schools, and in their communities in order to reach their long-term goals for their children. The *Meta/Goal* tool in Appendix 6 will aid you in helping families identify how to leverage resources at all levels to support their children in reaching the goals they have set.

Summing Up: New Beginnings Together

Teachers face an increasingly complex and challenging role: not simply teaching what they know works but also becoming more active and involved with a very diverse population of children and families. The dilemma is to reach each and every child. There are so many aspects to teaching, from guiding the child, to extending the program to the homes and communities, as this chapter proposes. What I suggest here is to focus on caring, bringing back the heart and the relationship as the *basis* for teaching. Think back to how we learned to talk and walk. What motivated us? Do you remember your favorite teacher? What was it that endures in our memories? It's our inspiring relationships that spur us on, that model for us the next step to take, that guide us, and that hold our hands as we sharpen our skills and knowledge.

As in any venture, an investment in building a meaningful and equitable relationship with the child and the extended family is a time-consuming and formidable task. Now, early education teachers have to deal with the demands of accountability and testing and all the paperwork associated with these measures. Teachers and administrators, especially at the preschool level, are hard-pressed for time and energy to fill all the responsibilities of providing a quality, stable education to *all* children. After all, most came to this career not for the money and glory, but for the children.

Teachers who open their hearts and respond to the whole community surrounding the child create lasting and supportive relationships. For Latinos, as for many others, the extended family and its circle of friends and *gente*—people—are key to the child's upbringing. *Compromiso*—commitment—means to be bound in a promise to others. It is a mutual act. A committed teacher will engender committed families. A culturally and linguistically responsive teacher therefore:

- Understands that to know a child, she must know the child's community
- Extends her work to reach the child's family circle and neighborhood
- Welcomes members of the child's extended family as co-teachers, co-planners, and initiators of activities
- Is prepared to work with parents when there are disagreements
- Provides opportunities for intergenerational engagement that mirrors *la familia*

The next pages of this chapter offer some reflection questions and resources to help you put into practice some of the principles reflecting the values of *la familia*. The following chapter will lead you to incorporate what you've learned through your involvement with families and their communities into the environment and climate you create in your classroom.

Reflection and Discussion Questions

Intergenerational Interactions

1. What in your program do you see as valuable intergenerational interactions?
2. As you think about your family engagement activities, where could you see opportunities for family members of different ages to interact informally?

3. What learning and value do you see in your activities for which both children and adults gather, converse, or play together?

4. How do children in your program receive cues about the social consequences of their behavior and develop a sense of responsibility towards others?

5. Are there informal or formal ways that young children in your program can observe and "apprentice" from older peers?

6. What features could you put in your program to strengthen intergenerational bonds?

7. How has an extended family's involvement made a difference in the life of a child?

Strengthening the Home–School Connection

1. What options do you have to reinforce and build on what the child is learning at home?

2. What experiences could you include in the classroom environment that would echo some of the child's favorite activities at home?

3. How can the home vocabulary be expanded?

4. How will you measure the child's progress in reaching the goals the family has set?

5. How can the behaviors and cues the child hears at home be reinforced in the classroom?

6. What channels are open for mutual contributions of ideas and practices?

7. How are the families and communities engaged in defining the direction of program and practice?

Action in the Community

1. What support do you get from and give to the communities from which the children come?

2. What pathways have you forged to coordinate resources and assets in the communities you serve?

3. How does your program build knowledge about surrounding communities?

4. How do you ensure that your community knowledge is tracked and used in your program and curriculum development?

5. How does your program contribute to community forums and to action plans that respond to the comprehensive needs and strengths of your families?

Related Resources

Intergenerational Interactions

Generations United

This membership organization is dedicated to providing support to intergenerational collaboration to improve the lives of children, youth, and the elderly. Programs include resources for grandparents serving as caregivers to young children, and for those working with elder caregivers. Access information and materials online at *<www.gu.org>*.

Zero to Three

Search the archives for articles on including grandparents in the classroom. For example, search for the words: resources and grandparents. See *<www.zerotothree.org>*.

Other Resources:

Booth Church, E. 1994. "Learning from Our Elders." *Scholastic Early Childhood Today:* 40–41.

Bouchard, D., and R. H. Vickers. 1990. *The Elders Are Watching.* Tofino, Canada: Eagle Dancer Enterprises. This illustrated poem presents indigenous views on elders and their roles, and it can be a useful tool to compare and contrast cultural views.

Ortiz, J. M. 1999. *Nurturing Your Child with Music: How Sound Awareness Creates Happy, Smart, and Confident Children.* Hillsboro, Oregon: Beyond Words Publishing.

In this book, speech, language, self-identity, play, and behavior are approached through sound relationships with peers, elders, and everyday home activities.

Strengthening the Home–School Connection

Some children's books that portray Latino and other families in non-stereotypical ways:

Alma Flor Ada's and Gary Soto's books and poems for children also offer realistic snapshots of everyday life for children of Latino ancestry. Dr. Ada has pioneered programs and materials for working with families using children's literature and family stories. Visit their websites: *<www.almaflorada.com/>* and *<falcon.jmu.edu/~ramseyil/soto.htm>*.

Garza, C. L., Harriet, R., and D. Schecter. Spanish translation by Francisco X. Alarcón. 1996. *In My Family/En Mi Familia*. San Francisco: Children's Book Press/Libros Para Niños. A family album that lovingly shares the artist's memories of the Hispanic cultural experience as lived in the Southwest.

Garza, C. 1990. *Family Pictures/Cuadros de Familia*. San Francisco: Children's Book Press/Libros Para Niños. Growing up in Texas and fully immersed in her family's Mexican traditions, the author presents her recollections of being a child.

Lists of books for young readers that can serve as a source to early childhood professionals' understanding of the real life of Latinos in America can be found at *<www.eou.edu/~clauritz/hispanic.html>*.

The National Center for Culturally Responsive Educational Systems (NCCRESt) has information regarding the overrepresentation of culturally and linguistically diverse learners in special education, including *Addressing Culturally and Linguistically Diverse Student Overrepresentation in Special Education: Guidelines for Parents*, written by Alfredo Artiles and Beth Harry and available online at *<www.nccrest.org/Briefs%5CParent_Brief.pdf>*.

Ada, A. F., and R. Zubizarreta. 2001. "Parent Narratives: The Cultural Bridge Between Latino Parents and their Children." In *The Best for Our Children: Critical Perspectives on Literacy for Latino Students*, edited by M. L. Reyes and J. J. Halcón. NY: Teachers College Press.

Building Strong Programs for Strong Families, available online at *<www.head startinfo.org/publications/hsbulletin77/cont_77.htm>*. This website from the Head Start Bulletin, Issue 77, provides information, activities, and ideas for enhancing father involvement in your program.

Action in the Community

For an example of teaching ideas based on public art, go to *<www.cambridgeartscouncil.org/public_art_tour/map_06.html>*, where you will find sample fact sheets, neighborhood maps, and activity sheets for various grade levels.

The *Parent Services Project* is an exemplary program that extends beyond the early childhood center to a variety of activities and collaborations involving parents. Information about programs, training, and materials are available at *<www.parentservices.org>*.

Facilitating Community Change, by Darvin Ayre, Gruffie Clough, and Tyler Norris, is an extensive manual that provides a flexible model for working in partnership with communities on any issue, and it includes a wide variety of tools, especially graphic planning tools, to engage in assessing, preparing, tracking, and implementing a collaborative action plan. Available from Grove Consultants International, (800) 49GROVE, and through their website *<www.grove.com>*.

Endnotes

1 Schonkoff, J. P., and D. A. Phillips. 2000. *From Neurons to Neighborhoods: The Science of Early Childhood Development.* Washington, D.C.: National Academy Press.

2 Fuller, B., C. Eggers-Piérola, S. D. Holloway, X. Liang, and M. F. Rambaud. 1996. "Rich Culture, Poor Markets: Why Do Latino Parents Forgo Preschooling?" *Teacher's College Record* 97 (3): 400–418.

3 Delgado-Gaitan, C. 1990. *Literacy for Empowerment: The Role of Parents in Children's Education.* London: Falmer Press. *Goals 2000: Reforming Education to Improve Student Achievement.* April 30, 1998. Washington, D.C.: U.S. Department of Education, *<www.ed.gov/G2K/>*.

4 Fuller et al., "Rich Culture, Poor Markets."

Bernhard, J. K., M. L. Lefebvre, K. M. Kilbride, G. Chud, and R. Lange. 1998. "Troubled Relationships in Early Childhood Education: Parent–Teacher Interactions in Ethnoculturally Diverse Child Settings." *Early Education* 9 (1): 5–28. Shannon, S. M., and S. L. Latimer. 1996. "Latino Parent Involvement in Schools: A story of Struggle and Resistance." *The Journal of Educational Issues of Language Minority Students* 16: 301–319.

5 Vidal de Haymes, M., and I. Medina. 1995. "Latino Families and Child Welfare: Engaging Informal Supportive Cultural Practices." *Empowerment and Latino Families.* Chicago: Family Resource Coalition, 13 (3 and 4): 26–29.

6 Eggers-Piérola, C., S. D. Holloway, B. Fuller, and M. F. Rambaud. 1995. "Raising Them Right: Individualism and Collectivism in Mothers' Socialization Goals." Paper presented at the Annual Meeting of the American Educational Researchers' Association in San Francisco, April 18. Etzioni, A. 1999. "The Good Society" *The Journal of Political Philosophy* 7 (1) 88–103.

7 *Comadre* and *compadre,* literally "co-mother" and "co-father," are reserved for the closest friends, who, although not related, are considered family. *Padrino* or *madrina* are the godparents.

8 Vidal de Haymes, M. and I. Medina. These networks serve as economic and social supports and can be instrumental in the advancement and survival of the family.

9 In this publication, I have chosen to use *teacher* to encompass all those who care for a young child in a structured setting, including early childhood program directors, center and kindergarten through grade three teachers, family childcare providers, assistant teachers, and kith and kin caregivers.

10 The factory.

11 Generations United Report. *<www.gu.org/projg&ointro.htm>* Last modified June 29, 2004.

12 Holloway et al., "Rich Culture, Poor Markets." Greenfield, P., and R. Cocking. 1994. *Cross-Cultural Roots of Minority Child Development.* Hillsdale, NJ: Lawrence Erlbaum. Eggers-Piérola, C. 1993. "Beyond Inclusion: A Review of Ethnographies of Latino Students." Unpublished Qualifying Paper, Harvard University.

13 Northwest Regional Education Laboratory. 2000. *Improving Student Success Through School, Family, and Community Partnerships: Where Do We Go From Here?* Conference Proceedings. Downloaded June 11, 2004 from *<www.nwrel.org/cfc/publications/improving_student.html>*.

14 Shannon & Latimer, "Latino Parent Involvement in Schools."

15 Bailey, D. B., D. Skinner, P. Rodriguez, D. Gut, and V. Correa. 1999. "Awareness, Use, and Satisfaction with Services for Latino Parents of Young Children with Disabilities." *Exceptional Children* 65 (3): 367–381.

16 U.S. Department of Education, National Center for Education Statistics. 2003. *Status and Trends in the Education of Hispanics (NCES 2003-008)*. Washington, D.C.: 12.

17 Bernhard, J., J. Pollard, C. Eggers-Piérola, and A. Morin. 2000. "Infants and Toddlers in Canadian Multi-age Childcare Settings: Age, Ability, and Linguistic Inclusion." In *Research Connections Canada* IV: 791–85. Ottawa, ON: Canadian Child Care Federation. Gonzalez-Mena, J. 1997. *Multicultural Issues in Childcare.* Mountain View, CA: Mayfield Publishing. Gonzalez-Mena, J., and D. W. Eyer. 1989. *Infants, Toddlers, and Caregivers.* Mountain View, CA: Mayfield Publishing. Derman-Sparks, L., and the A.B.C. Task Force. 1989. *Anti-Bias Curriculum: Tools for Empowering Young Children.* Washington, D.C.: National Association for the Education of Young Children.

18 Evans, J. L. 1997. "Both Halves of the Sky: Gender Socialization in the Early Years." Coordinators' Notebook No. 20. Washington, DC: The Consultative Group on Early Childhood Care and Development.

19 Erickson, M. F., and K. Kurz-Riemer. 1999. *Infants, Toddlers, and Families: A Framework for Support and Intervention.* New York: The Guilford Press.

20 Ibid., 131.

21 Zeanah, C. H., J. A. Larrieu, S. S. Heller, S. and J. Valliere. 2001. "Infant–Parent Relationship Assessment." In *Handbook of Infant Mental Health,* second edition, edited by C. H. Zeanah, 222-235. New York: Guilford Press. These authors write about the importance of knowing the context surrounding choice, decisions, and process in child rearing from how the parents talk about the child to what they do when a child is upset or misbehaves.

22 Gonzalez-Alvarez, L. I. 1998. "A Short Course in Sensitivity Training: Working with Hispanic Families of Children with Disabilities." *Teaching Exceptional Children* 31 (2): 73–77.

23 Eggers-Piérola, C., S. D. Holloway, B. Fuller, and M. F. Rambaud. 1995. "Raising Them Right: Variations in the Socialization Concepts of Ethnically-Diverse Mothers." Paper presented at the Annual Meeting of the American Educational Research Association, San Francisco, CA.

24 Eggers-Piérola, "Beyond Inclusion."

25 Chud, G., and R. Fahlman. 1995. *Honouring Diversity Within Child Care and Early Education.* Vancouver, Canada: Ministry of Skills, Training and Labour.

26 Magdalena Rosales-Alban.

27 Generations United Report, 45. 2004.

28 Rodriguez, G. G. 1999. *Raising Nuestros Niños: Bringing Up Latino Children in a Bicultural World.* New York: Fireside.

29 See the Self-Assessment Toolkit for Head Start and Early Head Start Programs. May 2002. The Self-Assessment Toolkit for Head Start and Early Head Start Programs for Region I (New England) is available in electronic format at <*www.acf.dhhs.gov/programs/region1/hsh.htm*>.

CHAPTER

3

Pertenencia/Belonging

Welcoming All Children

Focusing on *Pertenencia*

The moment you open your door to a child you have a chance to welcome her, as well as her family, into the fold and deliberately make a space for her in your classroom. As soon as the child enters your room, a whole new and exciting world opens up before her. This world can also be foreign and fearsome to enter, at times.

An Invitation In

Imagine you are walking into a classroom for the first time. You feel nervous, but the first thing you experience is smiling faces all turning to welcome you. *"¡Hola! Como está?"* the teacher greets you in your mother tongue. *"¡Hola!* Hi! How are you?" chime in the children in the midst of the activities. And there is so much going on! Just like a Sunday gathering of *la familia*—your extended family—back home in Colombia. And so many vibrant colors, you really feel like it's spring, although it's snowing in this foreign place where you've settled. You see a garden in the middle of the room where two toddlers are watering and spritzing some lush green and purple plants; a pair of young children carefully planting seeds; a teacher, kneeling and pruning seedlings with a teenager, while keeping a watchful eye over the room. Other children come and go; they stop to watch or to join the gardening party. Surrounding the garden—just like the *plazas* you left back in Colombia—there are *tenderetes,* markets stalls stacked with pyramids of oranges and guayabas and many other fruits made of plastic. Your eyes are drawn to a corner of the room by the fragrant aroma of toasted bananas, reminding you of those delicious *tostones* of your childhood. Eight preschoolers and a grandmother are gathered around the kitchen area, helping another teacher set up for a "formal" lunch around the big, low table where everyone eats together daily. Even the youngest child—barely a toddler—is involved, playing with different ways to fold the napkins with one of her friends. Two other young children are in the block area, in the process of building a sprawling village, as a third, younger child joins them and launches a toy car down a ramp the others just built. In your town in Colombia, schools did not have those big blocks in the classrooms, nor had you ever played with them, but you couldn't wait to try. Immediately, one of these children comes over to you and invites you to help. You're going to like being in *this* classroom!

What makes a new place feel welcoming? The sometimes-elusive sense of belonging—*pertenencia*—is usually at play. In the example above, the hypothetical "you"—a new teaching assistant of Colombian background—saw a myriad of activities that were interesting in themselves, but also led to interactions that build relationships and shared experiences. You saw vibrant reminders of the colors and places dear to you. You got a whiff of a familiar smell. You saw how the group prepared to come together for lunch and how people helped each other. These were things you could connect with or that you wanted to connect with, like the building block activity. You also saw the different ways children and adults initiated and joined interactions. Some, like helping fold the napkins, may have been typical of your own upbringing. And, more importantly, you were personally invited to come in and take a role in an activity; there was a place for you in the group, and the group reached out to help you feel at ease.

Before any of us can learn, we must feel supported and comfortable. This provides the ground that enables motivation, learning, and success to take place and, at the same time, allows learners to risk learning new things and to thrive in a new environment. Making the home–school connection is essential in providing a foundation for transitioning into new situations. Cultural competence and caring should be visible and palpable from the start. A culturally responsive program, as shown in the example above, is a place that radiates a sense of family. Children can see themselves and familiar ways reflected in the classroom and feel safe to be themselves and to grow, protected, finding many ways to interact with others and with the things in the environment.

Belonging implies a relationship beyond comfort, however. When we feel a sense of belonging somewhere, we want to stay, and we want to come back.

A combination of the familiar and the new and stimulating contributes to this desire. This balance between the familiar and unfamiliar pushes learners beyond their own limits of understanding and makes a learning program a productive and enriching place for all, including the adults. Some children may want to just watch and *not* be part of a group, especially at first, when they are newcomers and the group is an unknown. So, particularly for those who come with a different experience of home, teachers may need to think about what it means to keep a balance between the known and the unknown.

This chapter is about building a classroom culture, climate, and environment that echoes positive relationships within extended families and fosters group cohesiveness and caring within the program. At the same time, this chapter offers ideas for supporting the child's individual and cultural identities as well as for the formation of an inclusive group identity. In other words, this chapter strives to answer the questions: How can classroom rules, routines, and environment contribute to an inviting, nurturing climate and a sense of belonging in the Latino child? And, how can the classroom culture transform and be enriched by the differences each and every child brings?

Educators can use this chapter to begin to untangle the different values and contexts embodied in *pertenencia*—translated as *belonging* in English—and to consciously put in place elements and relationships that enable the classroom to be a welcoming place where *all* feel a sense of belonging. Ideas in this chapter encourage teachers to integrate the different influences on a child's identity, including family, group attachments, mother tongue, and cultural ways of communicating. I also suggest ways to prepare spaces where children see themselves and their families reflected throughout the environment, as well as how to gain an understanding of what others bring from their home and culture. Along with some activities to bring *pertenencia* to life, I include snapshots of model programs, reflection and discussion questions, and a sampling of relevant resources.

Latino Views on *Pertenencia*

Dime con quién andas, y te diré quién eres.
Tell me who you go with, and I'll tell you who you are.

This Spanish proverb, commonly used throughout Spain and the Americas, puts a different spin on the English equivalent—birds of a feather flock together—suggesting how personal and group identity are interwoven. Another saying, "*Dime de dónde vienes y te dire quién eres*"—Tell me where you come from, and I'll tell you who you are—refers to the importance of origins and history in shaping identity.

In Latino cultures, *pertenencia* means identifying as part of a group, as more than an individual. This value is especially important in a culture where social contacts are the key means of access, support, and information. Many Latinos' identity is closely linked to their sense of belonging and allegiance—to their native and adopted countries, to their culture, and to their families and communities.

While many cultures may have common perceptions of belonging, the English translation of the word doesn't adequately convey the full meaning attached to *pertenencia* in the Spanish-speaking world. Whereas the root of the word belong refers to being suitable, or suited to a group, *pertenencia* emphasizes the interactive phenomenon of belonging: to pertain to, to be obligated to, to relate to, to be an integral part of something. Within Latino and other group-centered cultures, belonging implies commitment and obligation to others—*compromiso*—a value I discuss in more depth in Chapter 5. Belonging to the extended Latino family or community means helping and respecting each other, as well as sharing experiences and responsibilities.

A Dominican *conocido*[1]—acquaintance—told me: "*Para mi, sentir pertenencia es sentirme dueño*"—for me, feeling belonging is feeling ownership. This intriguing remark made me think about the complex relationship between one person and the place, people, or things that make him feel empowered, thus investing him with a stake, a responsibility, and a role that ownership entails, as well as the benefits. Giving and getting are interlaced in the Latino concept of *pertenencia*. At the core of *pertenencia* is duty to others. In other words, *pertenencia* speaks of a reciprocal relationship that benefits both individual and group. Feeling connection with others gives individuals support, models, and power in pursuing their lives and contributing to society. On the one hand, the family clan provides shelter, guidance, protection, and love—the basis of trust. On the other hand, children are socialized from a very early age to care for others and to contribute to the household. Thus, children's awareness of self and belonging is built on having a purpose and an active role within the family and the community.

Marjorie Orellana describes how a young child, already at age six, shows the sequence of her life in the past and the future by depicting herself in a timeline of helping acts, with captions like: "I want to help wash the dishes for my mom… I want to help my mom and dad paint a house for them… I want to buy clothes for my brothers. I can work to buy them things… I will make the bed and help my brothers to get dressed."[2]

Developing a sense of belonging in the early childhood setting helps children from any culture transition more smoothly into a new, supportive learning "family." A commitment to the group builds upon and refines the interpersonal skills and ways of learning that are so vital in the functioning of the family network. Feeling a sense of belonging is particularly key to newcomers and children of migrant workers. Without the support of the extended family and community, these children may feel isolated from others. Their mobility causes a lack of ties in the new community and interrupted school years and relationships, thus making them more vulnerable without the connections and supports needed to transition well into school and neighborhood. They may then have a hard time finding footing and inspiration in the new culture or setting. Educators play a vital role in giving each child a chance to make connections and develop a sense of belonging.

Creating a Climate for *Pertenencia*

In many ways, the values that will enable you and your program to inspire a sense of belonging in all children are already part of your implicit mission as educators. Mindfully focusing on these, making them more visible from the very first contact with families, and developing strategies based on these values will engender an atmosphere where each and every person feels welcome. As I present *pertenencia* in this chapter, these values can be summed up as follows.

Values in *Pertenencia*

respecting and trusting others	being respected and trusted
appreciating others	being appreciated
sharing with others	benefiting from what others have
helping others	counting on others

These values suggest that culturally and linguistically responsive learning programs and schools adopt the following principles in the classroom:

- Nurture the development of individual, cultural, and group identity in each child
- Create an atmosphere that is familial and echoes solidarity, where the group of children and adults form trusting connections and strong commitments to one another
- Consciously integrate cultural ways of expression, learning, and relating in order to facilitate the integration of the diverse children and the transformation of the class culture

Creating a climate of *pertenencia* that celebrates the strengths of our multicultural society helps educators assure positive outcomes for children.[3] Yet, it can be difficult to do and requires educators to sensitively reconcile and integrate cultural differences.

What these principles may look like in action will depend on the setting and capabilities of your program or school. Do you have a home child care, where substantially changing arrangements or modifying certain routines may be difficult? Do you run or teach in a center that is part of a franchise where the physical environment is set up the same in each classroom according to program requirements and materials? Do you have limited contact with families? Is your kindergarten through fifth grade program attached to a high school or a residential facility where mothers work and study? You may think of creative ways to adapt some of the ideas in this chapter, and the following chapters will help build your program's capacity to reach out to families and communities, to create opportunities for children and staff to learn together and to learn from each other.

Throughout the following sections, the activities and ideas will echo various ways to nurture a sense of *pertenencia*, from bridging cultural identities to creating a sense of belonging through daily rituals, rules, and routines. The social skills so important to bonding with a group are threads throughout this chapter, including fostering relationships and connections, nurturing through verbal and nonverbal expressions of caring, and building pro-social skills such as respect and responsibility for others. In the following pages, I also give some ideas for setting up the learning environment with spaces where the whole group or small groups can gather, as well as a way to introduce individuals to the classroom in a comfortable, welcoming way.

Bridging Cultural Identities

Identity is first shaped at home. Young children observe models and then make choices based on what and whom they relate to, as well as on their personalities. As we grow and move into different worlds, identity also transforms into new, more complex identities, taking on new dimensions. Children of different cultures may very well encounter a classroom culture that unwittingly denies or devalues what has shaped their identities and way of life. Instead of forcing each child to conform or to choose between one or another of these identities, imagine how rich our learning communities could be if each child's multiple origins were honored, and each had the opportunity to develop bicultural identities. As one mother said, "Being bicultural means being able to choose the best of both cultures." As educators, we can help young children in this critical period of becoming bicultural. We can help them build bridges between cultural identities. In this chapter, I offer some ideas you can use to begin to explore the challenges and opportunities that names, identity, and being bicultural might present to a Latino child.

Naming Who You Are and Discovering Identity Through Others

I began this book with a story about a teacher's unwillingness to use a child's name, Asunción, in favor of something "easier." A person's name in many Latino cultures symbolizes how individual identity is intertwined with group identity and values and is often a complex combination of maternal, paternal, and baptism names. When introducing a child to the group, the teacher can acknowledge that the child is already a member of a group and include family information in the introduction. Use the richness of names to explore meaning and connections. Is the child's first name handed down through the family? Does the name have a special meaning or express a quality the parent values? Does it refer to an ancestral town? Does it embody a particular hope or value of the parents, or is it a way to honor a loved one? What significance is there in the children's nicknames or the terms of endearment that parents call them? Consider the first-day experience of Asunción and how her teacher got her name wrong. Perhaps the next idea will help you and your teaching team think further about the connections between identity and belonging.

BRINGING IDEAS TO LIFE
What's in a Name?

Use personal stories and children's literature to explore the importance of names. Alma Flor Ada's story, *My Name Is María Isabel,* dramatizes some of the issues newcomer children face, and it can be used by teachers to generate awareness and activities based on names and their meanings. We all have first-day and name stories to draw on that help us understand how identity and belonging are entwined in our name. When someone remembers our names, we feel acknowledged, visible.

The following questions, adapted from Ada's and Campoy's book, *Authors in the Classroom: A Transformative Education Process,*[4] can help teachers reflect on the immigrant child's experience. Please go back to read the story at the beginning of Chapter 1, first.

- Why do you think Asunción—from the story in Chapter 1—or other newcomer children may not correct others when their names are mispronounced?

- Your program may have rules about calling children by their given names. Families and those intimate with a child may use different names and nicknames. What do you feel about calling children by nicknames? Can you think of both positive and negative effects of certain nicknames? In Spanish, for instance, two common terms of endearment are *gordita*—little chubby one—

and *reina*—queen. How would you discuss the use of these nicknames with children? With parents?

- In what ways could you help children explore their own and others' multiple identities? Can you think of activities involving self-portraits, art, musical expression, or autobiographies?
- Does your own name reflect a special meaning or family member?
- How do you feel when someone gets your name wrong?
- Are there times when you enter a new situation and do not know how to behave or what is appropriate? What do you do in that case? What helps? What makes things worse?

 ## Did You Know?
Multiple Identities Means More to Choose From

Did you know that Latinos in the United States are not only a heterogeneous group, but may even bring multiple identities that reshape the cultural heritage each brings? Although most share a language, Spanish, we can't assume that it is their native tongue. Many come to the United States already having moved from one cultural and physical environment into another, acquiring two or more languages—Spanish and perhaps one or two indigenous languages. Gloria Anzaldúa, a well-known Chicana poet, writes in her text about this crossing of borders, of her *mestiza*—mixed European and indigenous—identity, as well as her identity as a woman, moving from the indigenous Nahuatl, to Spanish, to English, and to the Tex-Mex dialect, honoring the origins of all her ancestors and influences.

 ## What Would You Do?
Reconciling and Integrating Cultural Differences

Latinos from different countries, different generations, and different economic and social backgrounds bring with them expectations that may not all harmonize with the anti-bias and gender equity standards that quality education should uphold. Not all culturally valued ways are reasonable to enact in your classroom. Read these two perspectives that follow, and think about how you would handle a similar situation.

A teacher's view:
It's not all rosy and quaint, making a classroom multicultural. And supporting Spanish in the classroom, well, all's not positive there either. What does it say about

a language when the plural of everything with mixed gender is masculine? In Spanish, a boy child is *niño*, and a girl, *niña*. So, if you want to say children and there's a mixed group of children, people say, *"Niños."* What kind of message does that send to the girls? And what do I tell my girls who want to play with trucks and my boys who want to play with dolls when their parents discourage this? I see this every day. One day, when Manuel's father came to pick him up, he was in the dress-up corner playing with his best friend, Claire, an older girl who had adopted him from the first day. They really enjoy playing house together! You should hear them. They chat away all the time, and it's good for Manuel, since he's a little shy about talking. Claire had dressed him up with a frilly apron, and he was pretend cooking with her. His father hit the roof. "Why do you let my boy get dressed like a girl?" I tried to explain that the children all choose their activities, and that Manuel loved to play dress up, as his friend Claire spent much time there.

A parent's view:

How can the teacher not understand that Manuel needs to know that he's a boy? In a parent workshop, they tell me that now, the children at his age are already "exploring their gender." Well, I don't want my boy to "explore" being a girl! I remember how I used to be teased when I was little because I was always with my sisters' friends. I don't want that for my boy."

Your view:

- Can you think of ways to address this conflict with sensitivity?
- What would you say to this teacher, to help her move beyond her frustration?
- It is not enough to say, "We do things differently here." What would you say to this parent?
- How about Manuel? How do you think you can present the situation from his side? Or from Claire's side?
- Can you think of a time and place in which it might be safe and productive to have a discussion with the parent about this? Some centers use puppets to role-play situations, inviting parents to the event and discussing as a group some of the different perspectives.

Honoring the varied influences on children's lives visually is a powerful way to say, "We accept you, and we know you and who you care about." Try the activity below to create this feeling of acceptance and intimacy.

BRINGING IDEAS TO LIFE
Who We Are Webs

From the very first day, you can create a powerful visual of each member of the program community. With photos, maps, and illustrations from magazines, create a web, a visual representation of each child and the different people, places, and things that are part of her world. The purpose of this activity is to recognize that each one's identity is made up of many parts: where she came from, what she experiences and feels, and what she chooses.

First, take photos of each child. Throughout the year, collect different photos of the child and the family to add to the web.

1. Begin by creating a web for each child with string glued to a large piece of poster board. Older children can create their own web.

2. Paste a photo of each child in the center of her web.

3. Explain to the children that they will be making a web of their favorite people, places, and things.

4. Ask children and/or families to bring in photos or draw representations of their cherished family members and dear friends and pets or cut out magazine illustrations of favorite toys, places they go to, or favorite places in their homes. Paste these visuals onto the string web around the child.

5. Display the web prominently on the walls, and take it down for children to add pieces to it once a week.

6. Set aside a time once a week during circle for children to explain what they added and why it's important to them. In this way, you are helping children see how all the things and people around them impact who they are.

? Did You Know?
What's in a Word

Did you know that in Spanish, as in other Western languages except for English, the "I" is not capitalized? On the other hand, the written short form of the formal "you" is capitalized (*Vd.*, for *usted*). Among many Latinos, *usted*—instead of the more familiar *tu*— is used to address not only strangers but also respected and loved family members, including parents and grandparents. The use of language is very telling of our values. The role played by respect for elders and hierarchy among Latinos has influenced the survival of this polite custom through the centuries.

Offering Role Models

Role models serve to bridge cultural identities and extend the home–school connection. A role model from a similar culture who speaks the child's home language presents a touchstone for both the child and family. In particular, Latino adults at programs or schools can serve as a bridge to home. They can facilitate communication and transition into the educational culture and also serve as role models with whom children can identify.

You must, however, pay special attention to not use one particular adult as representative of Latino culture and to not assume that any one Latino's beliefs and practices—even communication styles—are indicative of all the Latino children and families in your center. Find ways to present different role models, whether from real life, from myths and stories, or from history, that represent Latinos with varying looks, experiences, ways of interacting, views, and identities. Children can be inspired by the achievements of the various role models you provide and the dignity and expertise with which they approach an everyday task. Make sure you represent role models who cross traditional gender boundaries, for instance, a female carpenter or a male nurse.

"Insiders" from the culture can help the family feel comfortable, an asset when teachers need to resolve disagreements or explain policies that may be contradictory to parents' wishes. An insider, in the family's perspective, may better understand where they are coming from and perhaps can help interpret their views to other staff. In Chapter 2, I describe how to reach out to extended families and communities so they will be an active presence and influence in your program or school. In Chapter 5, I also point to some ideas for enhancing the program's cultural responsiveness by drawing on the strengths of Latino staff as role models and professionals.

 ## What Would You Do?
Invisible Differences

Latinos have a wide variety of dialects, customs, and even appearances. We may assume that Latinos have olive or darker skin and *mestizo*—mixed European and native—features. We may rely on our ears to pick out the cadence and accent of newcomers to identify where they come from. Sometimes, the differences are not visible.

A teacher's view:

I'm worried about Mark. He's been in the classroom for over a month and has not yet bonded with any of the other children or with me. I have tried, and I'm quite aware of giving each child touchstones in transitioning to this new learning environment. I tried to pull Mark into activities, but he's so shy... Still, Mark has not said a word and doesn't seem to understand when others talk to him. I was becoming concerned about his hearing and language ability, and I called in the parents. When the parents came in, I realized they are newcomers from Mexico and speak Spanish. Since he was white and blue-eyed, I hadn't suspected that he could be Latino. It's a shame. I usually assign children who come from a different background a "buddy" who speaks his language and whom he could connect with, an older child to draw him out and introduce him to some toys. But in this case, I didn't. I made the wrong assumption.

A student's view:

Looking back on my childhood, my Latino identity has impacted my life. Because I don't *look* like what others see as Latino, I wasn't recognized as Latino, not even by other Latinos. Growing up with one foot in my Latino home and one foot in my American world, I was able to coexist in both with relative ease. However, creating a bridge between the two worlds has not been possible. I passed, but I did not fit in with the mainstream. I needed to see somebody who looked like me and felt like me and recognized who I was. I feel I am missing a part of myself.

Your view:

When incoming children enter our schools and our centers, they may come without a file of information, like many immigrant children. Their intake forms may be incomplete or missing. The parents may not be the ones who drop off and pick up the child.

- How do you identify the background of a child?
- What assumptions and expectations do you have of children from different ethnicities? Of children with limited English?
- Could you provide a role model that this child could identify with?
- What are some ways in which you could capitalize on this situation to help others see beyond superficial similarities?
- How can you ensure that a child like Mark develops bonds with the other Latino children as well as with the mainstream children in the program?

Connecting with Families and Connecting with the Group

We often hear the expression "safety in numbers." Part of daring to grow and do something different—that is, to develop—is feeling safe, and feeling safe in a group happens when both the individual and the group are vested in each other's survival and find points of connection to build this investment.

Group gathering places in which to share stories, to play, and to practice the skills of working in a group are vital for creating a sense of belonging in the class.

The placement of activity centers, even the design of the center, can be thought out to present opportunities for connecting with others. Center director Yvette Rodriguez shares how she began planning for this:

> Think about what happens when you enter a building… whom you see and how they greet you has everything to do with how you approach your relationship with the people inside the building. In our center, since we had the luxury of designing our new building, we explicitly asked for a director's office surrounded by glass, right next to the entrance. This alone increased the center's contact with the whole family, especially those most reluctant to enter, such as a grandfather dropping off a child, as the Latino propriety dictated they greet the director, and the accessibility of the center leader made them feel more visible and heard. Now they say, "*Hola*, there's the *directora*. Let me tell you what happened this morning with Pablito." They come in to talk, and sometimes they stay.[5]

The plan for this center was designed so an open kitchen and the placement of the bathrooms lead to many opportunities for the children and adults to cross paths with adults and children from other classrooms. There's more community, and everyone knows each other.

Think of ways to enrich the activity centers you already have in your program in order to enhance connections with home and with peers. A kitchen play area with equipment and materials such as plastic food and dinnerware as well as dress-up areas are favorites in many preschool activity centers. Children can interact around a familiar routine, role play, and begin to negotiate socially, as well as practice familiar vocabulary and take on different identities in these areas. Be flexible. Let the children keep their dress-up costume throughout the day if they like. Rotate the materials on an ongoing basis, asking families to contribute old clothes and objects that are appropriate for the centers.

The organization and arrangements in the learning environment can be consciously adapted to favor group-centered instruction. For instance, when setting up an activity table, placing materials in the center of the table instead of parceling them out in individual portions will encourage negotiating and sharing skills. Learning centers can be designed to replicate familiar neighborhood environments where people interact naturally as they go through their daily activities, like in the *plaza* in Chapter 2. A *placita*—small town square—can be created with centers depicting homes, gardens, markets, a school, and a bank, all surrounding a common play area or a circle space where whole group activities can occur.

Perhaps you can give children opportunities to create their own spaces, like the Mayan-inspired pyramid created by a group of kindergarten through third graders who shared a classroom (see Figure 3–1).

Figure 3–1 *The Putney School Maya Project* (Photo by Costanza Eggers)

Once inviting environments have been created, you may want to work out an orientation process to introduce each new child to these special places. Greeting routines are also important for establishing a sense of courtesy, respect, and belonging.

BRINGING IDEAS TO LIFE
Tour Guide in the Classroom

This activity involves a ritual for introducing each new child to the classroom; engaging a "buddy" to serve as the guide, point person, and informal host of the new child and introducing him to individual children during a classroom tour. Even the youngest children can take part, for instance by offering a hand and a walk-through or by participating in a choral greeting. Some possible components:

1. A "train the trainer" session facilitated by both teachers and children comes up with a plan that is put in action for each new entering student.

2. This plan may involve a "welcome basket" with art materials, books, and a photo book of the children in the classroom involved in activities (see the alphabet book idea in point 4).

3. Negotiate a process with which the children in the classroom feel comfortable, making sure each child has a say and a role in the welcoming routine.

4. Can you think of ways to include the children and families in your program in a book or video that you could show new families? One center I visited created a beautiful alphabet book with photos and text that showed the children in the center in different group activities, such as "N: nursing *niños* at naptime; W: waving wildly at the waterfall!"[6] The book was "published" and distributed to families and sold throughout the community.

Building Pro-Social Skills: Ownership and Obligation

In group-centered cultures, an important part of a child's development is learning how to be an active member of a group. As I show throughout this book, many Latino cultures prize children's cultivation of respect and loyalty, obedience to elders, understanding limits, and attention to each other's needs. By helping children build their pro-social skills and ability to function well within a group, teachers can help them build bridges between cultural identities. The idea is to convey that the children are not alone, that they are cared for, but also that they are accountable not just to themselves, but also to others. The cohesiveness in the learning environment that responds to this cultural principle emanates from interdependence.

A cohesive learning environment that creates a sense of belonging is reflected in children's and adults' interactions: they care for each other, learn from each other, teach each other, and play together. For the teacher, creating an optimum learning environment translates to creating a social context where children and adults feel invested in each other. To foster such an environment, provide many opportunities for children to identify with the group, develop pro-social group skills, and form relationships with peers and adults in the program.

Building relationships and exercising the skills and joys of living together as a group are the first steps towards building a sense of belonging. Therefore, this section also incorporates ways to create a culture of caring, from building socio-emotional skills basic to the child who is *bien educado*—well educated and socialized, empathetic, and giving.

Strategies for teachers to promote pro-social qualities include:

- Modeling empathetic responses
- Modeling consideration of different points of view
- Guiding children to express their own feelings
- Encouraging children to support others

- Helping children understand another's perspective
- Providing children with opportunities to explore alternative solutions[7]

For some time now, we have known that children develop deeper bonds in small groups than in large groups, that there is less aggression, and more interaction, and that in large groups children will tend to divide into smaller groupings by gender.[8] Developmentally, according to some, young children also have a harder time staying within a large group for an activity. As a result, our preschool and kindergarten classrooms in the United States have often been designed around small group free play or structured activities, and we may neglect or avoid organizing large group activities that may cause problems or be frustrating to young children. And yet large groups, often deemed inappropriate for very young children, can also be sources of many subtle and rich language and other learning experiences as well as the basis for a sense of safety that an accepting group can afford.

In some cultures, large groups are occasions when young children learn to be *bien educados*—well-brought up; that is, socialized and educated at once. As they participate in a church service, in an extended family meal, in festivities, or join family members as they harvest a crop, young children learn to look and listen, to do things, to behave in a group, to be attentive, how to show appreciation, and many other complex lessons that provide a foundation for success in the future.[9] These experiences can be recognized as *funds of knowledge*[10] to be shared with others through storytelling, illustration, and dialogue; this builds understanding, literacy, and inquiry skills in a natural way.

We know that the pathway to literacy is language and that relationships lead to conversations. In Chapter 4, I will discuss language and learning in more depth, but let's begin by looking at the role of language in building a sense of *pertenencia*.

Connecting with the Mother Tongue

"Ethnic identity is twin skin to linguistic identity—I am my language. Until I can take pride in my language, I cannot take pride in myself."[13]

Native language is essential in building a sense of belonging, identity, and solidarity, as well as in providing continuity with the home. In Spanish, the term "mother tongue"—*lengua materna*—is the most-used translation of native or first language. However, in contrast to "native language," which implies the language acquired at birth, "mother tongue" suggests the relationship between mother and child, the language the mother speaks, a connection with an experience even before birth.

Children and adults in the child care environment need to be able to use the language they are most familiar with in order to fully express their needs and wishes and in order to better understand others. Making efforts to pair Spanish-speaking adults and children will facilitate this process. Does your program offer incentives for siblings to enroll? Even when this is the case, programs often separate siblings to avoid sibling "rivalry," punishing the connection rather than building on the positive elements and possibilities inherent in a sibling relationship. As I observed often in my visits to exemplary programs and read in teacher and parents' reports, pairing siblings in groupings or activities allows young children to build on their familiar modes of communicating and relating. The older sibling develops empathy and complex ways of communicating faster, and the younger sibling develops language and literacy faster, not to mention social and transitioning skills.

 ## What Would You Do?
Group Dynamics

Building group identity can also take a wrong turn, and a mindful balance between individual development, self-esteem, and group belonging needs to be kept at all times. Children's great urge to belong can exert undue pressure on them to conform, rather than fully develop their sense of self. The repercussions of giving up part of one's identity or language in order to "fit in" can follow children throughout their lives, creating a "cultural split."

A teacher's view:
I really want my bilingual children to belong, and speaking their own language just separates them from the group. These two Hispanic girls are always together, holding hands, chatting away in Spanish, they're their own little group. I really want them to fit in, and speaking Spanish just shuts other children out.

A student's view:
My friend and I were at recess and speaking Spanish when a teacher who was on duty came to us and told us to speak English, that we were in America. I didn't know then that it was language discrimination. I thought she thought I was so dumb that I didn't know where I was living and born. I told her that I knew where I was, but she told me to speak English, because it was a waste of time to speak a language that nobody spoke. Of course, I was very upset, because everybody in my family spoke Spanish, and they weren't nobodies.[11]

Your view:
- What does "fitting in" mean to you? What do you think it means to the teacher above? To the Spanish speakers?
- What would you do if you were in the teacher's shoes?

- What do you think are signs that a child is not feeling a sense of belonging at your center or feels left out?
- How could you engage teachers and students to come to an understanding about how to best "fit in"?

My Tongue Is Like a Map

Mami said yes, Abuelita sang sí.
They said, Two languages make you a rich man,
But words never paid for my penny candy.

Agua, water. Arroz, rice. Niño, me!
Arroz con leche, sang Abuelita
As my mami said, A is for Apple.

My ears were like a radio, so many stations.
Sometimes I would dream in English and Spanish.
I was a millionaire each time I said yes and sí.

Rane Arroyo[12]

 ### Did You Know?
Losing Language Means Losing Family Ties

Did you know that, in the case of many extended immigrant families, losing the native language creates a generational divide? Family relationships based on respect for elders and the oral transmission of their wisdom, stories, and heritage can be weakened because elders may have less opportunity to develop the second language and the younger generations lose the ability to communicate with them because they are not proficient in the native tongue.

If you have the resources and the will, encouraging children's first-language development can be enhanced by the following practices:

- Learn greetings and songs in the children's native language.
- Have bilingual books available and share them with families.
- Encourage families to use their native tongue in many different ways, including conversations, poems, sayings, reading, storytelling.

- Use the children's first language to help them transition from one activity to another. Ask bilingual staff and families for appropriate phrases, such as "*¿Tienes hambre?*" (Are you hungry?); "*Vamos al baño.*" (Let's go to the bathroom.); "*¿Quieres jugar afuera?*" (Do you want to play outside?).

- Translate directions and key phrases into the children's first language.

- Pair children with bilingual peers in activities.

- Invite guests and volunteers who speak the children's language.

- Label common objects and toys around the room in two languages.[14]

- Have children talk about and represent favorite animals, like the "bunny story diorama" in Figure 3–2, taken from an activity led by artist and teacher Susan Thompson.

Cariño—*Caring and Tenderness: Family Ways of Caring*

Non-verbal communication is rarely dealt with in teaching preparation programs. Amazing, considering that many skilled teachers I spoke to alluded to the fact that "teaching from the heart" is what drives them. Since a sense of belonging to a group

Figure 3–2 *Bunny Story Diorama* (Photo by Susan Thompson)

is cemented by demonstrative caring—*cariño*—you could consider ways to appropriately and frequently use physical contact and even certain cultural terms of endearment and expressions.

> I love my children so much, I'm always calling them "*papito*," "*tesoro*," and "*amiguitos*." And they call me "*missy*." But my lead teacher says I shouldn't do that; that it's demeaning and denies their individuality! How can she say that?[15]

In fact, for Latino children this may well feel comforting, as when a teacher says *mis niños*—my children—and makes them feel included. Rather than emphasizing the individual, these terms remind the children they are part of a group, and the *mis*—my—speaks not of ownership, but of a relationship. Anglo American teachers who understand this dynamic do indeed use Spanish and use these terms successfully in the classroom.[16]

Nonverbal gestures and behaviors are also frequently culture-specific, for example, the distance between people when they are interacting or the rhythm and tone of their voices. Nonverbal shows of disapproval or affection—such as touching and lap sitting—are frequently sensitive areas to broach in educational settings. *Cariño* is a vital part of communication and development in Latino cultures. It evokes not only a sentiment of caring for someone, but also a way of treating someone, so being a caring person—*cariñosa*—is understood as a positive, physical demonstration of caring for others in general, not just in particular.

Amazingly, although much is known and touted about infants' brain development via sensory experiences, including touching objects, the extension of the sense of touch into the caregiver/child relationship remains a controversial subject. We know from research that touch, from both a therapeutic and an affective standpoint, is elemental in the socio-emotional development of young children.[17] Positive effects of touch reach beyond the infants to the adults or peers who engage in touching, including grandparent volunteers in infant care, interrelations between caregiver and child, and fathers' expression of emotion and bond with child.[18] Unfortunately, early care and education settings do not routinely encourage physical contact that shows affection.[19] Sadly, the lack of physical contact affects the children's social comfort and behavior well into adulthood, thus also impacting how effective they are as caregivers when they are adults.[20]

At the same time, parents, teachers, and service providers need to be prepared to approach and discuss with each other the negative aspects of touching and where to draw the line. Inform yourself and communicate with staff and parents about the different possible consequences of certain behaviors. Speak directly to the point, while letting primary caregivers know about the interpretation of the law or regulations in your state or program. For instance, if a young child kisses another, the child may face sexual assault charges, and parents can face negligence charges. Police may be called if fights erupt between children. Teachers may be admonished not to allow young children to sit on their laps, and they need to know the laws about reporting any suspected abuse to social agencies, even if the abuse does not occur in the center or program. A good beginning point for a discussion on boundaries can be found in Spanish and in English at the following web page: <www.ocfs.state.ny.us/main/prevention/assets/Pub1154-S-SayNO.pdf>.

 ## What Would You Do?
Touching: A Teacher's Challenge

In this urban, multicultural child care center, many of the teachers and the children are Latino. The teachers very often hug children, hold them on their laps, and kiss them. The children are also very affectionate with each other. At an open house for families, one of the teachers noticed that an African American mother was standing on the sidelines and seemed to be watching with concern as a father was giving kisses to his child and his child's friend. The teacher approached the concerned mother, and explained, "Isn't it nice to see the relationship that father has with his little girl? That family is very loving, and they open their arms to all their children's friends as if they were their own."

- What would you have done in the same situation? What are some alternative approaches?
- What would you need to do with your teaching team to address the issue of touching when people from different cultures may have opposing views and experiences surrounding the subject of demonstrating affection to children?

Perhaps at a meeting you can bring up the issue, drawing on some of the following questions:

- What is the bottom line? Who defines this?
- What concession do you make for family/child preferences and how do you establish what these are?
- At what point do you seek outside guidance? Where do you go?
- How do you advocate for the needs and preferences of the family/child when a situation arises? What are the resources or data that would enable you to make a decision or support an existing regulation in a way that is fair and respectful of the family?

Rituals, Rules, and Routines for Bonding

What a child experiences every day not only becomes a strong shaper of identity, but also provides a ground for understanding language, actions, behaviors, and the social context surrounding that routine, whether that be a greeting song, a clean-up task, or a bathroom break.

How do people come together as a group? Historically, we create rituals, actions, symbols, words, and sounds that repeat and give us cues of what is coming next, or they mark a special event. Ritual is really about bonding. Sharing a moment in a special way with others many times connects us with our heritage, with our families, with happy times. I remember rushing to eat twelve grapes as the clock struck twelve on the last night of the year. I remember the whole extended family going out onto the patio to clang pots and pans to scare off the old year. But most of all, I remember the people who were around me when I was gulping grapes and clanging pots, and who are still by my side, helping me celebrate each new occasion.

Routines are daily necessities, things we do again and again, perhaps without thinking, and the transitions into these routines are also references that connect us with our families and the way things are done at home. In the classroom, there are opportunities to establish routines that will also eventually serve as familiar references to young children. You can help make these transitions smooth by instilling a bit from each of the children's family life. You can try to:

- Establish routines that include teaching methods used traditionally in families. Mealtime rules, sayings, refrains, cooking together, tidying up, or morning greetings can incorporate some of the verbal and nonverbal cues the child gets at home.

- Make frequent references to family (by name) in daily interactions, such as "Your grandmother would be proud of the way you helped Johnny today." When disciplining, you can also draw on the values a parent places on sharing without necessarily shaming the child.

- Use familiar stories and books, as well as literature from the Americas, including poems. Invite authorship from the classroom members and their families, as well as other teachers and community members who volunteer in or visit the program.

Daily routines can be infused with structured and unstructured group activities that foster group identity and a sense of belonging as well as informal opportunities for building friendships. Mealtimes, for instance, are key routines in the socio-personal—as well as language development—of young children. These periods provide rich opportunities for the center community to bond and share meals as a group, and they also enable participation of even the youngest in informal dialogue with others.

Connecting with family routines is a good way to build a sense of belonging in your children. A rich store of ideas can emerge from some family practices. For instance, one family reserves dinnertime to touch base on the days' successes and issues, going around the table to even the youngest member to share their daily experiences. Another brings the young children along in their migrant work, encouraging the children to learn by observing and hearing the daily work of the family. This "witnessing" and sharing in family tasks contributes to a child's development in a natural nondirective way, like the apprentice model, that can be echoed in the classroom. Early childhood programs based on models like Reggio Emilio and Open Circle have a social meeting time where young children take an active part in sharing their personal issues and experiences as well as in making decisions together.

Mealtime

Many Early Head Start and Head Start programs emphasize family involvement, even instituting "family-style" meals and inviting parents to join their children for lunch. This is a great idea and very in keeping with the value of *la familia*—the extended family—that I discuss in Chapter 2. To train staff to use the practice effectively, however, programs need to be aware that mealtimes may look quite different in the homes of some families. For example, some programs encourage self-feeding, choice, and taking what you want from the table, and these behaviors may clash with parents' preferences. Some practices, such as allowing a child choices or mannerisms that parents discourage at home, may cause parents to scold their children.

In one instance, Latino families raised red flags when their children came back from an urban, multi-ethnic center with bad table manners and growing demands and resistances to certain foods. Taking advantage of the fact that the family-style meal is part of the center's routines, the staff heard the parents and negotiated some acceptable accommodations to mealtime rules, while at the same time encouraging the development of self-help skills. Through dialogue with the families, staff became aware of the following behaviors that were important to many of the parents:

- Portions are not controlled because feeding until the child is satiated is valued.
- Food is brought to the table on serving plates, and seconds and thirds are allowed.
- Children do not help themselves from serving plates on the table, as the adults' attention and protectiveness is seen as important in avoiding bad table manners, such as reaching, and teaching portion control so food is not wasted.

- Children are not encouraged to pour their own drinks, as spilling or clumsiness may embarrass them.

- Reaching and talking above others' voices is considered bad manners for children of all ages and therefore discouraged at the meal table. Dialogue and listening are modeled by the adult and encouraged among children.

- Food is not wasted or thrown out thoughtlessly, since food is valued as much as money. Hygienic conservation of food is encouraged in different ways.

While accommodating to the rules and expectations of all families—either in the case of mealtime, as above, or in other aspects of the daily life of the program—is neither desirable nor possible, honoring both the program guideline and the choices a family makes in raising its children is fundamental, as is opening a dialogue that will lead to compromise. The following activity, which you can engage in with parents and with children, can help you come to some common understandings about what it takes for each child to feel safe and part of the group. So the "spin" on rules is that they are not to control individual behavior, but rather to learn to live harmoniously in a group—*convivir*.

BRINGING IDEAS TO LIFE
Rules to Live by: Conviviendo

This activity, adapted from a Reading the World VI Conference workshop ("Teaching Cultural Respect and Wisdom Through *Dichos* and Multicultural Literature," presented by Miguel López and Yuyi Morales) involves children and families in defining what matters to them in classroom behavior by employing popular sayings—*dichos*. If your group of children is older, you may want to do this in separate groups for children and adults.

1. Prepare lists of popular sayings from different cultures and in different languages.

2. Post these lists and use them to encourage family members to generate other sayings they have heard that are meaningful to them.

3. Say you will be all coming up with classroom rules based on these sayings.

4. Take turns reading these sayings aloud.

5. Have each participant pick one of the sayings. An adult helper can copy the saying onto oak tag, while you encourage the children to share why it is important to them and illustrate the saying.

6. Come up with classroom rules or routines that respond to this saying.

For example, at the end of this chapter and in Chapter 4, there are a number of teacher resources that have *dichos*. Use these to discuss what's important about the sayings chosen. For example, *Mira y verás*—look and you will see—speaks of the value of observing to learn, instead of asking. What would you suppose the following sayings convey about Latino culture or about what a parent wants? Explore the meaning of some of your own favorite sayings and other traditional sayings from the Americas with the children and families, such as:

- *Beneficios son cadenas de obligación*—Profits lead to a chain of obligations.

- *Quien de los suyos se separa, Dios lo desampara*—Whoever isolates herself from her people will be forgotten by God.

- *Con obras la buena fama se labra*—Fame is forged with good deeds.

- Use videos, illustrations, songs, and books that capture dichos in different media, like Ralfka González and Ana Ruiz's book, *My First Book of Proverbs: Mi Primer Libro de Dichos* (see Figure 3–3).

Figure 3–3 *Mi Primer Libro de Dichos/My First Book of Proverbs*
(Reproduced with the permission of the publisher, Children's Book Press, San Francisco, CA. Art © 1995 by Ralfka González and Ana Ruiz.)

Enriching the Physical Environment
Through Cultural Sensory Experiences

Most teachers spend a long time setting up the classroom so it is inviting and stimulating to children. Children need spaces for whole-group as well as individual and small-group spaces, so they can engage in a variety of formal and informal interactions that allow them to share experiences and aspects they bring from their roots.

Reflect on the impact your own environment has on your disposition, on your sense of connection. Light, color, and landscape exert a powerful effect on everyone. Imagine being transported from one environment into the total opposite. While adapting to the new environment is, of course, the desirable goal, we must recognize that different environments yield a different aesthetic and a different outlook, which we can easily explore in our classrooms to the advantage of all of our students—and colleagues.

> Closing my eyes I see palm trees swaying.
> Seagulls circling. Haciendas, pink and green.
> Still, sí, sí, with eyes open I taste salty, saffron Cuba.
> Muchas gracias, mama cubana, for cooking up an island
> in your tiny New York kitchen.

> Mimi Chapra[21]

The sounds, colors, sights, aromas, foods, and cadences of our early years stay imprinted in our minds, transforming the idea of home into a palpable, multisensory experience we use as a reference for the rest of our lives. Mimi Chapra writes about the "clicketty clack" of her mother's bracelets sliding up and down her arm as she chops onions for the meal. This sound alone evokes deep memories connected to the values and practices passed down through generations. In my own culture, the "slave" bracelets that grace the arms of many women in my family stand for duty and mark the development of a woman. We are to receive one, ceremoniously, when we reach puberty, another when we marry, and one for each child born. The soft "click" of these bracelets, like those of the *mamá cubana*, are comforting reminders that I am part of a family.

The words and rhythms connected to childhood delights are also anchored to memory. Just by hearing the word *dulce de leche*—a delicacy eaten by the spoonful in my native country—I begin to sense the thick, sticky substance, like peanut butter, filling my mouth. And I can't think of characterizing my mother without recalling her evening prayer ritual, which included a trance-like recitation where no word could be distinguished, only the rising and falling, pious, and suffering rhythm she intoned as she rubbed her rosary beads.

BRINGING IDEAS TO LIFE
Colors, Sounds, and Smells

Many early childhood programs have units on color, growing plants, and music.

Unfortunately, art materials, toys, and equipment in classroom centers often rely on strong primary colors, rarely including the rich pastels, ochres, and other hues that are prevalent in Caribbean and Latin American environments. We know that color and light exert profound effects on human beings, and yet few environments in many parts of the United States offer the variety of colors that reflects different cultures, except perhaps in the Southwest or in ethnic restaurants. Newcomer, migrant, or low-income families may not have the possibility to exercise choice in filling their home with familiar color, but our programs can enrich their appearance by making the effort to find and use a spectrum of objects and experiences:

- **Color:** Collect photos of architecture, textiles, and interior and exterior settings in different Latin American countries. You can glue them onto playing cards and cover with polyurethane, or you can have children make a collage. As you begin color exploration in your program, you can encourage children to compare and contrast by placing photos or objects from different countries of the same color, but varying hues. For instance, the strong, deep green in some African cloths compared with the Caribbean yellow-green and the Irish Kelly green provide young children with a deep, subtle experience of color.

- **Smell and Taste:** Researchers believe that the sense of smell is the strongest link with subconscious and childhood memory. Go regularly to markets in ethnic neighborhoods to find different fruits, vegetables, and canned goods. Wash and cut one or two of these every now and then and use them in different ways. You can pass the food around in circle, include it in a snack or meal, have children use it as a source for art projects like stamping, or, for older children, as a source for a poem or a still-life painting. Florists are another source of aromas that trigger familiar memories and senses, and the beauty and color of flowers can recall many of the exuberant landscapes many Latinos born outside of the United States have experienced.

Cut out photographs from magazines, seed catalogs, and supermarket flyers of different fruit. Have children pick out which of those they are familiar with, they have eaten, or seen on a tree or in the ground. Make a list of all the names of fruits and vegetables that you know and the children know from their home or from the country from which they came. What a rich vocabulary of poetic words you will collect! Maize, corn, guava, guayaba, mango, membrillo (quince), papaya, fruta bomba, limes—which in some countries are called lima, in others limón—all offer a variety of textures, smells, tastes, and colors for the children to experience.

Treasures and Objects That Warm the Space

Many may conceive of cultural awareness as posting depictions of people in traditional dress, displaying folk arts and crafts, or including traditional food and festivities. However, simply enacting a "tourist curriculum" has generated much criticism. While exploring the roots of different cultures may enrich teachers' knowledge, a culturally and linguistically responsive program should represent the children and families as they are *today*, and not simply through stereotypical, folkloric references that are not explored in depth or in their variations. Some activities in this chapter and subsequent chapters guide you in this journey to compare, contrast, and extract personal meaning from the outward signs of culture or experience. For instance, those of you who have children of Mexican background can investigate some ancient birth ceremonies, such as that of the Maya, and enlist the families of the children in sharing what they do in their families when a new child is born and named. You can then compare and contrast these present and past customs cross culturally, helping the children make connections with their culture's past while at the same time validating their present and also helping them see other approaches to this vital passage in a family's life.

Most importantly, your program can ensure that what the children see and touch daily allows them to connect with their own experience and family, as the model program described below has done.

 Programs That Inspire
El Centro's Families Are Present

At this school that reaches from Pre-K to third grade, the family is made visible as soon as you enter. Professional photographs of each family line every hallway. These large, black-and-white photographs show the pride the center takes in its community. A common reading area, or "library," has hanging textiles and quilts borrowed temporarily from families. Families are welcomed to this space to view and borrow books and other materials, as well as to admire and contribute to the regularly rotating exhibitions. The large entrance and patio have a variety of comfortable seating arrangements and decorations—like a living room—that encourage parents to linger and chat with others as they drop off or pick up their children. Children, as they go through the halls, can notice each others' families, comment, and share information about their own families, as one young child I observed did. He pointed to the photograph of his friend's family and said, "I saw your baby brother today ... he has hair now! See, he didn't in that picture ... Maybe my baby sister soon [sic] have hair."

In order to avoid inequities or conflicts around sharing a particularly treasured toy or object, some programs might have policies about what a child can bring from home. However, familiar objects and routines are key in helping any child transition from a home environment into a classroom. Something concrete to hang onto ties the child to the new setting. Program staff, together with families, can brainstorm ways to bring the home into the program. What materials are especially meaningful? How can similar materials be integrated into the environment? Later on, I give an example of an activity to encourage the sharing of these precious things that families collect.

You may find that children and parents alike will bring in materials or objects that your program feels are not developmentally appropriate. As an example, in a family day care setting, four-and-a-half-year-old Carmen's favorite activity at home was to sort and stack a collection of large Mexican coins her grandfather had given her. This activity can be valuable to bring into your program's learning centers, as it provides a foundation for developing mathematical skills in all the children, and allows the child to serve as "expert" and model for the younger children exploring this new way of playing with a material. The family child care provider, whose licensing supervisor told her the size and material of some of the coins were inappropriate in her mixed-age setting, copied some of the designs and numbers on the coins onto large plastic disks of different sizes and colors she had collected from the Children's Museum's recycle bins. She set these disks inside a play cash register drawer in the "market" play area, and watched as Carmen told the younger children in the group about the coins and showed them how to stack and sort them.

Many teacher resources from the United States and from the Americas are also a source of visuals and activities that can expose all the children to places and landscapes from Latin America. One example, in Spanish, presents a unit on creative expression and cultural identity carried out in Santo Domingo. In this unit, the community process for defining and designing the workshops is also represented visually in photographs, giving a rich experience of the rural context, the modern dress, and the look of the community, as well as the sense of artistic expression there. One activity involved painting the trunks of trees in vibrant, richly patterned colors. Another project was to depict indigenous houses on a mural. See the *Aspectos Culturales* web page at the end of this chapter and review the resources throughout this book for many other sources of information and visuals. You can access a Resource List of English and Spanish language materials at <*www.edc.org/ccf/latinos*>.

Objects have meanings attached that tell much about a culture. The *rebozo*, a Mexican scarf used for a variety of purposes, calls to mind the *chador*—head covering—in Arab countries.[22] Much more than a garment, it serves as a carrier for infants, as a pouch for gathering fire sticks, as a towel to dry off from a cleansing in the river, as a cover-up, and as a tablecloth for meals outdoors during harvest.

For me, the *mate* gourd on my shelf conjures fond memories and practices from my own culture. I see my grandmother sipping through the silver filigreed straw, passing it to each of us little ones and to the rest of the family when we were gathered together. As the *mate* is a very bitter herb, the ritual consisted of my grandmother passing the small gourd and straw to the adults first, then filling it repeatedly until the bitterness was washed away, then letting the children sip the sweetened herb. Taking on the task to periodically fill the gourd with piping hot water was like a rite of passage to which each of us looked forward. This *mate* time symbolized for me a warm sense of family, of others partaking in the same activity, of adults protecting and preparing us young ones from the bitterness, and of symbolically acknowledging our maturity as our task and our resistance to the bitterness dictated. Even to this day, in my town of birth, you can see people strolling on the boardwalk with the ever-present thermos and the *mate* gourd under their arms, stopping on the boardwalk to sip and look out to the water.

As part of your daily rituals and routines, you can prepare the children for the *Museum of Our Homes* activity described below by telling stories of your own special objects. Bring a keepsake or meaningful object from your own home or from your classroom to circle time. Tell a story about why you treasure the object, what memories it holds, or what association it has with your family. Take inspiration from the work of artists like Margaret Stratton, whose *Inventory of My Mother's House* consists of snapshots of a collection of her mother's possessions, from the onion flakes she bought to the thrift store lamps, all symbolizing her mother's constant collecting and rearranging of her home.[23]

BRINGING IDEAS TO LIFE
Museum of Our Homes

The traditional show and tell at morning circle can be modified to good use if you set up a daily "ritual" to bring in and tell about a special object and then exhibit it for the day in a display case. Prepare for this during the family's orientation to the program, giving parents possible examples and having them encourage extended family members to also contribute a favorite object.

1. Explain to families that the purpose is to help the children express themselves and to help them get to know each other and their families and what they do at home. You can encourage conversation between the family and child and also help the child connect words and story with an object or visual representation. Some examples could be a photograph of a pet, a sweater knit by a grandmother, a tool used by the father, even a favorite toy figure. You need not think it has to be a cultural "artifact," but rather an object the child cherishes, or feels has particular meaning to a family member.

2. Establish a clear routine for turn-taking that doesn't rely on the teacher, such as passing a ball or rolling a toy vehicle to the next speaker.

3. Decide where to place the objects after circle time so the children can begin to learn that some objects that have meaning to others may be so precious that they cannot be shared, or that they would cause someone distress if lost. You can designate a place as the "museum." It could be shelves at a high level, or a display case visible to all who walk in the room. Rotate the objects frequently, returning them to families as needed.

Respect for objects, whether they are playthings, books, or works of art is intrinsic to many Latinos. Children can learn this respect without feeling denied.

Turning Challenges to Opportunities

In some of the chapters in this book, I have ended with a section of *Questions for Reflection and Discussion*. Here, I try something different: I start with a sensitive issue that might prove challenging for teachers. Following a poem that presents a particular aspect of the issue, I suggest some dialogue triggers to ignite personal reflection, as well as some scenarios and questions for your work in the classroom.

Symbols of Beliefs or Symbols of Caring?

Religion and spirituality are taboo subjects. Whether teachers are equipped or encouraged to deal with it, the reality is that faith and religion have an enormous impact on many cultures' values, practices, and even objects and keepsakes associated with childhood memories. Find a way to brainstorm with peers what to do in these situations. The poem below can serve as stimulation to broach both your own feelings and how to deal with situations that arise in your classroom with families and children.

The associations even young children make can be complex, as the following poem indicates. The statuette of the virgin, an ever-present figure and model in the religion and lives of many Latinos, here symbolizes for this child a supportive presence, a love, not necessarily a religious or spiritual one:

"My mother also *me enseñaba* [*would teach me about] *La Virgen.* I dreamt *La Virgen*, ate *La Virgen*, talked *La Virgen*, dressed *La Virgen*... *La Virgen* was in keychains, on money, in wedding rings, in childhood pictures next to me, on the trees, in the mirror, sleeping next to me in bed... *La Virgen* was my mother because she taught me what it meant to be a girl, a Xicana, a Latina... Invasion of the heart, the mind, the soul, the body, *La Virgen* has claimed me hers. There is no going back to the old *sabeduras* [wisdom] and the hand-me-downs. *La Virgen* has handed-me-down the one thing that was never there, love... *Como mi madre que me acariciaba con ternuras tan preciosas, como su cara, su cuerpo, manera de vestir, como el paradiso que nunca existio, ese amor.* [Like my mother who would caress me with precious tenderness, like her face, her body, her way of dressing, like the paradise that never existed, that love.]"

[*Translated by the author.] Excerpts from *Querida Lupita* by Dinah Consuegra.[24]

Reflection Questions for Teachers

Depending on who is in your teaching team and your school policies, broaching the subject of religion may be inappropriate to do in a group, but perhaps paired up with someone you trust, or individually, in your journal, you can explore your own associations. One positive and broadening way to approach the subject is to focus on the senses, memories, and sentiments, not on what you perceive to be the religious aspect. The beauty of the poem above is that it does just that. Many of us have strong memories that come to play in the whole *ritual* surrounding religion. Across the world, a wealth of sensory experiences overlap the practices of different religions: the smell and clang of the incense burner, the dressing up on Sundays or Saturdays, the special foods and words, the rules that guide the way you listen to elders, the group chanting, the silence. Some feelings and memories may be positive and some negative. Some rituals and songs may be shared across some cultures, others may be markedly different, like the structured call and response contrasted with the exuberant witnessing that spills across the aisles in some churches. Many of these rituals and experiences are very tied to our identities and our connections with family and home.

- Call up memories and experiences related to religious activities and explore how you felt, who shared those moments with you, what you saw, heard, and felt.

- Have you ever been ridiculed or have you heard someone ridicule something that you value, like your language or your religion? What would you say now in that situation?

- Do you exhibit objects in the classroom that have special spiritual or religious meaning for you?

- How did you come about your definitions of right and wrong?

- Are there particular aspects of your own or another religion that rub you the wrong way? Why? How do you deal with these feelings?

- Are there particular groups from which you have felt excluded? How did they exclude you?

- Think of a time when you felt different and that you didn't belong, or when you didn't know how to fit in or behave in a situation. What stopped you from fitting in? What would you do differently now? What do you wish the person in charge or with power had done in that situation?

- Are there places that feel particularly welcoming to you? What are the elements that make it so?

- How do you behave differently in these places compared to where you don't quite fit in, or where you feel uncomfortable?

- When you are in a group, what makes you feel cared for?

In Your Classroom

RELIGIOUS CONFLICTS AND PREJUDICE Be prepared with some strategies to deal with the subject of religion or prejudice when it comes up in the classroom. Children between two-and-a-half and four years old are already shaping their awareness of race, differences, and exclusion, and may even begin to label, reject, or even show signs of hostility towards individuals and groups that they have begun to perceive as different.[25]

- If a Muslim father brings his child to your classroom with her head covered, how would you handle this? This is a hot issue now in many parts of the world, even among Muslims. Do you know the issues? Can you understand the parents' views? How can you balance being respectful to the parent's beliefs and assuring the child will not be excluded?

- A family of Jehovah Witnesses does not want their child to celebrate holidays. Do you eliminate any holiday celebration from your program? If not, how do you make a safe space for the child not to feel left out of a group celebration?

- Can you create group rituals, as suggested in previous pages, that can help all the children share some common cherished memories and experiences that make them feel safe and protected, such as making hot chocolate whenever it rains, playing the flute to signal naptime, or dancing in a circle three times before sitting down at morning circle time?

- What if a child exclaims, "Hell!" and another responds, "If you say hell you'll go there"? Do you say, "We don't say that here," and that's it? What are other options?

Don't shy away from these challenges. They are bound to occur in our multi-cultural world. Turn them into opportunities for your own learning, reflecting on what you bring of your own beliefs to teaching, including the way you talk to children, the way you dress, and the routines you follow. Open yourself up to seeing other perspectives and become an expert mediator. You probably do this every day when there is conflict between children.

A very useful curriculum for dealing with some of these issues with your peers speaks volumes just with its title: *More Is Caught Than Taught: A Guide to Quality Child Care* by A. Jack Guillebeaux. The curriculum has various modules, including Vision, Internalized Oppression, and How To Be Together, each offering activity ideas and agendas for discussing the hard questions.[26]

GROUP IDENTITY AND INCLUSION Fostering group identity is just as vital as self-development. Go beyond the usual focus on the social development of individual children and discuss with colleagues some of the following questions:

- Can you define the "culture" of your program? What do the routines, schedules, ways of doing things convey to someone looking in from the outside? Is it inviting? What makes it so? Does it change from day to day, or as adults or children come and leave the group? Can you re-imagine the "culture" of your classroom to reflect each and every child? What would you see, and what would each of the staff and children do differently in your imagined classroom?

- How do the adults and children in your program behave when a new child or adult enters the room or becomes part of the program?

- What are some strategies you use in your program to help a child become part of the group?

- What do you do when you see a child being left out or standing apart from the group for extended periods of time? Note: Sitting silently on the sidelines is sometimes an important developmental stage for newcomers, who may rely on observation to make sense of the new cultural norms.

- What do you do to acclimatize children to be an active part of the group at their own pace? Are there multiple ways of joining in? Is it okay for a child not to join in?

- Developing empathy and caring for others is essential in forming a group edentityk as well as respect and sharing. How do you frame your intervention when a child disrespects or refuses to share with others? Do you help the child see the situation through her own eyes ("Do you remember how you felt…") or do you encourage the child to become aware of the other's perspective ("See how sad he looks. What could you do?")?

Summing Up: It's in the Relationships

To establish a sense of belonging, children need to recognize themselves and their families in the classroom. Identity formation involves developing a sense of self and of place within a community. As bicultural children grow, they take on multiple identities—that help them define themselves, what they do, and where they belong in different ways, and these should be encouraged. The bilingual, bicultural child has the advantage of choosing the best of both cultures. As educators, we can encourage this blending or contribute to their sense of being divided. In her book, *The Inner World of The Immigrant Child*, Cristina Igoa writes about what she calls the "cultural split" immigrant children in her class felt as they tried to fit into American society. Behaving one way at home and another in the classroom may cause disconnection with parents, as well as cultural split. Igoa presents an insightful and dedicated teacher's reflection on the learning experiences of newcomer children, following them across the years to determine what impacted them in their schooling. She recommends an approach that is cultural, academic, and psychological (CAP) to ensure that a cultural split does not pull apart immigrant children.[27]

Shared experiences that are punctuated with trust and respect provide a ground for the growth of a truly inclusive collective. The garden I described at the beginning of this chapter is symbolic of the possibilities for interacting, belonging, exploration, and stewardship. These experiences provided occasions for the children to observe and participate in growth and to learn to care for the environment they share. An arrangement that favors interaction, collaboration, negotiation, exploration, and solidarity reflects what each child brings and stimulates each to grow both as an individual and as a member of a community, taking them beyond self-development, beyond empathy. Keep in mind that cultural competence is not what is on the four walls, or the types of books, or strategies, but rather in the relationships, in the conversations, in the interest each shows for the other's thinking, and in the way one builds on another's idea. As a teacher, you can encourage this dynamic co-construction. In the next chapter, I describe ways to design group projects and learning experiences that build on this foundation of bonds and connections.

Related Resources

Aspectos Culturales

This website provides resources and ideas for teachers to integrate and raise their awareness of Hispanic culture and language, including ideas for books, games, music, resources, and activities: <*www.aspectosculturales.com/*>

Consejos de mi Tia

This booklet, available in Spanish and English, was created by the National Latino Children's Institute. Included in their Words for the Future CD-ROM are learning situations that are culturally relevant under the guise of advice from an aunt. Sticky note pads with typical *dichos*—sayings—are also included in the kit. See the Connections and Commitments web page: <www.edc.org/cof/latinos> for resource information.

Authors of Note

Alma Flor Ada, Isabel Campoy, and Suni Paz have teamed up often to produce quality Spanish and English materials that make a special effort to connect children with family, past, and issues of migration and culture. For instance, Ada and Paz'*¡Pío Peep!* is a book and CD of nursery rhymes from the Americas put to song in both languages. Ada's *A Magical Encounter: Latino Children's Literature in the Classroom* is dedicated to giving guidance to kindergarten through upper-grade teachers about the use of quality literature in their classrooms, including recommendations, resources, and activities, as well as background understanding about the history of Latino literature, oral tradition, and culture.

For children in kindergarten through third grade, *The Upside Down Boy/El Niño de Cabeza*, by J. F. Herrera (2000) tells the story of a boy feeling "upside down" when he goes to a new school. The teacher works to make the boy feel a sense of belonging by involving the family and bringing in the boy's talents to share in the classroom. San Franscisco: Children's Book Press. Other useful sites:

- The Center for Multicultural Literature at the University of San Francisco. <*socrates.usfca.edu/new/institutes/childlit/index.html*>
- Yuyi Morales' colorful and creative web page opens to a variety of features that can be helpful in a classroom with Latino children, including "Abuelita's wisdom." <*yuyimorales.com*>

Endnotes

1 Julio Saldana.

2 Orellana, M. F. 2002. "The Work Kids Do: Mexican and Central American Immigrant Children's Contributions to Households and Schools in California." *Harvard Educational Review* 71 (3): 372.

3 Derman-Sparks, L. 1990. "Understanding Diversity: What Young Children Want and Need to Know." *Scholastic Pre-K Today*, Nov./Dec.: 44–50.

4 Ada, A. F., and F. Isabel Campoy. 2004. *Authors in the Classroom: A Transformative Education Process.* Boston, MA: Pearson Education, Inc.

5 Yvette Rodriguez, director of Ecuelita Borikén, Boston, Massachusetts, in a personal communication.

6 Ryerson Early Learning Center, Ryerson Polytechnic University of Toronto, Canada, 1998.

7 Adapted from Slaby, R. G., W. C. Roedell, D. Arezzo, and K. Hendriz. 1995. *Early Violence Prevention: Tools for Teachers of Young Children.* Washington, D.C.: National Association for the Education of Young Children.

8 Smith, P. K., and K. J. Connolly. 1987. *The Ecology of Preschool Behavior.* Cambridge, UK: Cambridge University Press.

9 Barbara Rogoff describes this apprenticeship in her work, Rogoff, B. 1990. *Apprenticeship in Thinking: Cognitive Development In Social Context.* New York: Oxford University Press.

10 Moll, L. C., C. Amati, D. Neff, and N. Gonzalez. 1992 "Funds of Knowledge for Teaching: Using a Qualitative Approach to Conect Homes and Classrooms." *Theory into Practice* 31 (2): 132-141.

11 Wanda Rodriguez, a teacher taking "Supporting Preschoolers with Language Differences," a credit-bearing course offered through EDC, Inc.'s Center for Children & Families, described at <*www.edc.org/ccf*>.

12 Arroyo, R. 2001. "My Tongue Is Like a Map." In *A Tribute to Mothers*, edited by Pat Mora. New York: Lee & Low.

13 Anzaldúa, G. 1987. "How to Tame a Wild Tongue." In *Borderlands/La Frontera: The New Mestiza.* San Francisco: Aunt Lute Books: 59.

14 If there are a number of children with different languages, labeling everything in all the languages may not be appropriate. However, exposing children to a variety of languages in all their forms (oral, visual, heard, and written) is beneficial, as this builds language awareness.

15 Anonymous Latina teacher assistant.

16 Montero-Sieberth, M., and M. Perez. 1987. "Echar Pa'lante, Moving Onward: The Dilemmas and Strategies of a Bilingual Teacher." *Anthropology and Education* 18 (3): 180–189.

   Cazden, C. 1983. "Personalization of Instruction and Classroom Management: Features of Cariño." In *Social and Cultural Organization of Interaction in Classrooms of Bilingual Children,* edited by Erickson et al. Final Report NIE G-78-0099. Washington, D.C.: National Institute of Education.

   Eggers-Piérola, C. 1993. "Beyond Inclusion: A Review of Ethnographies of Latino Students." Unpublished Qualifying Paper, Harvard University.

17 Pelaez-Nogueras, M., T. M. Field, Z. Hossain, and J. Pickens. 1996. "Depressed Mothers' Touching Increases Infants' Positive Affect and Attention in Still-Face Interactions." *Child Development* 67: 1780–92.

18 Field, T. M. 2000. "Infant Massage Therapy." *Touchpoints* 7 (1).

19 Field, T., J. Harding, B. Soliday, D. Lasko, N. Gonzalez, and C. Valdeon. 1998. "Touching in Infant, Toddler and Preschool Nurseries." *Early Child Development and Care* 98: 113–120. Cigales, M., T. Field, Z. Hossain, M. Pelaez-Nogueras, and J. Gewirtz, 1996. "Touch Among Children at Nursery School." *Early Child Development and Care* 126: 101–110.

20 Fernando-Trujillo, J. 2001. "Estudio Multicéntrico Sobre el Empleo del Tacto Como Forma de Comunicación del Profesional de Enfermería con los Pacientes." *Revista Metas de Enfermería* March. *<club.telepolis.com/torrefdz/enfermero_y_profe3.htm>*

21 Chapra, M. 2001. "Mi Mama Cubana." In *A Tribute to Mothers,* edited by Pat Mora. New York: Lee & Low.

22 As explained by Suzanne Fisher Staples in March 2004 in her keynote speech at the Reading the World Conference, University of San Francisco, San Francisco.

23 Stratton, M. 1994. "Inventory of My Mother's House." *Imagining Families: Images and Voices* by Willis, D. Exhibition catalogue. Washington, D.C.: National African American Museum.

24 *<chicanas.com/poetas.html#Dinah>*

25 Derman-Sparks, L., C. Higa, and B. Sparks. 1980. "Children, Race, and Racism: How Race Awareness Develops." *Interracial Books for Children Bulletin* 2: 3–9. Kalin, R. 1984. "The Development of Ethnic Attitudes." In Samuda, R. J., J. W. Berry, and M. Laferrière, editors. *Multiculturalism in Canada: Social and Educational Perspectives.* Boston, MA: Allyn & Bacon.

26 Guillebeaux, A. J. 1998. *More Is Caught Than Taught: A Guide to Quality Child Care—Developed for Early Childhood Parents and Teachers.* Federation of Child Care Centers of Alabama (FOCAL). *<www.focalfocal.org/focal.htm>*

27 Igoa, C. 1995. *The Inner World of the Immigrant Child.* New York: St. Martin's Press.

CHAPTER
4

Educación/Education

A Holistic and Relational Approach to Teaching and Learning

Todo lo que aprendí, todo lo que se me quedó, y todo lo que me sirve en la vida, lo aprendí de niña, a los pies de mi abuelo, sentada en la falda de mi madre, mirando todo lo que veía alrededor, corriendo por los campos, yendo al mercado, peleando con mis primos, ayudando a los vecinos. Esos momentos fueron mis ventanas al mundo, y lo que ví por esas ventanas me empujó a buscar las destrezas para entenderlo.

Everything I learned, everything that stayed with me, and everything that helps me in life, I learned as a young girl, at my grandfather's feet, sitting on my mother's lap, watching everything around me, running through the fields, going to market, fighting with my cousins, helping the neighbors. Those moments were my windows to the world, and what I saw through those windows compelled me to seek the skills to understand.

Focusing on *Educación*

What stays with us from our childhood is not so much *what* we learned, but *from whom*. The strength that many Latinos bring is their tight bond with *la familia*— the extended family, as I described in Chapter 2. Our families are the first hands that "guide our feet," to paraphrase Marian Wright Edelman's prayer.

As we face a new century and a new millennium, the overarching challenge for America is to rebuild a sense of community and hope and civility and caring and safety for all our children. I hope God will guide our feet as parents—and guide America's feet—to reclaim our nation's soul, and to give back to all of our children their sense of security and their ability to dream about and work toward a future that is attainable and hopeful.[1]

Now, more than ever, we need to be mindful of how to bring alive the caring and safety that each child felt at grandfather's feet and on Mama's lap. And—as in the spiritual that inspired Edelman's prayer—we must search their hearts, stand by them, and hold their hands as we "guide their feet."

Just as the population of Latinos is growing, the youngest are already lagging behind peers in preliteracy and numeracy as measured by conventional tests.[2] Educators urgently need to understand the causes of this gap as well as how to bring out the best in every child, regardless of background.

Children do not fail—schools fail children by not providing experiences that are consonant with their needs and their families' goals and that engage them in meaningful activity that builds on their own cultural capital, experiences, and interests. Teachers play a vital role in making these links that support the development of the whole child.

In group-centered cultures, such as the Latino cultures, *educación*—education in Spanish—is not anchored solely on academic knowledge. Rather, the emphasis is on the development of the whole child. Children acquire an ethical and civic consciousness that takes them beyond individual achievement to reaching their potential as members of a community.

In this chapter, I focus on this fundamental basis of Latino and other cultures throughout the world: the development of the individual as a responsive and responsible member of a society. Looking beyond a framework based solely on individual achievement and attainment of knowledge, this chapter discusses a relationship-based, holistic approach to teaching and learning that connects the child with real-life situations and with the thinking and expertise of others, matching home knowledge with classroom work. I pay special attention to nurturing family literacy experiences both in the home and in the program or school. I also introduce issues and strategies related to second-language learners, because language is the key component in learning, communicating, and connecting with others. Throughout the chapter, I provide examples that illustrate life-long learning strategies that build capacity to learn, act, and solve problems individually and in interactions, drawing on multiple ways of knowing and multiple perspectives.

In previous chapters, I shared strategies to support children in developing their own and their group identity by creating a climate for *pertenencia*—belonging, and

I wrote about partnering with the extended *familia* as a vital contributor and resource for every child's learning. This chapter is dedicated to building on these two dimensions—individual and group—and applying them to teaching and learning.

As we know, teachers now must be prepared to teach children who come with different languages and ethnicities, because more than half of them will have such children in their classrooms. However, few currently receive any specific and comprehensive training towards that end.[3] Although this whole book is designed to support educators in this engaging and challenging work, this chapter specifically focuses on a model for teaching and learning that builds on the strengths and addresses the challenges of Latinos in the United States, supporting them in their path towards becoming fully participating, bicultural, bilingual citizens.

Once you have transformed the educational climate and environment into welcoming places for all children, families, and staff, the next step is to create learning opportunities that explicitly draw out what each child brings, is interested in, and needs to grow, gain mastery, thrive, and have a place in the world.

In this chapter, I highlight what many Latino families want for their children, discuss the role of *educación* through a cultural view on success, and share a snapshot of a memorable learning experience for a Latino child. In the classroom, children move between roles as apprentices and experts. As they become invested in each others' learning, children begin to know in a new way, creating a group dynamic that stimulates learners beyond the scope of their own thinking. They do this by solving a problem together, conveying to others their own knowledge and experience, by building on what they each bring, and by helping others learn. Although delving deeply into specific content is beyond the scope of this book, I suggest some approaches and ideas to enhance the literacy and learning of Latino children, as well as others, in ways that build on their cultural and linguistic ways of learning and language development

At the end of the chapter, I invite you to reflect on *educación*, and refer you to some resources to support you in continuing to explore the concepts of relationship-based and context-rich learning.

Being *Bien Educado:* Well Brought Up and Well Educated

In any culture, education is a means to developing the tools, knowledge, and capacities needed to succeed in life. In Latino culture, however, the concept of *educación* also encompasses ethical and social development.

Educación and Success

The definition of *educación*, "dirigir, encaminar, doctrinar," refers to the act of guiding, and indoctrinating in spiritual values just as much as teaching a discipline.[4]

This definition speaks of influences from spheres beyond school, encompassing family duties, beliefs and customs, and service to the community. *Educación* attends to the spirit as well as the mind of the child. Being *bien educada*[5] is being a centered, responsible, moral, knowledgeable, and *respected* individual. Having *educación* means knowing how to behave in society, how to be respectful, cooperative, and considerate towards others, as well as how to be part of a group—a loftier view of success than individual accomplishment.[6]

To those belonging to a group-centered culture, educational success and career advancement are not ends in themselves, but rather a path to achieving a fuller potential as a human being, enabling each to better contribute to the good of the group. "I studied and worked hard so I could give back to my community," is a common claim for Latino achievers. From a Latino perspective, taking this responsibility to "give back" and to be responsible for others is one of the highest priorities in raising a child, as this Puerto Rican mother articulates:

> I want them to be aware of all the things that are around them. I want them to be active. Well, you know how some people live in a place and they don't care about everyone else and the betterment of their surroundings? They just say "Okay, I'm going to be here, I'm going to take care of my little corner. But I won't care whatever happens to anyone else." I want them to be aware of everyone else's feelings.... I want them to be out there taking care of the children, of their surroundings, of the schools.[7]

For Latinos, then, the lifelong aim in being educated and a "success" is tied to being the best that you can be in order to fulfill your calling and contribute to your family's heritage and to your society. Sayings and stories, grandparents, and schools teach this calling and duty. However, *educación* does not mean replicating the older generation's path, but forging new ones. Like many immigrants coming to this country, Latinos' expectations for their children involves bettering themselves, but without losing the sense of duty towards others in the scramble to take advantage of the opportunities in the United States. In the children's book *Bizcochuelos*, for instance, a young boy, tired of filling family expectations and doing household chores, runs off to find his own true calling, lured by a mythical butterfly, and then creates a family tradition that is passed down and shared symbolically from generation to generation. Latino myths, stories, and sayings teach the children to be proud of their heritage as well as to honor the humanistic values that their forebearers hold to. *Más vale persona que hacienda*—a person is more valuable than a possession—teaches us to put worldly gains second to others. *Quien de los suyos se separa, Dios lo desampara*—those who abandon their families and friends will be abandoned by God—speaks of the essential moral learning of *educación*: service and obligation to others.

Successful modes of learning for Latino children in early education settings involve matching school and community approaches, group tasks and play, interpersonal experiences that entail oral and nonverbal communication and shared problem-solving, all of which, and more, are present in the recollection below.[8]

Memorable Learning

I'll never forget when I first learned to measure. Back home, Missy[9] Rodriguez *nos educó*—educated us—very well. She was very strict, but I remember she used to think up fun things for us to do together. One day, when I was five, she divided our class into two groups. She gave each group a map of the field and the woods behind it, with a little drawing of a house at the other end of the woods and of our school building in front of the *fútbol*—soccer—field. She said the house on the other side was hers, and that she was inviting all of us to listen to music in her living room. She said each group had to work out a way to get to her house, but without getting in the way of the game of *fútbol*, and without getting lost in the woods. Oh, and she said, "Don't forget Rafaelito," the youngest of all of us.

Missy Tati, who was Yashira's grandmother, took my group, and we all talked at once: "Let's walk around the edge of the field." "No, let's climb that rock and see if we can see the house first. My Papi is a farmer, and that's how he checks on his crops." "I'll hold Rafaelito's hand." "Me too, we'll put him in the middle so he can run faster." "Let's get yarn to tie on a tree so we don't get lost." "My tia told me a story about breadcrumbs to show the way."

Oh, the fun we had, all together, running through the woods, searching for Missy's house! Then when we all got there, Missy was there with the other *compañeros*—classmates, who had waited for us at the door, and said *"Bienvenidos!"* [welcome], served us *aguita de tamarindo* [a refreshment typical of Puerto Rico], and we all chattered excitedly as we told her about how we decided what was the best and fastest way to her house. We were careful not to put our feet on her couch and we didn't break a thing, not even Rafaelito! For days afterwards we talked about our different ways, drew maps, replayed several approaches with our toy animals and with string, and tried again our way, but without Rafaelito, since we thought he may have slowed us down...but it wasn't as much fun without his giggling. Finally, we decided a good way to see which way was the shortest way was to use the yarn to "measure" each way. Then for weeks Missy had us talking about different ways to get to places, what made each way faster, harder, slower, more fun. We began measuring everything wherever we were, and we came up with many different ways of measuring, with our feet, with our hats, with paint brushes, with books. "Mira Rafelito, you are three Cinderellas long!"[10]

What does it mean to teach in a culturally and linguistically responsive way? First, consider what makes a memorable learning experience for you. What comes into play that makes for an exciting, yet safe, exploration?

In the vignette above, the teacher and the assistant teacher spearheaded a real life experience that engaged the minds and bodies of the children, and the children took it from there, working together to achieve a palpable goal: getting to the teacher's house. They enacted, without teacher intervention, the best of *educación*: being responsible for each other, being respectful of the teacher's place, building on group ideas, playing, drawing on home and family knowledge. These modes of learning, linking relationships with learning and real-life tasks, have been proven successful for language minority students.[11]

Sometimes we teachers think of teaching as something more conscious and constructed than the experience above, but delve a bit further into your own past to identify how what you were taught and what you learned connect with and feed what you do now.

Questions for discussion and reflection:

- Think about something you know how to do well. How did you learn to do it? What did you learn?

- What do you like about what you do well?

- What has had the most impact in making you feel successful?

- How do you get past being uncomfortable with what you *don't* know?

Keep in mind the answers to these questions as you engage in teaching and learning with Latino children. As a teacher, you have learned to recognize children's personalities, learning styles, and needs. You are aware, of course, that the more you know the children, their families, and their backgrounds, the more you are able to reach and support them. Skilled, culturally responsive teachers are constantly preparing themselves and re-inventing what they do in order to give their students what they each need in order to thrive. But beyond looking at the individual child, they strive towards understanding the overarching view of what learning means for people of different cultures, as how we teach and how we learn reflects our values more than our dress, our food, or any other outward aspect of culture. In the next section, in order to contribute a bit to this view, I tell about cultural ways of learning that are in harmony with the value of *educación*. The following model summarizes the approaches I suggest.

Educación in Action: Relationship-Based and Context-Rich Learning

To be consonant with the value of *educación,* the skillful and responsive teacher approaches teaching holistically, encouraging learning relationships, helping children make connections across the curriculum, and building on the experiences and skills they bring from their communities and culture.[12]

This section is devoted to outlining some concepts and guidelines to help teachers and programs provide opportunities for children to learn through culturally-responsive methods that allow them a variety of ways to latch onto a learning experience, including individual and family learning and inquiry, apprenticing and mentoring, and participating in collective learning and meaningful activity. A reflective teacher clearly articulates why she uses an approach and how she pursues a child's thinking. Hopefully, the material here will help teachers shape a rationale for the best practices they may already use, and help them see how essential and effective these approaches are for Latino children.[13] Figure 4–1 represents the cultural ways of knowing that I've gathered here.

Inquiry: Context-Based Learning

Academic learning relies on significant amounts of information presented in abstract—rather than concrete—paths to learning. Perhaps because of the connotations and limitations being encased by four walls, even in preschool and kindergarten classrooms a great amount of knowledge and skills is still presented out of context or in highly structured ways.

The emphasis on text-based knowledge in the education field could leave some assuming that home environments without a rich store of books and writing experiences are deficient as compared to those where books and reading are visible daily.[14] But, after all, each child enters the classroom with a wealth of knowledge reaped from the people, stories, activities, and surroundings they come into contact with daily. Teachers need to be inquirers into the lives of children and families, and into children's minds and hearts.

When we were young, it was the three Rs: "readin', writin', and 'rithmetic." Speaking from a teacher's perspective, as much as we know and feel that learning should be much more than that, we're still deeply enmeshed in very structured programs pushing *reading first,* literacy, and the creation of environments that foster literacy. One program has kindergarten kids doing mostly "sit-down" work from two to three-and-a-half hours a day, and this approach is seeping into preschools. How can we squeeze in time to follow the children's thinking then? What happened to play? We know children are natural inquirers. They learn from their curiosity, from their excitement at doing things, ordinary things, like answering the phone,

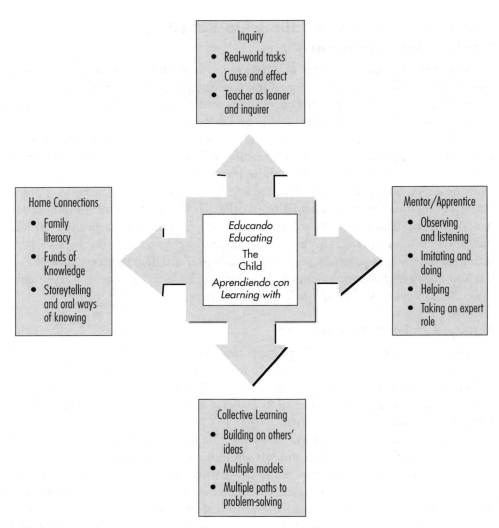

Figure 4–1 *Cultural Ways of Learning*

opening a door, pressing a button to make a sound… We are there to guide, translate, and extend those experiences with ordinary things, make them "aha!"[15] moments—when learners have an enlightening discovery—and use them as platforms for reaching benchmarks. Our world now needs children to grow to be thinkers, doers, and explorers. The three Rs we teach should be, "responsive, receptive, and responsible."

Inquiry into meaningful and concrete events, experiences, and phenomena, whether through guided discovery or through play, and approaching real life problems or challenges grounded in everyday experiences will provide a concrete context for children's learning. Although it sounds easy and natural—like riding a bike for most of us—in fact, teachers may indeed face challenges following a child's thinking and understanding how to uncover the expertise they bring. As an example, read the case of Elvira's teacher, whose best intentions bore no results until a peer unlocked a way.

 ## Building on Strengths
Finding a Way

Elvira sat in the corner of the room when she arrived in an American first grade classroom. Newly arrived from Salvador, she was placed in a bilingual Anglo American teacher's classroom. This teacher was tremendously dedicated to her students and always extended her learning beyond what was called for. Having had long exposure in her training to inquiry-based, hands-on learning, the teacher set up rich opportunities in her room for children to do interesting things, although most of the activities were heavily language-based. However, Elvira was not engaging or responding. One day, the teacher heard a classmate ask Elvira, "*¿Y que hacías en tu país?*—So, what did you do in your country?" Elvira didn't answer. "*Y cómo era tu escuela?*—What was your school like?" Elvira blushed when she shared that she had never been to school before, but that she helped her family in many ways.

Her peer continued to ask questions, and little by little, the teacher and children learned how Elvira had never sat down at a desk, but spent much of her time outdoors in the orchard and standing at her father's workbench. She used to help her father take apart pistons in engines and clean them with a broken ring. "Really?" joined in another classmate at the sound of the word *motor*—engine in Spanish—and soon a small group was gathered, hearing all about what Elvira did, and asking her to draw the "pistons" she talked about. The teacher followed up, exploiting this hands-on know-how by introducing the unassembled parts of a simple wave machine donated by a university lab. Elvira listened as the teacher told her in Spanish that the machine made waves in a tank of water and "drew" the waves it was making on a graph. Without ever having seen a wave machine, Elvira organized all the parts on the ground and proceeded to try different ways to put all the pieces together, with her classmates watching and helping under her direction. From then on, the teacher had a hook to bring Elvira into classroom experiences, and Elvira's interests and expertise—as well as her status—grew through sharing and inquiry. The teacher then had rich fodder for engaging Elvira and her classmates in meaningful conversation and related literacy activities such as labeling, illustrating the class' explorations, documenting directions to put together and take aart objects, and "writing" in their journals.

Even in young children, inquiry begins by observation. Taking in "data" from all sources, in complex forms, creates a backdrop of information that children can choose from when formulating their first question. Cause and effect is one of the first inquiries infants explicitly explore. When children see that their cry gets a response, they have already begun to make the connection between cause and effect. This discovery is a result of interactions. This is the beginning of communication: expressing needs, being understood, and understanding others. The next activity suggests one way to begin to explore a physical phenomenon that fascinates young children and is inspired by a "character" in a book. Making associations between a story and a hands-on activity will help second-language learners develop a vocabulary to talk about their explorations.

BRINGING IDEAS TO LIFE
Cause and Effect: Wind, Breath, and Motion

Many quality books are available to specifically expose young children to the values and knowledge of different cultures and countries, such as scientific and folk wisdom generated from observation and lore. Draw on cultural literature to inspire investigation.

As an example, introduce Alma Flor Ada's *Medio Pollito/Half-Chicken*, a bilingual book based on a Mexican folktale that tells about the rooster on a weathervane. Enlist a Latina staff member or family member to read the book in Spanish as well as to assist in follow-up activities, such as making the "wind sticks" described below. Breath and motion are simple cause and effect explorations that fascinate young children.

Prepare an outdoor table with drinking straws, tape, and long strips of tissue paper in different colors. Model a couple of different ways to attach the strips of tissue to the straw. Then watch how children experiment moving the "wind stick" to get the tails moving. Encourage children to hold the straws in different ways and facing different directions. Watch and note what the children do so you can talk about it later with them. Some may run, like with a kite, some may blow, some may help each other find ways to increase and decrease the movement. Let the children play without interference. Be prepared with appropriate questions that will help them think about what they are doing. You can follow up by making a chart about what you think the children know, and note what resources you and they would need to deepen their exploration.

You can adapt this activity for older children by providing other material that the children can experiment with, including light cloth or gauze that they can pierce through with the straw or tie to the straw or paper. Follow-ups can include different materials and equipment, like making a wind sock out of paper to place on a pole in the playground, blowing bubbles, or fanning feathers across the room.

These explorations will help children investigate the impact of force, weight, and direction on the distance an object travels. As they investigate, you can keep in mind some key questions that will help you see what the children are learning and how you can best guide their exploration further. For example, the following general questions address language, math, science, social, and artistic understanding:

- What patterns are the children seeing as they repeat a motion, a stroke, an experiment?
- How do they introduce variations into their patterns?
- What connections are they making?

Taking a common example, children often make rainbows. They may begin by copying what a peer has done or a decal they have at home. At some point, they may reverse the order of the colors, make an upside-down rainbow, make smaller rainbows in order to add a landscape, or begin to blend the hues with watercolor. When they see oil in a puddle, they see rainbow colors. If the child's thinking is pursued in each of these instances, it may very well lead to new paths of discovery and more significant understanding.

The Head Start on Science and Communication Program and the Early Learning Program have a variety of units on physical, earth, and life sciences that may be helpful to teachers of young learners, as does Ingrid Chaufour's and Karen Worth's *Discovering Nature with Young Children*.[16] The following web page for parents also has activities and questioning suggestions that can be useful in a preschool classroom or in a family child care setting: *<www.kidsource.com/kidsource/content/learnscience.html>*.

In many cultures, physical phenomena are strongly associated with spiritual and life lessons. While being careful not to foster misconceptions in science, you can help children make imaginative associations by finding out more about wind and breath and their meaning in various parts of the Americas. Many myths, folktales, mores, and rituals include the elements of fire, wind, water, and earth, and they have rich symbolic references to values and learnings for the holistic development of the child.

Making Home Connections

Skillful teachers define what and how they teach based on what each child brings, and they understand that the ultimate goal is to build curriculum and methods that draw on the children's past, heritage, present life, and vision of their place in the future. Because we know the impact of the home and a child's first teachers—their families— valuing and using home ways of learning are being discussed more in our field. What the parents want for the child, how the child fits in with the community, and what children are exposed to in the first few years shapes their minds and their futures. Throughout the developing world, successful alternative models of schooling have generated a shift in the thinking about children's outcomes. The focus of teaching has to move beyond making children literate. The questions should be: How can children's well-being be enhanced? How does the child's learning relate to the community's needs? And how does the learning experience enrich children's relationships with peers, family, community, and the adults around them?[17] These questions are inherent to a focus on *educación*—learning in a social context—which begins in the home, with *la familia*.

Challenges to Opportunities
Building Bridges

Home customs and parental beliefs—from discipline to gender expectations— need to be understood and discussed respectfully. A father might balk at seeing his son playing with dolls, for instance. Find ways to discuss these issues with your peer teachers and then broach the subject in a non-threatening way with parents. For instance, "You know, I see Pablito likes to play with all the toys we have here, and he uses the dolls especially to role play, making up complicated dialogue that shows he is learning much vocabulary and how to use it, as well as practicing how to clothe himself, share, and work out conflicts." Then, broaden your own understanding of the issues involved: "How does he do this at home? Are there particular things that worry you about how he plays with dolls?" Take the occasion to tell him about the role models of both genders you bring to school, and invite father, mother, or other kin to come to show or tell about what they value.

Programs That Inspire
Going Home Book[18]

A group of four adult Latina students and teachers set out to create a bilingual children's book that would capture some of the experiences of the Mexican American "transnationals" who cross the border regularly to visit their ancestral towns in Mexico. These young women, who presented at the Reading the World Conference V in San Francisco in March 2003, were looking for a way of not only investigating their heritage but also helping the newcomer child or the child of immigrants reflect on the impact of coming from another land and culture, as well as see how being in the United States has changed their lives and the lives of those who were left behind.

They began by interviewing their own families to find out what brought them to the United States and what they remembered about where they came from. Then they went to their hometowns to do an "ethnography" of the place, people, and happenings. They each made lists and described their towns' "characters," took photos of the town, and made schedules of the lives of some townspeople to see in the smallest detail how each conducts their lives. "See that photo where my grandmother's hair is wet? She just came out of the shower in my uncle's house, that's where all the family and neighbors go to bathe, since he has plenty of running water."

They looked for similarities in the four places and in the village life, especially around the plazas and the rituals, looking for a common symbol to merge the essence of the four communities into one book. They organized and compared the four places and their populations, including stores, plaza, churches, families, homes, roads, landscape, and then made a composite of the four villages to dramatize in their book. They illustrated how the life in the town changes when the transnationals go back and forth, painting a lively scenario of the *quinceañeras* where all the neighbors and families chip in to organize the festivities, contributing their skills in dressmaking, decorations, and food. The *quinceañera* is an important passage in the life of a young woman of Mexican descent, and the typical cost for the event is equal to that of a wedding, including dresses for the *quinceañera* and her attendants. In the four ancestral villages, the ceremony is not only more affordable for the transnationals, but actually contributes to the local economy and the life of the town. In the four villages in real life, and in the book, the event takes place publicly—in the plaza—with church bells ringing in celebration and the town crier inviting all to attend. In the interviews and in the book, the villagers rejoice in participating in the festivities and in contributing what little they can to mark this most important phase of a girl's growth.

The four young Latinas published the book and use it in their classrooms to give life to the continuous "going home" experience of many Mexican Americans, as well as of many Latinos from the Caribbean.

Transnationals are international ambassadors for the United States. They not only contribute to the U.S. economy, but also to that of their native countries. Salvadorans, for example, last year took back $2.1 billion to Salvador, and Mexicans $14 billion.[19] Our immigrant populations have a rich store of knowledge and experience that contributes to their resilience and their enduring impact on the shaping of the United States. Celebrate the special gifts they bring and encourage bilingualism and biculturalism. Becoming American should not mean giving up this richness, but rather adding to it. Choose children's books that speak to newcomer experiences and the immigrant journey from different perspectives, for example, *The Upside Down Story/El Niño de Cabeza* or *Esperanza Rising*. And, to further your own understanding, find books that put you in touch with the immigrant experience, like the story of the fictionalized "Garcia Sisters" by Julia Alvarez, or a teacher's story of how she created a space for immigrant children to shine and take pride in their origins.[20] Cristina Igoa's touching book, *The Inner World of the Immigrant Child,* relates how a class of newcomers learned to express themselves through visual storytelling using filmstrips they created and shared with each other. Despite the fact that the children are ten to twelve years old, Igoa's insights and strategies can be an inspiration and resource for teachers of younger children. The group process is intrinsic to the literacy development of the children in this story, as the whole class gathers to provide positive feedback and to plan sound effects for each filmstrip together, sharing and presenting their customs to each other, and making a class book entitled "Friends Forever." [21]

Much emphasis has been placed of late on promoting family literacy. When considering the lives of diverse communities, teachers need to broaden their views on what constitutes a language-rich environment. Oral traditions are strong in Latino cultures, and they can be a logical and natural stepping-stone to meaningful family literacy activities. Storytelling can take many forms in Latino culture. Sharing family memories and extracting lessons from these memories for the next generation is a time-honored custom. Read how one teacher exploited an opportunity to blend family stories, moral development, and intergenerational literacy in an exciting project that brought pride to the mothers and children who participated in making an unusual book extracted from authentic experiences.

BRINGING IDEAS TO LIFE
Mariquita la Traviesa

"I never misbehaved when I was little—*nunca fui traviesa*," one of the mothers in visiting artist Susan Thompson's parent group asserted, frustrated at her own child's behavior. All the other mothers joined in, "My mother would never allow me to question her punishment." "The kids these days, the trouble they're having in school, so young... I never got into that kind of trouble." "You were perfect children? Never any problem, ever?" Susan prodded. Then she told them a story about a time she got in trouble when she lost her mother's precious pin, and the mothers started to laugh, nodding. One mother started "*Sí, yo tambien hice algo así*—I also did something like that. I remember a time when I lost my brand new shoes. I hated to wear shoes, but when we went to church one day…" And one after the other, they began to open up and tell about the naughty things they did and how they got into trouble and were punished.

At this turning point, Susan asked the mothers, "Maybe we need to tell our children that we weren't so perfect, and show them how they can become responsible and overcome their naughtiness." Thus, *Mariquita la Traviesa*—Mariquita the Little Rascal—was born (see Figure 4–2). First, the mothers began by telling their stories to their children at home and talking about how they got past their childish mistakes. Then the mothers told the stories to each other as Susan audiotaped them. The mothers, together with their children, created a bilingual storybook. They created one composite character, *Mariquita*, who did all of their mischievous deeds. They soon realized that animals were often featured in these adventures, so they decided to end the book by making Mariquita become a veterinarian. Susan made sure that each of the mothers and children could participate, even if they didn't feel comfortable reading or drawing.

Programs That Inspire
Building on Family "Funds of Knowledge"

In a pioneering project in California, teachers become learners, visiting their students' homes, where, hosted by the family, they learn about the everyday activities and work of family members. The teachers then develop projects that integrated math concepts and language in a familiar context, based on aspects of the life of the families, such as designing a garden. In addition, beginning with the parents' interests and concerns, parent-teacher workshops continue the learning relationship by offering opportunities to engage together in hands-on activities in topics identified by parents and relevant to their lives, such as lunar phases and shopping, where conceptual understanding of science and mathematics come into play. This approach not only aligns with best practices that support inquiry, hands-on knowledge, and the principles of *Connections and Commitments*, but also serves to dispel any misgivings or assumptions teachers may bring about lack of opportunities in family life and about the relevance of routine tasks to learning.[22]

Build your own connections with families with the following activity, which can serve as both a family literacy activity and a shared experience for the young children in your program or classroom of different backgrounds.

Figure 4–2 *Mariquita la Traviesa* (Photo by Susan Thompson)

BRINGING IDEAS TO LIFE
Photo Stories

What could be more familiar and natural than looking at family photo albums? Family portraits are excellent conversation starters and can be just as effective, or more so, as formal reading or language activities in improving children's language development and literacy.

Many children have seen family members pull out photo albums or show visitors family portraits, at the same time telling the visitor about the photo and the family members. Valuable language skills are called into play during this "telling." In showing a photo, much information is conveyed, including name, action, place, sequence, relationships, description, as well as about family history: "This is Juana when she was nine," a parent may say, "Ay, she was curious as a cat! Here she is coming out of a tunnel she found under the road in our hometown when she was chasing a rabbit. And this is Uncle Jorge, reading a story to Juana and little Tom." Think of the stories and conversations that can emerge from just these few comments.

If you chose to adapt this idea for your classroom, find ways to encourage sharing of family albums, or you could request parents to put together an album of their latest family outing or event. During small group or circle time, for a week, have children take turns sharing their albums. Afterwards, keep the albums in the reading corner for children to look through. First listen as they show the photos. What literacy and preliteracy skills do they draw on as they flip through the photos? Do other children have questions or comments? These occasions can be very productive in helping children make connections and comparisons with each others' lives. What do they share? What's different? Perhaps some picnic in the same park every Mother's Day, or a couple have an uncle named Jorge. Maybe one's father comes from an Asian background and another's is a red-haired, blue-eyed Latino.

As you listen and observe, note for later what vocabulary children use that you could build on and what kinds of literacy skills they show that you can highlight. You can also develop a simple tool to compile information that you can use in your curriculum later. To keep the exchange less "teacherly" and more informal, take a step back, don't let children rely on you to direct the conversation. Later on, you could model more complex conversation using your own photos of a family trip. You can also ask questions to help extend the children's conversations about the photos. However, consider carefully when to intervene, so children don't necessarily experience this as a teacher-directed lesson.

You could ask, for instance: Who is that *in front* of your mother? Is your sister *between* you and your brother? What is *behind* that tree? Tell us where your trip started. And then what did you do? These prompts will help you enhance the child's concepts about time and space, as well as to know the family.

To follow up on these informal conversations, you can make a class album, involving groups of children in creating a "big book" of trips or events. You can use various materials, such as ticket stubs, Polaroids or digital photos, drawings, magazine photos, and brochures from your outings. Begin by "setting the stage" during circle time, that is, having the children recall the trip as you show them the Polaroids and other mementos. Set tables or floor space with a selection of these materials, glue sticks, and a big poster board taped to table or floor. As you visit the tables, make sure you don't stand, but sit at the same level as the children, maybe joining in as a participant, adding your own photos. In this way, the children may rely less on you as the expert, and look to their peers if they need help. Listen to the conversations of the children as they select and create with the materials. You can write their comments and explanations, which later on could be attached to the back of the album pages. After you put the book together, you can use it to "read aloud," with each group telling the story of their photo pages, and it can have a permanent home in the class library, where children can look at the albums on their own or show their parents the albums during family visits.

BRINGING IDEAS TO LIFE
Telling, Retelling, and Reading Stories About Food

Food is most assuredly a reoccurring theme in many multicultural children's stories, songs, and rhymes, and games. Try *Benito's Bizcochitos/Los Bizcochitos de Benito* by Ana Baca (1999, Piñata Books). This bilingual picture book by a Latina author from New Mexico is particularly useful for connecting with Latino children because it centers around the history of the *bizcochito*, a traditional Christmas cake in Mexico, that is now the "official" state cookie of New Mexico. This book shows how the grandmother passes down this tradition, weaving myth and reality, and concludes with a recipe for children and adults to make together. Suitable for children three to seven years of age, *Benito's Bizcochitos* can provide rich possibilities for conversations and allow children from different ethnic backgrounds to share stories about what their own grandmothers and grandfathers taught them. They can also compare and contrast what they eat and what they know as *bizcocho,* because all Latin American countries have their own version of a food by this name, ranging from a cake to a flatbread.

The side-by-side Spanish and English versions in this book equally value both languages and allow both teachers and families to read with the child.

Introduce the book and related activities, along with several other books with the similar theme of comfort food, such as:

- Bertrand, Diane Gonzales. *Sip, Slurp, Soup, Soup / Caldo, caldo, caldo*. Houston, TX: Piñata Books.

- Chavarría-Cháirez, Becky. 2000. *Magda's Tortillas / Las Tortillas De Magda*. Houston, TX: Piñata Books.

- Galindo, Mary Sue. 2001. *Icy Watermelon / Sandía* Fría. Houston, TX: Piñata Books.

- Heaslip, P. C. 1987. *Chapatis Not Chips*. London: Methuen Children's Books.

- Macaluso Rodríguez, Gina. 1994. *Tamales De Elote / Green Corn Tamales*. Tuscon, AZ: Hispanic Books.

However, don't just leave it at the food level. Teaching around themes, although easier to structure and schedule than emergent curriculum, is limiting in nature. Take a step beyond and see where it takes you and the children. Reflect on the different ways food is significant and is enjoyed in each of the above. Compare and contrast the different elements and "morals" of each of the different books with families on a family reading night. In the Bertrand book, for example, a rhythmic text with repetitive phrases relates how the children watch Mamá make soup (recipe included) and go with Papá to get tortillas before joining the family to eat this typical Mexican meal. As you read the book, or as children describe their favorite foods, have spaces for conversations and pose questions to spark dialogue. Do their fathers cook? Do their parents have their own specialties? In Chapter 2, I relate an example of a father who was a cook and gave a cooking lesson to all the children in the center, aided by the teachers, who followed up by making bilingual food lists and recipes for the children to follow. Encourage emergent writing by setting up materials in a natural setting, such as food lists that children check off in the kitchen play area and labels for fruits and vegetables in the market area.

Find ways of documenting literacy and language skills you see emerge from conversations, dress-up, and storytelling. This will help you track each child's milestones. The following chart can give you ideas on what to look for as you record your observations. You can also build a tool such as the sample observation tools in the Appendix *(Literacy Implementation Observation Tool* and the *Relationship Observation Protocol)*. In the chart below, one column lists speaking skills, the other audience skills. Audience skills are just as important in language learning as speaking and expression skills. Perhaps you can capture these capacities by video. On several action research projects I worked on, I videotaped interactions and conversations, and then showed the children the tapes. The children were transfixed, hearing themselves and others talking, revisiting an exploration from a different point of view, or observing something significant that had escaped their attention at the moment: "Oh, look! Ricky is putting a straw down the ant hill just before they moved their eggs." This prompted new and interesting rounds of comments, connections, and conversations. Both speaker and audience benefit from these conversations.

Speaker (Child talking and sharing)	Audience (Child listening and interacting)
• Oral expression	• Oral expression
• Nonverbal communication	• Nonverbal attention
• Description of persons, clothes, objects, places	• Listening
• Clarifying when others don't understand	• Learning about peers and their families
• Distinguishing action, time, space, and sequence	• Formulating questions
• Communicating and sharing personal experience	• Making connections
• Using and expanding vocabulary and knowledge	• Building on or completing others' ideas

 ### Keeping a Balance
Balancing Freedom and Support

Keeping a balance between the familiar and the new is essentially the best way to learn for most. Children love and learn from repetitions and routines, such as reading from the same stories over and over again. Second-language learners benefit because they are trying to assimilate and make sense of so many new stimuli, and repetition helps them begin to build patterns of language and understand the social expectations and discourse around what occurs in the classroom. However, freeing their creativity and imagination allows them to express themselves more intuitively and personally, as well as to push their thinking and skills beyond what is simply modeled and memorized. Find ways to both support the familiar and encourage innovative thinking and new words and experiences.

Figure 4–3 *Talk Book (Photo by Susan Thompson)*

Bring together the power of the visual and oral by starting a class tradition of making "talk books." These books without words (see Figure 4–3) free children to invent stories and make connections between words and meaning without being tied to a repeating storyline, and they also give them opportunities to practice pre-literacy skills such as page turning, sequencing, and describing. If you add sensory experiences, such as those I discussed in Chapter 2, you can trigger more memories and associations. Susan Thompson, the instigator of *Mariquita la Traviesa*, had her students do an interesting activity that could be easily adapted into a "talk book." She asked the children to make up a "poem" about their grandmothers using their senses, thus exposing them to metaphor as well as rich description. Building on the sensory activities in Chapter 2, you can suggest some beginnings: "My *Tati* smells like…"; Granmama's hair feels like…"; My Grandmother's voice sounds like…"[23] Georgia Heard's book *For the Good of the Earth and Sun* suggests many ideas for generating poetry from even the youngest children. Isabel Campoy's poetry books are particularly appropriate for children of different backgrounds, and will inspire you to find ways of touching on the imagery and values that children absorb from their upbringing and experiences.[24]

Considering the Needs of Second-Language Learners

Before I go on to describe the other components of this model of cultural ways of knowing, I'd like to explain why I've chosen to provide examples that begin with quality bilingual books.

Providing language and literacy experiences across the curriculum benefits all children, but is especially crucial for second-language learners, as discussed in the key points of the section below on *Understanding the Development of Language and Literacy.* To help children who come with little or only oral knowledge of English, always finds ways to support language and literacy in context, that is, connect the spoken and written word with a visual and with an experience, be it through arts and crafts, observation and discovery—such as the wind and breath activity described earlier—by discussing and doing, or by representing the word or the idea through the body, such as the *Tell It with Your Body* activity. In addition, for the culturally different, as well as for children with different learning styles, engaging the seven *intelligences*[25] in daily learning and teaching experiences is vital to their holistic development because they will have multiple ways to hook onto and benefit from the activity.

 Did You Know?
Why Bilingual?

Many of the activities in this chapter are drawn on books that are available in both Spanish and English. Although I discuss the rationale in more depth in following sections, I believe using *quality* bilingual books and books in Spanish will benefit the children in three mayor ways:

- Helps children develop skills in the mother tongue, which contributes to language development in the second language
- Gives children a corresponding vocabulary in both languages, which will allow them to draw on either language to build critical and conceptual skills
- Provides a platform for families to share the language experiences of their children, and, in the case of adults with limited literacy in their own language, promote family literacy

Children begin to think in the first language they hear. Just as children learn best when they are given a context in which to learn, the knowledge that children acquire and process in their mother tongue helps them learn in a second language.[26]

Whenever possible, use bilingual books to help young children discover phenomena in both their native language and English. Reach out to bilingual and bicultural teachers or volunteers who can help parents and children interact with the books. Bilingual adults can extend learning by participating in the small group discussions in their native language, drawing out conversation in the second-language learner. Alma Flor Ada's *Magical Encounter: Latino Children's Literature in the Classroom* is a wonderful sourcebook of essential knowledge, activities, and ideas, including a complete, categorized list of titles for kindergarten through the upper grades. As Ada recommends in *Teachers as Authors*, teachers should also pay attention to using books written by Latinos. Aside from sending a clear message about empowerment and voice, you are assuring that the children are exposed to values, culture, metaphors, and symbols from the firsthand experience and thought of a fellow Latino. However laudable and necessary it is for *everyone* to focus on cultural issues and to become bilingual, a cultural expert can provide the insider's perspective and share a tacit understanding that is not accessible to those outside the culture.

BRINGING IDEAS TO LIFE
Evaluate Your Bilingual or Spanish Language Books

Organize a workshop with other teachers in your program to assess the cultural and linguistic competence of books and materials you use daily or are considering using. Then you can try the same activity at a family night to get parents' perspectives.

Follow these steps to conduct an effective evaluation:
1. Ask each teacher to pick out two or three children's books they use regularly in the classroom with the Spanish-speaking children. Make sure you include some that you consider specifically *multicultural* children's books, so you can compare and contrast the strengths, themes, and illustrations.

    Perhaps your program or school classrooms already have an extensive selection of multicultural children's literature. In that case, you may pick out your and the children's favorites. If you are considering acquiring some new books, your local library may be a good resource. If your library lacks a quality selection of Spanish-language or bilingual books, you may be able to play a part in advocating for more. You can refer the head librarian to the Fairfax County Library's online list for ideas: *<www.co.fairfax.va.us/library/Reading/Elem/bilingual books.htm>*.

    In some cases, if you are part of a district school system or have a large population of children, publishers may send you review copies of books you pick from their catalogs.
2. *Alternative 1:* When all the teachers are gathered, brainstorm some simple questions to guide you in assessing the books. Questions could include:

- How do you think the book represents the feelings, values, and culture of the children in your class?
- How are landscapes, people, animals, plants, objects, food, or clothes that are familiar to children depicted in the books?
- What do you most like about this book?

3. *Alternative 2:* Download the Spanish-Language Materials Review Instrument from <*ccf.edc.org//latinos/id4.htm*>.

   You will find examples of how this instrument was used to evaluate teacher's books on the same web page. The tool is organized around this book's framework of values and can help you see how these values are infused throughout your books and also help you identify gaps.

4. Have enough copies of this blank instrument for teachers to work in pairs to fill it out.

5. After each pair has reviewed and discussed the contents of the book, share what you found in whole group and discuss where the books may fall short so you can consider carefully your next purchase.

6. Repeat the same process at a Family Reading Night. You can call it a Pajama Party for Families!

Programs That Inspire
Learning Through the "Practical Life" of Migrant Families

When the Foundation Center for Phenomenological Research in Sacramento decided to take on the task of responding to the needs of migrant families in Yolo County, California, they started with the needs and the wishes of the parents. The mostly Latino, migrant families, working up to twelve hours a day, had a desperate need for free day care for their young children. In addition, the parents were concerned that once in the schools, their children would face challenges and criticism when using Spanish and would also risk losing their respect for their culture.

The Foundation Center, under the leadership of Antonia Lopez, instituted free Montessori programs in the native language that would address the fears of parents. Extending to seven centers in 2000, this program is built around the concept of learning the "practical life" of the family. Where migrant families may not be able to engage in the kind of mentoring activities that allow young children to understand the meaning of the daily work and chores of the family, the centers build learning through daily activities that allow them to take pride and become expert in ways that contribute to the household, such as preparing food, washing dishes, washing and feeding themselves, and watching the growth of the fruits and artichokes their parents harvest. All this provides fertile ground for many kinds of conceptual understanding. Teachers were recruited from the migrant community, and a network of family child care programs was built across the region, making these programs particularly culturally and linguistically responsive, as well as accessible to migrant families.[27]

Learning Relationships

Much of what we know about best practices across cultures centers on social ways of learning. From birth through the adult years, others both motivate and help us to learn.[28] In addition, we learn when we teach others, clarifying what we know in order to be understood, rephrasing, refining, confirming or disconfirming, adding depth and detail, and integrating others' views and knowledge into what we understand.[29] Given the socially driven nature of Latino cultures, this is especially significant in our work with Latino children and families. The teacher aware of this dynamic will incorporate teaching methods and interactions that build on the relationship of the Latino child with others. In any given activity, outing, or play, many complex relationships are occurring at the same time. I highlight below some aspects of learning relationships that are particularly consonant with the values in *educación*: apprenticing, mentoring, and collective learning.

Beginning in 1993, I began to look closely at learning relationships in prekindergarten through third-grade classrooms. Inspired by my observations in these settings and confirmed in the research I did with a Ryerson Polytechnic University team[30] focused on quality multi-age relationships in diverse Canadian child care centers, mentoring as a valuable cross-cultural approach for teaching and learning became a thread throughout my work. As we saw in Canada, the variety of levels in a multi-age setting benefits the cognitive development of all the children because they are exposed to a broader range of stimulating activities and are inspired by the interests of both younger and older peers. We heard how older children's knowledge and expression sharpened and became more complex as they tried to tailor their talk and explanations to help others understand them. We observed younger, less-abled, and second-language learners all benefit from developmentally advanced activities that may not have been available in a more age-segregated setting. We watched as a younger child picked up the beat of a song intended for expanding the older children's knowledge of triangles, and we saw how a child with little English became interested in observing the development of insects and in books about insects as a result of standing over the shoulder of her older, English-speaking peers. Many family child care—now called in-home care—settings have the advantage of mixed-age groupings that foster such learning relationships. Our classrooms and centers in the United States are unfortunately less likely to accommodate mixed ages, although some examples exist that deliberately build on the benefits of having children of different abilities working together.

BRINGING IDEAS TO LIFE
Examples of Relationship-Based Learning

- Students with behavioral disabilities as well as those with language differences benefit from being assigned a "buddy"—an older or more experienced peer—to serve as a role model, help build confidence, and model the expectations and socialization rules in the classroom. In Chapter 3, we saw how this buddy could serve as classroom tour guide for a newcomer. [31]

- Project-based learning such as the Reggio Emilia model—an internationally recognized early learning program—centers around relationships between children and their peers, adults, community, and their environment. The approach favors a curriculum that emerges from the children and relies on shared decision-making and group problem-solving.

- *Success for All*, the Literacy Collaborative, and other early literacy programs include paired reading aloud and shared emergent writing as major components. Children can practice pronouncing words and letters and question meanings in safety before venturing to read aloud to a group or to the teacher.

- Choral reading or call and response are old standbys from the past that have been largely set aside, perhaps deemed too teacher-directed or not individualized enough. However, these practices are particularly helpful for second-language learners and Latinos, as well as African American children who enjoy this interactive, rhythmic, and predictable group activity. In a chorus, even the timid or the child who hasn't mastered the language can participate and practice sounds without standing out.

Apprenticing

Apprenticing is perhaps the most time-honored method of learning across cultures and across trades. Consider how you would learn to take a photograph, wire a house, mix paint colors, or make a peanut butter sandwich. Of course, many of these skills can be mastered through exploration, but imagine trying to follow directions or reading a book to accomplish these tasks. Apprenticing means watching and doing, led by an expert.

Apprenticeships can take many forms, from watching and imitating a peer's actions in the dress-up corner to apprenticing with a trusted expert—be it an adult who models a task that the child later imitates and internalizes, or more or differently-abled peers who provide a range of models or a complementary approach to learning. This allows the learner to choose from a variety of approaches and skill sets.

In the following story, Carlota and Josefa exemplify a traditional approach of apprenticing that is echoed throughout the world—learning from an elder. The observation of John and Clara that follows shows apprenticing from peers by watching and experimenting.

> Six-year-old Carlota and her four-year-old sister Josefa spend the hours after school and before dinner in their grandfather's workshop. There, sitting quietly, Josefa draws in her notebook, and Carlota draws on a gourd, as Don Andrés carves intricate markings on gourds that grow on the trees outside his window. Some of the symbols are age-old, passed down through generations from his Mayan ancestors. Others he or his daughters make up, metaphors for something they hold dear. The breeze flutters the leaves outside, the roosters crow, and the sounds of neighbors punctuate the silence, but few words are spoken between Don Andrés and his granddaughters. Every now and then Carlota brings Don Andrés her gourd and asks a question so softly that even I, sitting in a nearby corner, cannot hear. Josefa comes over and sits on his lap, picking a new symbol to draw in her notebook. For three days, this family opened their door to this stranger who had come to videotape, drawn by the mysterious and beautiful symbols in gourds carved by Don Andrés. The atmosphere of the three days was relaxed, almost meditative. The rhythm and focused activity were so transfixing that months later, when I showed a group of rambunctious American third graders one hour of uncut footage of Don Andrés' workshop, you could hear a pin drop. They absorbed the energy, as well as the skill and symbology that the gourds represented. With no instruction and little support from me, the children proceeded to make their own symbols and decorate their own clay pots with the care and respect they had witnessed in the video. My research trip to the Yucatán has reaped its reward: bringing back the spirit and the ways of learning of another culture into the life of a busy American classroom.

Learning from differently-abled peers also helps children with special needs. Simply seeing something done, without complex directions or words, allows special needs children, such as those with autism, to absorb the gist of an activity without the pressure of performing for the teacher.[32] Then a teacher, or peer mentor, can explicitly model a step of the process, giving the child a chance to imitate and better internalize the activity. For example, for Spanish speakers, you can use these simple lines and add a jump as you say the word *salta*:

> *Yo soy el coqui que salta, salta, salta*
> I am the little frog that jumps, jumps, jumps
> And later you can add the words *here* and *there:*
> *Yo soy el coqui que salta, salta, salta, aqui*
> *Yo soy el coqui que salta, salta, salta, alli*

Learning Through Play and Discovery: Bubble Making[33]

I observed an activity involving younger and older children playing outdoors. A group of twenty children gathered and waited around a small, child-size picnic table while teachers filled it with various kinds of bubble-making materials. This activity was accessible to different levels and held children's attention throughout an hour. I am not surprised that what we learn about developmentally-appropriate attention span is constantly disproved when the situation is rich, enjoyable, and socially mediated. The older children used various ways to blow bubbles, from strings to hoops dipped in vats and bottles, exploring different ways of producing the bubbles: blowing, running with the strings, or moving wands through the air. A pair of children dipped a hoop in a bucket of soapy water and jumped up and down from a bench. Two-year-old John stayed at this activity for over an hour, and two-and-half-year-old Clara joined off and on, between swinging with her friend. Both maintained focus for a very long time and kept trying without reaching frustration levels, perhaps inspired by the other children around them. John succeeded in making bubbles by jerking his arm upward rather than by blowing, having observed the older children doing this previously. Both were eventually able to blow bubbles, verbalizing their mastery joyously and loudly. Mission accomplished!

Can you think of an outdoor activity that can be accessible to all, yet could engender excitement and challenge and provide multiple ways of arriving at the same end? These experiences are especially useful to young Latino children trying to make sense of how things are done in their new environment. They witness that there is no one "right" way, and that creativity and trying new things will take them to new paths to discovery.

At the beginning of this chapter, I ask the reader, "How do you get past being uncomfortable with what you don't know?" What might that mean to a child who hasn't yet grasped the basics needed to function in an American classroom, for example, knowing how to ask to go to the bathroom? Watching others play and navigate the classroom gives children important cues for understanding the new culture and ways in the early childhood environment.

Cultivating a Mentor Role

Mentoring provides an opportunity for the learner to be the expert and engage in both pro-social and responsive practice, just as a teacher does when adjusting lessons or modeling to the level and interest of the learner. Mentoring both contributes to self-development and social development, but more importantly, to the growth of the learning community. Mentoring is the educational facet of helping, an essential social behavior that I discussed in more depth in Chapter 2. Empowerment, agency, and social responsibility associated with *educación* come from cultivating a mentor role in the young children we guide.

Being a mentor requires social and expressive skills that you can help the children groom in many ways. Often, nonverbal skills so important to building word understanding are not cultivated extensively. The following activity ideas can be useful.

BRINGING IDEAS TO LIFE
Tell It with Your Body

Use books and your own storytelling to engage the body and motor development of the children, helping them link their kinesthetic know-how with the vocabulary of the story. One of the favorite ways young children who are beginning to learn language interact with stories is through songs with gestures. In a safe group, they learn to recognize the meaning of certain words as they visually see them acted out. Like Itsy Bitsy Spider, nursery rhymes from the Americas guide children's understanding in fun ways, using gestures, expressions, and characters that are familiar. The following resources and others listed in the last part of this chapter will be helpful.

- Delacre, L. 1989. *Arroz con Leche: Popular Songs and Rhymes From Latin America.* NY: Scholastic.
- Griego, M. C., and B. Cooney. 1988. *Tortillitas Para Mama and Other Nursery Rhymes.* NY: Holt.

These two books are of Latin American nursery rhymes and suggest finger play activities.

Or, you could use books on animals, many of which are available bilingually, to tap into the young's natural interest in animal behavior. Encourage them to move like the animals you are reading about and use these occasions to explore the lives of animals. For instance, ask children: Where do you think birds sleep? Where does your dog or cat sleep? What about these fishes we just read about? Where did they get their food?

You can make up a tale where you model the actions, encouraging children to imitate repetitive actions associated with the words. For instance, try Antonio Frasconi's *The Snow and the Sun/La Nieve y el Sol.* Acting out being cold and hot comes easily to young children and is a great source of vocabulary and sounds.

Look to library sites for ideas, as well as multicultural book distributors such as Del Sol Books <*www.delsolbooks.com*>, Santillana Press <*www.santil-lanausa.com*>, and Children's Book Press <*www.childrensbookspress.org*>—all excellent places to find a variety of quality books by Latino and other authors.

Next, an activity and a book geared to building the helping and empathy skills necessary to be a good, caring mentor to others.

BRINGING IDEAS TO LIFE
Helping Hands

Building on what can occur naturally when children of different abilities and interests play together, use books to bring home the idea of helping. For example, try Gloria Anzaldúa's *Friends from the Other Side/Amigos Del Otro Lado.*[34] A renowned Chicana poet and writer, Anzaldúa offers many strong bicultural and humanistic metaphors, as well as evocative language, to touch on issues of identity and values of the bicultural child and adult.

This story tells about the journey many Mexican families make across the border, and also illustrates the commitment of a young Mexican child who takes a risk to help another. This book can lead to discussions, role playing, and story-telling about empathy and helping. I suggest using books from other cultures, including Anglo American, so you can show how these humanistic values present themselves throughout the globe.

Arnold Loebel's classic friendship tales in *Frog and Toad* accentuate empathetic and selfless giving. You can ask the children to tell about a time that a friend helped them, and how they felt, as well as a time they helped someone, and how the other person responded. These experiences are what cement the value of helping without regards to getting something in return, a requisite for developing a sense of commitment to others. Many teachers introduce empathy by asking the children to imagine how the other person feels, and yet the culturally responsive nuance of this skill involves children in seeing beyond their own needs and feelings. As a follow-up, create a visual "culture of caring." Show photos of young children helping each other.

Figure 4–4 *Sister Reading to Younger Brother* (Photo by Costanza Eggers)

Make a running list of "good deeds" that you update regularly—perhaps labeled *Helping Hands*—where you ask children to tell about ways they helped others recently. You can have some cut-outs from magazines handy that they can pin up to represent what they did to help, or you could list the ways or have children dictate captions. This can be effectively done when the children are all gathered in a group, whether at circle time, before nap, or during lunch. Include yourself. Say how you helped someone, then encourage each to add something they remember they did, such as, "I helped my baby brother eat his cereal," "I helped my mother wash our car," or "I helped my friend put away the blocks." Watch for helping behavior on the part of children who don't verbalize much or are shy, so their *helping hands* can be represented as well.

Designing Collective Learning

Group play and projects are key modes of learning for young children. Teambuilding, complex and critical thinking, negotiation, problem-solving, collective gathering of knowledge, and achieving collective goals can be a part of many group activities.

However, keep in mind that some children may be reticent, shy, or solitary, and they should not be forced to participate, whether it's circle time or a game of ball. For these children, and for those with special needs, devise various ways of entering a group project. For instance, you can tape a long roll of paper on a hallway wall at children's' level, and attach with string various drawing instruments, such as fat pencils or crayons at different points, as well as different shapes and toys. As they walk by, individual children are tempted to play with the toys and shapes, or trace them, or use the drawing tools in different ways. As crayons and pencils are attached by strings, this allows them to explore possibilities that are different from those available to them when drawing on individual pieces of paper. They can make circles, experiment with using both hands and arms at once, and swing arcs.[35] Each individual's experimentation then yields one large piece that can be referred to later in discussions: "I saw Leo doing an interesting thing: He first traced the toy dinosaur that was hanging on the wall, then he leapt to the next crayon, roared, and made a big arch. He did this three times. Leo, tell us about that, please."

Collective projects can be encouraged a variety of ways that can fit into the philosophy of your program. While I strongly believe in curriculum that emerges from what the children bring and what they choose to pursue, many programs may not have the freedom or flexibility in their schedules and curriculum to embrace project-based, child-initiated learning and play. In play, children make their own decisions and negotiate steps and rules. This kind of agency is important to their individual and group growth. Some of the activities in the "Bringing Ideas to Life" boxes have suggested structures and follow-ups, but I encourage you to investigate your own ways to engage your students in relationship-based learning that places them in a position to make decisions about the direction of their learning.

BRINGING IDEAS TO LIFE
The Games We Play

Many years ago, as a consultant and visiting artist, I developed three different intergenerational mural projects that involved young children aged three to twelve working together with community members, aunts, grandmothers, and teachers. The themes of the murals were family stories, favorite places, and games. In partnership with a community center, one of these murals, *The Games We Play*, explored the games that each of the children's families played, from adults to the youngest. Here are some ideas—which you can pick and choose from—to bring to life different aspects of this program.

- Prepare for this mural, playing, and storytelling activity by inviting everyone to a *Game Night*, where each family brings something they use in their play. Some may bring dominoes, others a jump rope or a ball, a top, cards, or even a hand-held video game. It doesn't matter if it's a cultural artifact or modern equipment; the point is to enjoy playing together.

- At the *Game Night*, which can be held outdoors and indoors, take slide photos of everyone playing. Slides will allow you to project and enlarge the images on a wall later on. If you have a digital camera and an LCD projector, that will work as well. Make sure you have some interesting and recognizable shapes in your compositions. These photos will form the basis for the mural.

- Hold a *Games Brainstorming* session with teachers and families at your center or school. Make a list of all the types of games you each remember from your childhood and the games played by the children. Revisit the Game Night, asking families to tell what they enjoyed doing and what they observed their children and others enjoying. Use this occasion to recruit a small number of adults to participate in the mural activity.

- Organize two weekend family workshops or various afternoons to complete the mural. You can follow these steps for a simple approach:

  a) Project the slides and have children and adults choose some silhouettes they would like in their mural.

  b) Pin large pieces of paper on the wall where the slides are projected so the participants can outline the figures and play equipment projected onto the paper. You can play with the size of the outlines by moving the slide projector back and forth. Use a variety of sizes, as the mural can represent games in the foreground as well as in the background (see Figures 4–5 and 4–6).

c) Ask the adults to cut out the outlined figures and give a small mixed-age group some cutouts to decorate with paint, stamping, and collage.

d) When the figures and outlines are dry, have the families and children talk about and create a background on a large roll of paper that will accommodate all the figures, and have the groups experiment with different places to put their decorated figures and game equipment. The background could be a landscape, a field of patterns, or simply glued material or wallpaper samples. If you have many materials handy, participants will be more creative.

e) Once everyone agrees on the placement, glue the figures, and cover with a couple of layers of polyurethane when the families have gone. The mural from this project was exhibited in Boston City Hall and then used in the classroom to generate storytelling and game activities.

Figures 4–5 and 4–6
Stages of "The Games We Play"
Mural, Roslindale, Massachusetts
(Photo by Costanza Eggers)

For follow-up activities, you can ask families and children to bring a commonly used toy, such as a ball or a top, and compare the different kinds and how they are used. In Mexico, for instance, there is a simple top that is wound up like a yoyo and then released. Jumping rope is also virtually universal, but each culture generates a diverse variety of songs, rhymes, and synchronized actions all excellent ways for second-language learners to grasp the nuances of culture and language.

A Note on Individual Versus Collective Inquiry

Skillful and culturally competent teachers design and assess learning activities in a way that invites and captures children's attention, celebrates the messy path to discovery, as well provides rich opportunities for collective problem solving. What may at times seem "off-topic" will help children connect their thinking with others' and follow multiple directions that lead towards more complex understanding and answers.[36] For instance, in interaction, children mix and match their ideas and theories, challenging and pushing each other's thinking beyond what they already know and understand in a natural way, similar to the way scientists debate.

However, not all means of designing and evaluating a group project are effective, as witnessed by the following teacher's dilemma:

> In our K-3 classrooms we use structured cooperative learning, which can at times work against some of the children's learning. The roles and questions are "assigned," even though they are rotated. I see children falling into the same roles over and over again, you know, the bossy child tells everyone what to do, the shy one, or the second-language learner who doesn't quite understand or speak up gets assigned a non-thinking role, like picking up the crayons or coloring the borders... and the activity doesn't engage everyone equally. It may be fun and look good in the end, but the final product is not truly representative of each of the children in the group's learning. I can't give a group grade for that kind of work.

Clearly, teachers need to be researchers in their own classrooms, seeking ways to understand and document what and how children really learn in groups. Academics without recent field experience may not be able to design an instrument that is adequate for the complex interactions that occur in an early childhood education setting. At the end of this chapter, I offer two sample pages of tools that you can draw on to better capture learning milestones in interactions. In the section at the end entitled *Lessons Learned About Teaching Latino Children*, I also provide some further considerations for assessing collective and cultural ways of learning.

BRINGING IDEAS TO LIFE
Storytelling Skills

Take advantage of the innate skills of young children to imagine and invent. Nurture their storytelling skills both by highlighting their skill when they tell a story and by providing opportunities and places in your read-alouds and in your own active storytelling for children to focus on their nonverbal enactments. Try the following ideas to sharpen observation skills, body coordination, vocabulary, improvisation, and understanding. All are more fun performed in a group!

- Try warm-up, transition time isolations, or yoga poses that focus the children's attention on one particular body part at a time, or on balance. You could say, for instance, "Stand like a flamingo on one leg."

- "Action Mirror" is a game for circle time where you invite two children at a time to come to the center to "mirror" each others' movements, as if facing a mirror.

- Simple charades or action moves with a song, such as a popular Latinamerican song, *Arroz con Leche*, which you can translate and make up words for that are meaningful and fun for the children: *arroz con leche, me quiero casar, con una señorita de* San Rafael [say the name of a child's hometown]—rice pudding, rice pudding, I want to marry, a young lady from San Rafael. Then you can add different actions to go along with the melody: *que sepa nadar, que sepa cocer, que sepa abrir la puerta para ir a bailar*—Who knows how to swim? Who knows how to cook? Who knows how to open the door to go out dancing?

- Pantomime: in circle, whole group, or while you are reading a book, encourage performance skills by calling out different actions for the children to represent, like walking the dog, climbing steps, climbing rope, being a rock musician, going through a revolving door, moving furniture, washing dishes, directing traffic, hammering, running to catch a bus, and so on.

- Animal transformations: draw on children's observation and imagination. Whether animals are featured in a book or in a child's storytelling, model and encourage children to represent animals with sound and body.

- "Knotting" is a popular activity throughout the world. Children hold hands in a line, and then one end of the line begins to weave in and out starting at the other end, without letting go of hands, entangling all into a knot. Have children problem-solve by finding different ways to untangle the knot. This gives the sense of "ensemble" work and awareness of others so necessary for future playacting.[37]

Remember, you are also a model the children look to, so hone your own storytelling skills, and have many props and costumes in the classroom so they can engage in storytelling, scene setting, and role playing at will.

A Final Note about "Teaching"

One of the most significant learnings from our visits across Canada ten years ago was that in a multi-age environment, at times, the most effective way to "teach" is to simply be present and not intervene.

What brought it home to us was one particular exemplary program. During our observations at this welcoming and vibrant school, teachers were spread out through the area and were watchful, friendly, and helpful when the children approached them, every now and then making a brief comment on what they were doing (e.g., when a child made eye contact with her: "Oh, so you're swinging very fast."), but they didn't make an attempt to extend play, to find teachable moments, or to curtail the children's exploration of their limits. The teachers in this center believe in the value of learning through peers. This allows learning to flow naturally from their play and interactions. The idea is that children will learn from being part of the community, testing their own limits within a "safe" frame of reference: the watchful and caring eyes of others, coupled with freedom and support. Teachers there are resources rather than facilitators. They may set up and present material, but in a way that allows exploration and discovery not directed by the teachers. Even the behavior "rules" are assimilated by children quickly and passed on by them to newcomers with little overt cueing from adults. For second-language learners as well as newcomer children, this approach is particularly beneficial, as children learn by watching, imitating, and doing, especially when they have models of different levels to use as inspiration, even if it's the mistakes of others attempting the task.

In contrast, in many other early childhood settings we observed the adults tending to hover and intervene more deliberately in peer interactions. There, we saw fewer spontaneous conversations, and children seemed to use language less and rely on the teacher more to problem-solve or give directions.

The lessons learned: Do not neglect to leave plenty of "unscheduled" time for children to flow naturally between activities *they* initiate, and make sure to join in as a learner in those child-generated activities, at their level, so the children can teach *you*.

Keeping a Balance
Structure Versus Flexibility

The principles presented here may potentially conflict with what is planned in your program, because advancing learning within this framework does not depend primarily on a set of constructed activities in scope and sequence. It's based instead on a naturalistic learning collaboration that engages the teacher as co-constructor and inquirer, not manager and shaper of the program.

Since fluidity, not rigid structure, is needed for child-initiated, collaborative, inquiry-based learning, maintaining strict schedules and adhering to planned programming may interfere with optimum learning for some Latino—if not all—children. Much of the "schooling" children experience in our centers and our institutions is organized and bound by activity or content areas, age-segregation, activity centers, and scheduling. Therefore, the task of the responsive teacher is to search for a balance between organized and spontaneous activity in the program design. In this chapter, I've suggested some activity ideas that serve as a first step. Chapter 6, focused on program change, will provide more structural ideas to enable your program to overcome limitations and build capacity, partnerships, and initiatives that contribute to the stability and professionalism in the field that is needed to maintain the flexibility to let the children take the lead.

Understanding the Development of Language and Literacy

Activity ideas and exemplary efforts will not, however, prepare you to truly respond to the struggles and challenges, as well as the opportunities inherent in having a multilingual class. Thus, following I offer some issues to consider that can help you begin discussions with your colleagues and the families of your students.

What Behaviors and Skills Do We Encourage?

Literacy and language development extends to behaviors beyond what is usually measured or conceived of as reading and writing skills. Understanding and communicating the value of these activities to your fellow teachers, families, and children is vital. Being well-equipped with rich observations will enable teachers to discuss more productively the child's development at home and at school. When talking with families, teachers can begin by sharing some of their observations of the children's learning in these vital and natural ways, for instance:

> When we were outside, I noticed that Johanna was watching intently on the
> sidelines as two other children were throwing a ball. Then, when the two ran

off, she went over to the ball and tried several times to throw the ball. At first she was tentative, but then I could see that she used some of the techniques she saw the older children using, like reaching high with her arms to get the ball further. The next day, she just ran over when other children were playing ball and joined them, yelling "Catch!" when she threw the ball. She just seems to want to try on her own and succeed before she joins the others. Since she doesn't yet understand the verbal cues, this seems a very effective way for her to master her skills and then grasp the words and rules of the game.

At a staff meeting, family discussion group, or even at a specially organized session that includes both teachers and families, take a moment to brainstorm. Whether you are a trainer or a teacher, ask other participants to list what they see as indicators and behaviors that the children are acquiring language and literacy skills. Show how language is the basis for literacy. Prepare a list for yourself ahead of time so you can generate some discussion. Some recognized preliteracy behaviors that are effective include listening to conversations, stories, and instructions; pretending to read; turning pages; following text with eyes or a finger; responding to active songs; watching others writing; imitating sounds or gestures that are connected with meaning (such as "baaa" when seeing an illustration of sheep), and so on.[38]

 Key Points
The Functions of Language

- Language and literacy are not just talking, reading, and writing: "Language tells us who we are, where we belong, and where we're bound."[39]

- Literacy originates from communication: stories, role play, play, information seeking and sharing, verbal, and nonverbal. Two-thirds of language used in the world is social conversation.

- Families from different backgrounds communicate and support literacy in different ways, from the way they tell stories to the way they correct children's behavior.

- Moving from the informal, practical use of language in everyday experiences to the particular kinds of literacy activities in school requires an approach that is mindful of and builds on the child's experiences in their daily lives.

Explore the many functions of language in oral and written form. With your teaching peers, talk about what the children might see and hear at home and in their neighborhoods that can be used as a base for literacy. Start with these and fill in your own ideas, as well as ask children and families:

- making shopping lists
- signing forms
- reading signs
- giving directions
- repeating words to baby
- taking phone messages
- writing postcards
- telling stories
- looking at photo albums
- filling out a bank deposit slip

 Did You Know?
Views on Reading

Many Latino families are well aware of the demands on children in schools and are adamant that their toddlers and preschoolers receive the background needed to prepare them to succeed in these environments. Therefore, this implies that an early childhood program best suited to the needs of Latino families presents two parallel, and at times contradictory, approaches. According to many Latino parents and even low-income parents from any culture, as children develop their social competence and find a sense of belonging, they also need to be explicitly taught the three Rs. In the case of families with a language other than English as their home language, the division between parent and teacher roles may become more marked, as parents rely more on teachers' expertise in the mainstream language and methods. Parents expect their children to be "taught" to be ready for school. On the other hand, programs may not see direct teaching of certain competencies as developmentally appropriate for young children. Sensitive approaches to bridging these divisions will help you in guiding the literacy of the children.

Whereas we know from the past thirty years of research in early childhood learning that play and enrichment activities are the appropriate vehicles for language and literacy development, some parents may expect that centers and kindergartens will be *pre*schools, not *play* schools for their children. They know their children will face hurdles in transitioning to primary school if they are not well prepared, and their own experience of schooling may not have valued less-structured, non-directed, or hands-on ways of learning.

Consider, what would you do if you heard a parent say:

> Now I do a lot with him. We read a lot now. I joined a book club. I read to him about a half hour or an hour. I tell him, "Listen to me," but he always wants to turn the page. I've got me some flashcards I keep in my pocket-

Figure 4–7 *Teacher and Me* (Photo by Su Theriault)

book, when we're in the car, on the train, you name it. I was crazy with him! I take those flashcards everywhere. He's gotta learn his ABCs. When he's getting it wrong, I get nervous, so I stopped. But I'm not a teacher.[40]

How can you both affirm and guide this parent's valiant attempts? What tools do you have at your disposal for the parents to use at home? How can you show the parent what and how the child is learning in your classroom?

These questions should guide your approach to solving different perspectives on learning. For example, to solve the ABCs dilemma, expose families to *Gathering the Sun: An Alphabet in Spanish and English,*[41] an alphabet book that is beautifully illustrated with the daily lives of migrant families, where the English and the Spanish are side by side, using poems, familiar words, images, *and* sentiments:

Regar	*Watering*
Tus sonrisas son	Your smiles
Para tus amigos	To your friends
Como el riego	Are like water
Para las plantas.	To growing plants. *Alma Flor Ada*

Understanding Bilingualism and Biliteracy

The climate has been very controversial of late: As we see the very young Latino population grow, we also see a push for English only in preschools and an elimination of bilingual programs in schools. Just as the market media is beginning to understand and appeal to the Latino, Spanish-speaking public, we also see growing unease about losing an English-speaking, American identity.

Although there are still many unknowns and much debate about bilingualism in the United States, throughout the world, bilingualism, and even multilingualism is a reality and an advantage in a developing, mobile future. Perhaps you can use some of the following statements to explore what you, your peers, and your students' parents feel and know about bilingualism and biliteracy:

There is a logical progression from being aware of an object to making a word/object correspondence. I offer the following as a progression. Can you discuss with your peers what proof you see for these statements? What do you think you can look for to confirm or dispute these claims?

- Words organize concrete knowledge (objects, people, animals, experiences).
- Labeling begins with the first word-to-object correspondence.
- Mislabeling can happen when a child hears different labels for the same object, person, animal, experience (e.g., combining Spanish and English words).
- Children go beyond mislabeling and can learn in, and switch between, two or more languages with proper bilingual guidance.
- Phonological awareness in Spanish should precede phonological awareness in English.
- Children learn their second language best when their first language is also well developed.[42]
- When children learn to think and express themselves in their native language, these skills transfer to their second language.

If...	You can try...
• Some parents may be confused as to which language to use	• Acknowledging their opinions and providing information for possible advantages/consequences
• Children use both Spanish and English words to describe an object	• Documenting when the child code switches and watching how she progresses

If...	You can try...
• Only English is spoken in your center or school	• Seeking information and models from the community, e.g., dual language programs, and asking experts to come talk to your staff, share strategies, and invite you to visit their programs.
• Some parents want their children to speak only English	• Showing that you value bilingualism by learning and using another language daily. Becoming bicultural and bilingual is ideally a two-way commitment

Many feel that native language maintenance should occur at home. However, bear in mind that many factors affect literacy in the home.

Factors That Affect Literacy in the Home

- How much adults speak directly to children
- Parents' consistency in language choice
- Education and economic level of family
- Parental attitude about bilingualism; how they and others perceive the status of their native language
- Available stimuli and strengths (extended family, varied models, bilingual, bicultural, immigration experience, oral traditions and conventions)
- Environmental obstacles (hunger, illness, family stress)

Finally, ask yourself: What happens when the native language is not developed?[43]

Consider ways in which this may affect the child at home. For example, losing command of the mother tongue can separate child from family, especially grand-parents, the holders of culture. Thus culture and language are eroded, as well as the vital relationship with the extended family.

Factors That Affect Literacy in the Classroom

Carlos, a rambunctious four-year-old, would never slow down. He wouldn't sit still for a story, couldn't play with toys cooperatively, couldn't even respond to my questions. With no English and what seemed like no Spanish literacy skills, no matter what I tried, I couldn't figure out what he knew or even test his word knowledge or learn what would help him build skills. I tried songs with gestures, tried pictures with labels, tried repeating everything while maintaining eye contact with him, all to no avail. I later found out he had come from a particularly dangerous rural area in Central America and that neither he nor anyone in his family had ever attended school or had a toy or book. The violence and gunfire he had witnessed when the paramilitary entered his village home made him uneasy about being indoors and wary of looking at anyone in the eyes. Once I understood this, I was able to get support for myself and for him to deal with this.

Teachers often have newcomer and transient children who add challenging and enriching possibilities to their practice, even as they struggle to understand and serve them. We need resources, though, and we need each other. As there is no definitive way to handle any given situation, we need our colleagues and peers to consult with and to help us search for multiple ways to reach each and every child. Again, I refer you to Igoa's *The Inner World of the Immigrant Child* for a closer look at the possible ways to reach children who come with different languages, cultures, and poignant tales of friendship, hardship, and leaving behind a homeland.

The standards and outcomes of the Head Start Bureau—arguably the first and most comprehensive national initiative for young children and their families—include in their guidelines a convincing research-based argument and some recommended standards on the development of first language, recognizing that "learning to communicate is the result of cumulative experiences from birth on."[44] And yet, these recommendations are not extended to legislated mandates, as are other significant, research-based standards, and little support or knowledge is shared about bridging from Spanish to English. Therefore, those "cumulative experiences" in the first language are likely lost, and the young child, at an early age, will need to begin from scratch building an accumulation of experiences in English, with no connection to what he already knows about language. Teachers need support and ideas to help children bridge these two very different patterns of language.

> One-on-one or group activities are a great way for a teacher to introduce a child to language. I personally use this technique not only with ELLs but also children with English language. I try to introduce the English language to non-English speaking students by introducing words in Spanish to the whole class that have the same meaning. This helps a child that doesn't have the English language "break the ice." They see the picture, hear the word, and even though they might not be able to get the dialogue fluently, this helps them socialize with children through play and in time acquire more English language skills. Also, when I read in a group setting, I try to use props as visuals.[45]

How does your program measure up in supporting second-language learners? Teaching teams need to assess what is being done, what works, and what gaps and challenges exist. Innovative and effective standards and outcomes for young children—such as the Head Start Program Performance Standards and the National Association for the Education of Young Children (NAEYC) standards—include some criteria for cultural and linguistic responsiveness, as do some state and also Family Child Care Self-Assessment tools. Try some of these questions to evaluate your program's strategies and make an action agenda to address needs.

Examining Your Program's Language Assets

- Does your program's registration form elicit information about languages spoken in the home?

- How many staff and volunteers in your center or school program speak other languages? Are they encouraged to engage in first-language and literacy activities with bilingual children?

- What materials and resources do you have in your program in other languages? Have they been evaluated for cultural and linguistic responsiveness? A source for an evaluation based on the *Connections and Commitments* Framework—the Materials Review Tool—is available through <*www.edc.org/ccf/latinos*>.

- What materials and resources are available to you in the surrounding community? (For example, library, community center, parent association in the public schools, etc.)

- Does your program communicate with families in their native language? How? Written, orally, informally or through interpreters at center activities? Remember, the more channels for informal and formal communication are open, the more parents can be partners in helping their children learn and in helping you teach them effectively.

- Does your program have a vehicle for soliciting family preferences about bilingual development?

- How does your program integrate oral and other nonliterate ways of knowing?

- How do you collect and share strategies that have been successful in teaching bilingual children?

- What resources and supports do you need in order to develop and implement literacy and learning strategies bilingually or for second-language learners? For example, have you considered a two-way bilingual model? What strategies have you noticed are difficult or confusing for bilingual children? What does your program or school do to identify and deal with these issues?

Key Points
Phonics

Phonics-based programs may be confusing for young children coming in with a background in a language other than English, especially those who share the same alphabet and some of the lexicon of the English language. Young learners beginning to identify patterns in language may assume correspondences because of some of these similarities. Spanish-dominant children may have more trouble than Chinese-dominant children because there are less commonalities between Chinese and English. Spanish is a very phonetic language, that is, it is written the way it sounds. English patterns of language are more different and complex, from word order to conjugation and pronouns. The young child's work at making sense of the patterns can be aided by following through with phonological awareness and literacy in Spanish before passing over to English. Comparing and contrasting, looking at similarities and differences in root words and pronunciations in Spanish and English are techniques that are being explored by ESL and modern language teachers, as is the use of the arts as a vehicle to learn a second language. This will lead to developing phonological awareness in the first language and understanding about how to transfer language and knowledge skills to the second language.

Lessons Learned About Teaching Latino Children

Potential Stumbling Blocks to Teaching in a Culturally Responsive Way

> This added attention to culture and different languages is all well and good, but, in the end, they have to learn English. That's what's going to make them succeed when they go to kindergarten. And that's what we have to look at when we document learning outcomes three times a year. We're not ESL teachers here, and we have six different languages in the classroom... Some seem to do well in English, and others, even with native language supports, aren't able to recognize letters. What are we to do?

Despite any teacher's or program's best intentions to serve diverse children and families, our field is still stumbling in its effort to ensure quality education for *all* children. Our educational systems and knowledge are leaning towards more structure, more control and accountability, and less freedom and flexibility for teachers to be innovative and responsive within a tight curriculum and daily schedule.

In an age of testing, teachers of young children are being made more and more accountable for the literacy achievement of the children they teach. However, an emphasis solely on literacy and individual learning outcomes can cloud the true work of a teacher, which involves tuning into each child's needs as an individual and as a member of a culture, or, if you will, listening with the heart. This means grasping the needs and complete portrait of the children and their communities in order to design meaningful learning opportunities. All the measures and outcomes for which we are accountable should be a means to capture these needs and this portrait in a dynamic way that informs what comes next.

Are We Asking the Right Questions?
Language Placement and Assessment

> When it comes down to it, those kindergarten placement tests narrow our view of the child's capability.... You know, Raúl tested with 400 words in his vocabulary, since he's been *drilled* consistently by his mother and his teacher, but Manny, who came with no English, only has 200 words, and yet he knows those words inside out, uses them in his conversations with peers, in sentences, recognizes the pictures and the words even within a long text, and pronounces them perfectly. Raúl can't seem to connect meaning with half of the words he "knows" according to the test, and certainly doesn't use many of them in his daily conversations. So, how come Raúl just breezes by to kindergarten, and Manny has to stay here another year? Manny is curious and sharp. If he stays behind...3 will he continue to grow as well?

Wherever they come from, when many Latinos settle in the United States, their identity and their bonds with other Latinos are cemented in a common language, despite variations in dialects, accents, and vocabulary. Beyond this language, which is a richness, not a barrier to learning, there are cultural aspects of language that impact how children learn and what they bring that has not as yet been adequately examined. Remember the case of Elvira, who knew how engines worked but not how to talk about or use this knowledge until a situation was created where she could use her unusual skills? Supporting and measuring how language develops through communication and daily tasks, for instance, means also grasping and explicitly teaching and looking at the subtle discourse surrounding language.[46]

> With the families we have here—from seven different cultures, I make a point to learn about cultural differences in communication, like eye contact, touching behavior, tone, and the distance people use when talking with each other. One day, at a parents' night, I watched as parents greeted each other when they arrived, and noticed for the first time what amazingly different conventions they each had for greeting each other or greeting someone

from a culture not their own. Some gave each other three kisses on alternate cheeks, intoning the same greeting words; the same families simply nodded and said "Hello" when greeting someone from another culture. Others kissed on two cheeks, another pair of mothers by one kiss and a hug. The men in two of the cultures hugged and patted each other's backs. When they greeted children, I saw even more differences in style, although many bent down to the level of the children. When I brought this up at circle time and asked children to play act greeting different people in and outside of their families, even more differences in the "discourse" of greetings became apparent, such as the fascinating subtleties of rhythm of speech and movement as the children role-played the greetings.

Looking at Collective and Cultural Ways of Learning

With fifteen million second-language learners now in our schools, many are being funneled into special education or to inappropriate placements because of the nature or language of the test and its administration.[47] Objects and words being tested may not be familiar to the non-native child; test-taking in itself may not be in the child's experience. Even when orally fluent in English, a child may lack the English vocabulary for some items being tested. What a child with little exposure to American life may lack in experience can greatly influence her ability to understand a word, a visual, or a direction, and may also impact how the child tests. Commonly used illustrations in visual alphabets and picture tests, for instance, can include a slice of pie, or a loaf of bread, foodstuff that might not be in the daily diet of many Latinos.

Beyond the challenges inherent in measuring *what* a child with language differences comes with and learns through our teaching, we may tend to overlook the ways coming from a group-centered culture may affect *how* children learn.

Some examples of assessments that document relationships, interactions, and conversations that lead to learning include the National Association of Family Child Care's Self-Assessment tool, the *Literacy Implementation Observation Tool*, the *Relationship Observation Protocol (ROP)*, and the *Science Teaching Observation Rubrics* (STO)—draft tools used to observe the teaching of science, children's learning, and program effectiveness. Sample pages from these last three instruments appear in the appendix, and they might be helpful in formulating your own way to gauge the impact of learning interactions. The ROP was developed to capture verbal and nonverbal interactions among children, including helping, mentoring, apprenticing, and conversational behavior, as well as the role of teacher in the interaction. These observations, coupled with descriptions of conceptual tasks, give a fuller picture of a child's path to understanding. The STO, a tool in development at

EDC's Center for Children & Families, is specifically intended to evaluate science learning in preschool settings. Another system of assessment of child outcomes used in primary grades is the *Work Sampling System*, which, although geared to looking at individual growth, has indicators that set benchmarks for interactions with others from preschool through third grade, as well as a section dedicated to measuring understanding of human interdependence.[48]

Individually administered assessment and placement tests can be misleading. Upon entering the pre-K classroom, a child's vocabulary may be assessed by a series of visual stimuli presented by the teacher. This is in no way a realistic situation. Children—especially newcomers—may not be able to "perform" under these circumstances, and thus a true portrait of where the child is at the beginning of the year will be missing. Imagine an assessment that places the teacher in the background, as a listener who has provided a project-based, collaborative activity that engages children in dialogue and problem-solving, and where children both learn and show mastery of language in the context of a task. This would enable the teacher to not only record the vocabulary being used during a particular task but also gives the teacher a set of context-based language clues that emerge from the children's functional language and their interests that can be incorporated into planning curriculum.

As a teacher, how do you think some of the following are represented in the assessments you now use? What are the shortcomings of these instruments? What do they *not* capture?

- Native language development
- Cultural responsiveness
- Interaction
- Environmental factors
- Family context, communication
- Phonological awareness
- Understanding of meaning

An assessment that values and measures the kind of learning that I am espousing here would have to look beyond measures currently used, even individual authentic assessments such as individual portfolios and child observation surveys. Although each can be valuable in gauging a child's learning, there is an important gap in the perspective they give. The push for testing is rationalized as a means of formative assessment, that is, information for teachers to use to build their curriculum and determine the children's needs. Much as teachers hesitate to add more paperwork that gets in the way of teaching, assessments are also needed that will allow them to keep present in their minds the primacy of group play, conversation, and collective problem-posing and solving, and not just individual development.

Summing Up: A Shared Path to Learning

As a way to sum up this chapter, I offer you an idea to implement with your families and staff.

 What We Believe
Sharing a Vision of Teaching and Learning

This bilingual chart can be used as a starting point to share with your Spanish-speaking staff and families some of the key points in this chapter. You can create PowerPoint slides of your own based on the chart or on the values and principles you articulate as a group. I've suggested some ideas for the kinds of photos from your program you could add to make the presentation more relevant to your early education community. Visual images communicate values and ideas.

As you go through each slide, follow-up with discussion questions and provide some examples from your observations of the children.

Educación y educar	Education and teaching
Ejemplos en la práctica	Examples in practice
• Los niños tienen oportunidad de tomar el papel de maestro y de aprendiz y de responsabilizarse del desarrollo de otros niños. [foto de un niño ayudando a otro]	• Children have opportunities to take on the role of expert and novice (mentor and apprentice) and to take responsibility for the learning of others. [photo of a child helping another in a task]
• Respeto y cariño es una meta central del desarrollo, ya que el aprendizaje depende de la relación entre el maestro y el aprendiz. [foto del niño consolando a otro]	• Respect and caring is a central goal of development, since apprenticeship depends on the relationship between expert and novice. [photo of child consoling another child]
• El programa ofrece regularmente proyectos de grupo en que los niños pueden colaborar, aprendiendo a crear, a investigar y a descubrir juntos. [foto de un grupo de niños trabajando o jugando juntos]	• The program regularly promotes group projects where children can collaborate, learning to create, investigate, and discover with others. [photo of children working on a mural or other group project]

Educación y educar	Education and teaching
• El programa hace conexiones con las actividades, métodos y costumbres de las experiencias diarias y culturales del niño/a, facilitando el desarrollo en contextos familiares. [foto evento cultural o comunitario]	• The program makes connections with the activities, ways, and customs of the child's daily and cultural experiences, facilitating development in familar contexts. [photo of a cultural or community event]

Focusing on *educación*—beginning with the family *funds of knowledge*, and building a practice of relationship-based learning—can reach the whole child and can engage the children's curiosity and motivation as well as yours. Recapping some of the teaching points in this chapter, I outline below some of the key features of quality teaching that responds across levels to many Latino children's cultural ways of learning. These promising programs:

- Use dialogue to bring in the learner's knowledge and experience[49]
- Involve students in shared decision-making[50]
- Are characterized by familial relationships with teachers
- Involve program staff in the children's community and in advocacy
- Encourage both the Latino and the non-Latino children to use and develop the Spanish language[51]
- Create contexts where children can relate the word to actions, visuals, music or rhythm, games and concrete objects and experiences
- Offer many opportunities for informal conversation with peers and adults
- Develop and use both first and second languages fully[52]

Reflection and Discussion Questions

Language

1. Have you ever been in a situation where you didn't understand the language being spoken? How did you feel? What helped you understand what others were saying?

2. What was the first word you remember learning? Was it the name of a pet? A rubber duck in your bath? Papa? Ask the families to share the first word spoken by each of your students. What does that tell you about each child?

3. What are some songs you remember from your childhood? Can you think about who taught them to you and where and with whom you sang them? How do you make songs memorable for the children you care for and teach?

4. How was literacy present in your home when you were growing up? How about now?

5. Do you write for your own sake every day? Do your students see you writing and reading? What do you share with them about your own reading and writing?

Learning Context

1. What did you learn from others? How can you enable this kind of learning in your own classroom?

2. What long-term hobby or interest occupied your time when you were very young? Do you know what the special interests of your students are?

3. How do you see your mother, father, sibling, or grandparent reflected in how you relate and what you do for work or leisure? How do you include your students' families' interests and work in the curriculum?

4. How do you make the most of "teachable moments"? For instance, when a child is pushing a car down a ramp, pulling a wagon with a friend, negotiating roles in the play area? What conversations and activities would spring from these teachable moments? How would you link these with your curriculum?

5. What outdoor activities and games do the children engage in? How do you think these types of activities lead to learning for your students?

Related Resources

First and Second Language Development

Christison, M., and S. Bassaro. 1997. *Purple Cows and Potato Chips*. Alemany Press offers many language-learning activities using the senses.

Ada, A. F., and C. Baker. 2001. *Guía Para Padres y Maestros de Niños Bilingües: A Parents' & Teachers' Guide to Bilingualism*. Spanish language version. Clevedon, England: Multilingual Matters.

Asher, J. J. 1988. *Learning Another Language Through Actions: The Complete Teacher's Guidebook*, 4th ed. Los Gatos, CA: Sky Oaks Productions.

Nelson, G., and T. Winters. 1980. *ESL Operations: Techniques for Learning While Doing.* Rowley, MS: Newbury House Publishers.

These last two books, which may be out of print and hard to find, may be worth a search nonetheless, as they have a variety of hands-on ideas for teaching language to children.

For both Latina and non-Latina staff and families, videos are invaluable learning tools. For a wonderful glimpse into a diverse classroom, see Video Ethnography Case Studies available through *<creativeworks.byu.edu/beede>*. For example, the video on Sheri Galarza's classroom provides rich insights into second language learning and teaching activities and theories, as well as engaging the teacher's perspective. These may inspire teachers to build their own cases using the tools available through this web site.

Children's Literature

Many wonderful children's books have been compiled in several lists and web pages in the last chapter, but the following is a beginning list that builds on some of the concepts in this chapter.

- Ada, A. F. 1997. *Medio Pollito/Half-Chicken.* Random House.
- Anaya, R. 1995. *The Farolitos of Christmas.* New York: Hyperion.
- Anaya, R. 1997. *Maya's Children: The Story of La Llorona.* New York: Hyperion.
- Anzaldúa, G. 1995. *Prietita and the Ghost Woman/Prietita y La Llorona.* San Francisco: Children's Book Press.
- Lomas Garza, C. 1990. *Family Pictures: Cuadros de Familia.* San Francisco: Children's Book Press.
- Martel, C. 1976. *Yagua Days.* NY: Dial Press.
- Mora, P. 1996. *Confetti: Poems for Chidren.* New York: Lee and Low.
- Ortega, C. 1996. *Los Ojos Del Tejedor or The Eyes of the Weaver.* Santa Fe: Clear Light.
- Palacio Jaramillo, N., ed. *Las Nanas de Abuelita: Canciones de Cuna, Trabalenguas y Adivinanzas de Suramérica / Grandmother's Nursery Rhymes: Lullabies, Tongue Twisters, and Riddles from South America.*

Not to be missed: The Multicultural Literature List from the Read to Me Project, downloadable from *<www.lili.org/read/readtome/multiculturallit.htm>*, has an annotated list of excellent multicultural books, organized by age.

For the Teacher

Ada, A. F. 1988. "The Pajaro Valley Experience." In Tove Skutnabb-Kangas & Jim Cummins (Eds.) *Minority Education: From Shame to Struggle.* Philadelphia: Multilingual Matters Ltd., 223–238

Ada, A. F., and F. I. Campoy. 2004. *Authors in the Classroom.* Boston, MA: Pearson Education, Inc.

Rogoff, B., C. Goodman Turkanis, and L. Bartlett. 2001. *Learning Together: Children and Adults in a School Community.* New York: Oxford University Press.

Giudici, C. 2001. "Making Learning Visible: Children as Individual and Group." Cambridge, MA: Project Zero, Harvard Graduate School of Education.

For ideas, parent hand-outs, articles, and other resources on language, bilingualism, and identity, see *<www.rootsforchange.net>*, which includes articles such as *How Can Providers Prevent Inadvertently Sending Negative Messages About Home Language to Children?* By Hedy Nai Lin Chang, Amy Muckelroy and Dora Pulido-Tobiassen, and *Fostering Bilingual Development* by Pulido-Tobiassen and Janet González-Mena.

Three new web sites present information, activities, links, and resources on bilingual development:

<www.headstartinfo.org/infocenter/literacy_tk/links_jun04.htm>

<www.rif.org/leer>

<www.ncela.gwu.edu/pathways/reading/index.htm>

<www.nabe.org/links.asp>

Endnotes

1 Edelman, M. W. 1995. *Guide My Feet: Prayers and Meditations on Loving and Working for Children*, xxviii. Boston, MA: Beacon Press.

2 Buysse, V., D. Castro, T. West, and M. Skinner. 2004. "Addressing the Needs of Latino Children: A National Survey of State Administrators of Early Childhood Programs." Chapel Hill, NC: Frank Porter Graham Child Development Institute, The University of North Carolina at Chapel Hill.

3 McKeon, D. 1994. "When Meeting 'Common' Standards Is Uncommonly Difficult." *Educational Leadership* 51 (8): 45–49.

4 Casares, J. 1963. *Diccionario Ideológico de la Lengua Española.* Barcelona: Gustavo Gili.

5 *Bien educado* is the masculine construction for well brought up, and *bien educada*, the female. Throughout this book, I have attempted to keep a gender balance in my language, rather than saying, for example, "he or she" or *Latinas* or *Latinos*.

6 The concept of "manners" is echoed throughout societies where the kin network and interdependence make certain social rules logical and functional.

Reese, L., S. Balzano, R. Gallimore, and C. Goldenberg. 1991. "The Concept of Educación: Latino Family Values and American Schooling." Paper presented at the Annual Meeting of the American Anthropological Association.

7 Holloway, S. D., B. Fuller, M. F. Rambaud, and C. Eggers-Piérola. 2001. *Through My Own Eyes: Single Mothers and the Cultures of Poverty.* Cambridge, MA: Harvard University Press: 106.

8 Macías, J. 1992. "The Social Nature of Instruction in a Mexican School: Implications for U.S. Classroom Practice." *The Journal of Educational Issues of Language Minority Students* 10: 13–25.

9 In Puerto Rico, teachers are often called "Missy" as a sign of both respect and endearment.

10 This, like several others snapshots and quotes, are crafted from compilations from my own experience as a teacher, researcher, student, mother, daughter, and colleague. I've included citations as appropriate.

11 Macías, "The Social Nature of Instruction in a Mexican School."

12 Eggers-Piérola, C. 1993. "Beyond Inclusion: A Review of Ethnographies of Latino Students." Unpublished Qualifying paper, Harvard University.

13 Strickland, D. S. "A Model for Change: Framework for an Emergent Literacy Curriculum." In Strickland, D. S., and L. M. Morrow. 1989. *Emerging Literacy: Young Children Learn to Read and Write.* Newark, DE: International Reading Association. Experts agree that language development based on social and context-based learning approaches such as inquiry and problem-solving, including culturally responsive practices such as shared writing and reading, group oral presentations and responses, promote reading skills.

14 Goldenberg, C., R. Gallimore, L. Reese, and E. Lopez. 2001. "Using Mixed Methods to Explore Latino Children's Literacy Development." Paper prepared for Conference on Discovering Successful Pathways in Children's Development. Santa Monica, CA. <*www.childhood.isr.umich.edu/mmconf/goldenberg.doc*>.

15 Duckworth, E. 1987. *The Having of Wonderful Ideas and Other Essays on Teaching and Learning.* New York: Teachers College Press.

16 Hammrich, P. L., and E. R. Klein. 2000. *The Head Start on Science and Communication Program Manual.* Philadelphia, PA: Mid-Atlantic Laboratory for Student Success at Temple University, Center for Research in Human Development and Education.

   Chaufour, I., and K. Worth. 2003. *Discovering Nature with Young Children.* St. Paul, MN: Redleaf Press.

17 In communication with Ash Hartwell, presentation at EDC, April 27, 2004.

18 Presentation by Sanchez, P., T. Dueñas Contreras, T. Dueñas Tovar, and M. López. March 2003. "Recordando Mis Raices y Viviendo Mis Tradiciones: The Making of a Transnational Bilingual Children's Book." Reading the World Conference, San Francisco, CA.

19 Lloyd, M. 2004. "Salvadoran Families Look Wistfully at Their Migrants." *The Boston Globe.* April 11: A6–7.

20 Herrera J. F., and E. Gómez. 2000. *The Upside Down Boy / El Niño de Cabeza.* San Francisco, CA: Children's Book Press.

   Ryan, P.M. 2000. *Esperanza Rising.* New York: Scholastic Press.

   Alvarez, J. 1992. *How the García Girls Lost Their Accents.* New York: Plume.

21 Igoa, C. 1995. *The Inner World of the Immigrant Child.* New York: St. Martin's Press.

22 Cazden, C. 1992. "Visit to the Funds of Knowledge for Teaching (FKT) Project, Luis C. Moll, Tucson, June 15–16." *Focus on Diversity* 2 (1): 2–3.

   Civil, M., R. Andrade, and N. González. 2002. "Linking Home and School: A Bridge to the Many Faces of Mathematics." Center for Research on Education, Diversity & Excellence. *www.crede.ucsc.edu/research/md/intro4_2.shtml.*

González, N., L. Moll, M. F. Tenery, A. Rivera, P. Rendon, R. González, and C. Amanti. 1995. "Funds of Knowledge for Teaching in Latino Households." *Urban Education* 29 (4): 443–471.

23 It's fascinating to note how many different names children call their grandmothers. Make a list of all the variations and post them prominently to honor these elders and also to feature a source and reminder of a person who impacts the children's lives and can be featured in their stories, art, and talk.

24 Heard, G. 1989. *For the Good of the Earth and Sun*. Portsmouth, NH: Heinemann.

25 Gardner, H. 1993. *Multiple Intelligences: The Theory in Practice*. New York: Basic Books. The *seven intelligences* promoted through Gardner's work—linguistic, logical/mathematical, musical, spatial, kinesthetic, interpersonal, and *intra*personal—have recently been expanded to include naturalist intelligence. For further information and resources for teachers, see <*www.educationworld.com/a_curr/curr054.shtml*>.

26 Krashen, S. 1992. "Sink-or-Swim 'Success Stories' and Bilingual Education." In *Language Loyalties: A Source Book on the Official English Controversy*, 37. Chicago, IL: University of Chicago Press.

27 This profile has been gathered from Fillmore, L. W. 1990. *Latino Families and the Schools. California Perspectives: An Anthology*. Los Angeles: Immigrant Writers Project, 30–37; and Lalley, J. 1995. "Migrant Families Find Quality Preschool and Day Care." *Family Resource Coalition Report* 3, 4: 19–20.

28 Bodrova, E., and D. J. Leong. 1996. *Tools of the Minds: The Vygotskian Approach to Early Childhood Education*. Columbus, OH: Merrill.

Ginsburg, H. P., and S. Opper. 1988. *Piaget's Theory of Intellectual Development*, third edition. Englewood Cliffs, NJ: Prentice Hall.

Vygotsky, L. S. 1978. *Mind in Society: The Development of Higher Psychological Processes*. Cambridge, MA: Harvard University Press.

29 Eggers-Piérola, C. 1996. *We Haven't Still Explored That: Science Learning In A Bilingual Classroom*. Doctoral thesis, Harvard University.

30 The team included Judith Bernhard, June Pollard, and myself, along with colleagues from the Ryerson Early Learning Center, Ryerson Polytechnic University, Toronto, Canada.

31 Zimmerman, B. 2001. *Why Can't They Just Behave: A Guide To Managing Student Behavior Disorders*. Horsham, Pa.: LRP Publications, *www.lrpdartnell.com*.

32 2004. "Imitation Helps Children with Autism Learn to Play." *Early Childhood Report* 15 (4): 9. For other resources for play adaptations for young children with special needs, see <*melindasmith.home.mindspring.com*>.

33 This activity is based on observations during a multi-age research project in Canada directed by Judith Bernhard, Costanza Eggers-Piérola, and June Pollard. This study yielded many fine examples of mentoring, apprenticeship, and relationship-based learning.

34 Anzaldúa. G. 1993. *Friends from the Other Side/Amigos Del Otro Lado*. San Francisco, CA: Children's Book Press.

35 This activity was observed during field visits on a multi-age research project in Canada directed by Judith Bernhard, Costanza Eggers-Piérola, and June Pollard and is summarized in Bernhard, J., J. Pollard, C. Eggers-Piérola, and A. Morin. 2000. "Infants and Toddlers in Canadian Multi-Age, Childcare Settings: Age, Ability, and Linguistic Inclusion." *Research Connections Canada* IV: 79–185. Ottawa, ON: Canadian Child Care Federation. This study yielded many examples of mentoring, apprenticeship, and relationship-based learning.

36 Eggers-Piérola, C., "*We Haven't Still Explored That.*"

37 These ideas are part of a curriculum, *Books from My Head,* that I wrote in 1985 and that was implemented for the Neighborhood Art Center and the Boston Public Schools. Taught by a team of professional artists, storytellers, and writers, it integrates three disciplines—art, writing, and storytelling.

38 Pinnell, G., and I. C. Fountas. 1998. *Word Matters: Teaching Phonics and Spelling in the Reading/Writing Classroom.* Portsmouth, NH: Heinemann includes some of these behaviors. For more information and categories of literacy behaviors, see <*www.zerotothree.org/brainwonders/earlyliteracy.html*>.

39 Clear Blue Sky (Producer). 2001. "Evolution: Darwin's Dangerous Idea." Episode 101 of the television series *In Evolution.* Boston, MA: WGBH.

40 Holloway, S. D., B. Fuller, M. F. Rambaud, and C. Eggers-Piérola. 1997. *Through My Own Eyes: Single Mothers and the Cultures of Poverty,* first edition. Cambridge, MA: Harvard University Press: 146.

41 Ada, A. F., S. Silva (illustration), and R. Zubizarreta (translation). 1997. *Gathering the Sun: An Alphabet in Spanish and English.* New York, NY: HarperCollins Publishers.

42 Bialystok, E. 2001. *Bilinguism in Development: Language, Literacy, Cognition.* Cambridge, UK: Cambridge University Press.

Cummins, J. 1981. *Bilinguism and Minority-Language Children.* Toronto, ON: Oise Press.

Cummins, J. 1979. "Linguistic Interdependence and the Educational Development of Bilingual Children." *Review of Educational Research* 49: 222–251.

43 Fillmore, L. W. 1991. "When Learning a Second Language Means Losing the First." *Early Childhood Research Quarterly* 6: 323–346.

44 Head Start Leaders' Guide to Positive Child Outcomes. 2004. 37. Downloadable online from <*www.headstart-info.org/pdf/HSOutcomesguideFINAL4c.pdf*>. You can find this document in Spanish also, as well other standards, outcomes, and strategies developed by the Head Start Bureau at <*www.headstartinfo.org/publications/publicat.htm*>.

45 Wanda Rodriguez, a teacher taking "Supporting Preschoolers with Language Differences," a credit-bearing course offered through EDC, Inc.'s Center for Children and Families. *www.edc.org/ccf.*

46 Discourse includes nonverbal and other unspoken patterns and rules of communication that provide important clues to meaning.

47 Parsons, J. 2003. "Margins of Error: The Needs of Limited English Proficiency Students Put Special Education Assessment to the Test." *Teaching Tolerance* 24: 33–37.

Valdés, G., and R. A. Figueroa. 1996. *Bilingualism and Testing: A Special Case of Bias.* Norwood, NJ: Ablex.

48 Jablon, J., D. Marsden, S. Meisels, and M. Dichtelmiller. 1994. *Omnibus Guidelines: Preschool Through Third Grade. The Work Sampling System.* Ann Arbor, MI: Rebus Planning Associates, Inc.

49 Moll, L. C., C. Amati, D. Neff, and N. Gonzalez. 1992. "Funds of Knowledge for Teaching: Using a Qualitative Approach to Conect Homes and Classrooms." *Theory into Practice* 31(2): 132-141:

Tharp, R., and R. Gallimore. 1993. Rousing Minds to Life: Teaching, Learning and Schooling in Social Context. New York, NY: Cambridge University Press.

50 Cohen, E. G., and J. K. Intili. 1982. "Interdependence and Management in Bilingual Classrooms." Final Report II (NIE contract # NIE-G-80-0217). Stanford: Stanford University Center for Education Research.

Walsh, C. E. 1991. Pedagogy and the Struggle for Voice: Issues of Language, Power, and Schooling for Puerto Ricans. New York, NY: Bergin and Garvey.

51 Cummins, *"Bilinguism."*

52 Buysse, V., D. Castro, T. West, and M. Skinner. 2004. "Addressing the Needs of Latino Children: A National Survey of State Administrators of Early Childhood Programs." Chapel Hill, NC: Frank Porter Graham Child Development Institute, The University of North Carolina at Chapel Hill.

CHAPTER
5

Compromiso

Shared Commitment to Professional Growth

Focusing on *Compromiso*

One by one, each arrived, with a hot dish, with fragrant coffee, one with flowers from her garden, several with bags of materials gathered around their homes. The slow, early morning rhythm quickened when all the teachers arrived. Hugs, laughs, "How are your babies?"; "What's that you have in your bag?" More greetings were exchanged as others arrived and sat at our table. Then a look from Doña Carlota told us it was time, and the chatter subsided. She began with a story of her grandchild Robertito, who had jumped into the new bathtub with joy, saying, "Look Nana, I made more water," when he saw the water level go up, and then, "Where did the water go?" when he got out and saw it go down. Then we had a lively discussion on how their three- and four-year-old students could discover the same questions. Someone would say, "and what if…" and "What's next?" and "How can we?" Then we pulled out our teaching books to see what knowledge we were covering, and what could be missing. Of course, we could never predict where the children would take us, but we knew what the first-grade teachers wanted them to know. We met with the first-grade teachers once a month in their school, so we saw what the first-grade children were doing, all their work tacked up on the walls. We planned for the children, and then we planned for us. "I need to know more about how waves happen; I know Ana is interested in waves." "Jorge always looks at the toilet as it circles round… what can we learn there?" Someone got a bucket of water and a long stick, and we began. And that's how one of our typical planning and professional development meetings went.

There's such joy in teaching!

Well, no, this is not a snapshot of your usual planning or professional development meeting. Here in the United States right now, our work may not be so idyllic. What you don't hear in the constructed excerpt above are some of the day-to-day obstacles that these teachers in a poor, rural village may encounter. Doña Carlota, a grandmother who had been trained as a teacher in her youth, took over the preschool when she retired—without pension. She is worried about whether the food will arrive today on time, and she is worried about whether her health care will cover her latest needs. The teachers have few materials or toys for the young children, so they gather and barter for all kinds of materials they can use to ignite the children's learning. Many of these materials are probably discouraged in accredited classrooms in the United States. The region these rural Mexicans live in had a rigid curriculum and text that they had to implement, and yet there were not enough books for everyone. They were visited by overseers and had fingers wagged at them if one of their students did not have all the skills they had checked off on the list. When a teacher was out sick, she could not be replaced with a substitute. So, they found freedom and innovation where they could. These planning meetings were *their* time, not school time.

I asked many teachers I know if they had any examples of early childhood programs where teachers planned their own development. "Only in small ways, if at all," most said. Teaching can be very isolating and demanding, I've heard many teachers say. Even if you work in a team, you may rarely have a chance to stop and talk together about your teaching, much less plan together or define your own professional development needs.

Going to training is a task that is required of us as professionals in the early childhood field. But there's much involved in turning a task to joy. One, I believe, is a shared commitment and say in how that training happens, and where it leads. But the most compelling reasons that help teachers grow, blossom, and stay in the field is the laughter and freshness of the young children and their minds.

Early childhood educators' commitment to children's growth is unparalleled. Despite the lack of compensation and professional recognition for many, they are accountable for children attaining early learning outcomes as well as meeting all accreditation standards. They are also responsible for collaborating with families, communities, and schools to assure children's school success. Every day, they do their vital work in a political, economic, and social climate that challenges even the most resourceful of our legislators and leaders. The profession can be one of the most isolating, providing few opportunities to take stock of skills and knowledge or profit from the stimulating exchange of ideas with peers that other professions rely on. It is no small feat to keep morale and hope under such circumstances. Like all professionals, early childhood educators need support and guidance to take a step back, reflect on their work, and grow. They need time to share and learn new strategies to keep their work and their programs responsive to *all* children and families. Within this context, a shared commitment to ongoing professional development is essential.

This chapter will help all of the stakeholders in professional development—teachers, administrators, trainers, and technical advisors—plan, participate in, and provide responsive professional development. I offer a process and rationale to introduce and reflect on *compromiso*—that is, a promise made with others to achieve a common goal—part of our Latino-based framework. In previous chapters, *compromiso* surfaced in discussions on partnerships with family and community networks, creating a sense of belonging in the classroom, and supporting the early learning of Latino children. In this chapter, I present how *compromiso* can be applied to the professional development efforts that will help you improve teaching and learning for all in your program—children and adults alike.

Although this chapter is dedicated to examining the value of *compromiso in professional development*, the other values of the *Connections and Commitments* framework echo throughout this chapter as well. In terms of professional development, the values have an added dimension, as follows:

Familia Family	Training and planning that keeps the family's interests at the forefront, and aids in understanding the family's point of view in controversial issues.
Pertenencia Belonging	Creating a climate of collegiality among the adult as well as the children, welcoming diverse and new staff.
Educación Learning together	Building on cultural ways of knowing, training is relationship-based and planning is collaborative.
Compromiso Commitment	Becoming responsible for the growth of the program community as a whole.

In this chapter, I discuss principles and practices that can support directors and supervisors—as well as teachers and other practitioners—in embracing the spirit of *compromiso* in professional development. This includes broadening the definition of who plans, gives, and participates in the training. It also includes creating a professional development plan where *all* can have a voice. Thus, the principles and practices I share here help guide teachers in building their cultural competence by becoming proactive in their own and their program's development.

Throughout the chapter, I pay particular attention to the support of bilingual and bicultural paraprofessionals, since they can be a valuable resource to programs in centers and in school-based early education programs, and they serve as models and cultural liaisons for Latino families and children. I also include ideas for reaching out to home-based child care and informal providers of care in the community, such as kith and kin—who care for a large portion of Latino children—in order to share resources and training as well as espertise. These home caregivers often have more opportunities to get to know the families and can contribute to capacity building in the area of parent relationships.

The Spirit of *Compromiso*: Commitment in Latino Cultures

Commitment in English fails to reflect the complex facets of its counterpart in Spanish. *Compromiso* means a shared commitment, a duty towards others, literally, a promise made with others to achieve a common goal. *Compromiso* is also the translation of *engagement*, when two people prepare to join in a matrimonial union, signifying a promise to work towards a future together. *Una persona comprometida*—a committed person—is a most flattering description and an acknowledgment of respect and achievement among many Latinos.

Commitment to the group is valued highly by people from different cultures throughout the world, including newcomers to American society.[1] In Latino communities that are tightly knit and in cultures that are group-centered, *compromiso* means that everyone rolls up their sleeves to pitch in where needed, and to *give back* to their communities. In a *barrio*—neighborhood—people rally together when action and decisions are vital to the welfare of children or the people who live there. They seek each other's advice, summon each other's help, debate opinions, and join forces to act. Problem solving is not usually an individual activity. An individual's roles and responsibilities are not bound, and an individual is more accountable to the group than to personal interests.

Teachers have high status and are considered *comprometidas*. In the view of many Latino families, teachers, as authority figures to whom they entrust their children, are expected to go beyond the boundaries of their job descriptions in order to serve the interests of the children. Within a committed program community, they act as models, mentors, and advocates for children and their families.

In the largest sense, *compromiso* means attention beyond immediate and individual development needs to the development needs of the whole community. It means looking forward, beyond one's own vested interests and requirements, to a bigger picture of the quality of life. The following example of *Villa Victoria* illustrates how a group of people who were *comprometidos*—committed—came to address the comprehensive needs of their community as they pursued their own goals. I hope that reading about *Villa Victoria* helps you engage in thinking about how this process of working together, planning, and making changes to benefit all could be replicated in the center or school where you work.

Model of a Committed Community[2]

On any given day, stand at any point in the urban neighborhood of *Villa Victoria* and you will see and hear passers-by greeting each other warmly. While the *Villa* is located in one of our country's larger and more important cities, there is a strong flavor of a small town Main Street of America's past.

Villa Victoria is the physical and social center of the growing Latino population. Many small clusters of townhouses with tiny yards share a community vegetable garden. A bilingual afterschool and youth program, a credit union, a market, and a post office line a plaza. One old church has gained new life as a community center and affordable housing. An ethnically diverse "tower" for elders—the only tall building in the area—is strategically placed. Its residents enjoy a view of the hustle and bustle of neighborhood life from each side of the building, from the central plaza to the preschool, from the busy street to the homes and gardens. Framed by a richly evocative mural by Latino artists, the life of the *Villa* provides a moving canvas for the elders to enjoy and become involved in.

The *Villa* also serves as the hub of comprehensive services for the growing community and beyond. City agencies, a school, and businesses line the perimeter of *Villa Victoria*, as well as a Spanish-language community cable TV station. Run by mostly bilingual, Latino staff, the businesses and agencies provide arts and culture activities for the schools and the city, support for the elderly and families of children with special needs, and ongoing economic development programs. In the *Villa*'s community-based learning environments, families and individuals can access technological resources and financial empowerment tools that enable them to shape and support their own development.

The neighborhoods surrounding *Villa Victoria* are now full of chic restaurants, shops, and upper-middle-class townhouses. Yet, the *Villa* has retained its character and its population of proud, low-income Americans. This is not an accident, but the product of the thoughtful planning of a committed community.

Thirty years ago, Latino renters organized to respond to the urgent needs of the community. Rising rents were forcing families and elders to leave the *Villa*. Housing was neglected and crime was growing, putting children and youth—mostly Latinos—at risk. Concerned neighbors organized into the group *Inquilinos Boricuas en Acción (IBA)*—Puerto Rican Tenants in Action—that became the cornerstone of urban development in the area.

At first, the group focused on redeveloping *Villa Victoria*'s physical space to meet the needs of residents. To guide their efforts, they observed and experienced the life of the neighborhood from inside—rather than just surveying neighbors. Then, since the majority of neighborhood residents were from the Caribbean, the developers went to Puerto Rico to look closely at city life, and they began to redesign the *Villa* to echo the most vital city neighborhoods there.

Very quickly, though, the tenants moved beyond their original goal to reclaim and redevelop physical space. Looking to the future and to the long-term needs of the community, they expanded their focus to include the quality of life in the *Villa*. They organized and met with the business community, the Human Services department and other city agencies, and representatives from the school system. Together, they created the *Villa Victoria* that flourishes today.

Throughout thirty years of changing political landscapes there were challenges, and some of the *Villa*'s services and supports have waned or expanded, but the heart of the neighborhood remains the same. The community is currently going through a process of self-reflection and growth in order to be more inclusive of other communities of color. The strategic networks of commitments that a group of dedicated *comprometidos* set in motion are still going strong. The little two-room preschool—*Escuelita Borikén*—begun three decades ago has now grown into a state-of-the-art center with eighty children and twenty staff, the pride of the *Villa*. The support, resources, and power of the community played a key role in the success of *Escuelita*. But, more importantly, the same spirit of *compromiso* that guided the efforts of *Villa Victoria*'s tenant group guides the bilingual, bicultural program staff. Every day, they play an active role in improving their own and the whole *Villa*'s capacity to thrive.

Figure 5–1 *Unity Mural by Roberto Chao and a Group of Local Youth in a Boston Neighborhood.* (Photo by Roberto Chao)

Heart of a Committed Learning Community

In *Villa Victoria*, the tenant's group realized that succeeding meant committing themselves to addressing the long-term needs of their community as well as taking action to achieve their immediate goals. Here, I hope to engage you in considering how you can become *comprometidos*—committed—to professional development, working together to plan, design, and participate in a committed learning community that responds to the needs of the community of children and families you serve.

Thoughtful attention to developing a committed, inclusive learning community helps keep programs strong and staff engaged and personally rewarded. Educators greatly benefit from professional development that engages them deeply in their own as well as others' learning and that supports them in integrating new knowledge and understanding about differences. In the pages that follow, I highlight three types of commitments that form the heart of effective, culturally responsive professional development. These commitments are essential in a heterogeneous environment where people bring very different values and practices. However, they are also simply good practice, sanctioned by all our knowledge of professional growth and promoted equally by pre-K and K-12 professional standards.

 Did You Know?
Characteristics of Quality Culturally Responsive Professional Development

- Offers ample opportunities for ongoing, evolving dialogue across classrooms and collaborative learning, as well as more structured planning and training venues within and outside the program.

- Is tied to goals and assessment, that is, teacher-assessment processes include peer collaboration and are adapted individually to accommodate self-defined goals and monitoring.

- Includes individual and peer-mentoring opportunities in both literacy and practice development, e.g., support and discussion groups to do assignments, observations, portfolio work, and so on.

- Features an inquiry approach, using child observation, listening, classroom and program documentation, and question posing. Uses developmental theories as a point of contrast and discussion, not as a universal standard of development.

- Makes standards and competencies from early childhood to pre-K to elementary education visible to teachers so they can see what will be expected from the children the following years, thus helping them identify steps towards final goals at the same time as they account for the families' goals.

Commitment to Lifelong Learning

You may have heard trainers speak of "life-long learning" or "habits of mind." One of the pillars of lifelong learning is *learning to be.*[3] For practitioners, learning to be, in the fullest sense, means being committed to self-development and contributing to the development of others. In Spanish, the word *realizarse* captures this concept of development.[4] *Realizarse* is seen as a personal responsibility: to better oneself not just to accomplish personal goals, but to be better prepared to give back to the community. This is a high priority and honor, not just a duty for Latinos.[5] The essence of the global movement to redefine education as lifelong learning is to actively choose what to learn, how to learn, and when to learn. This means individuals take an active part in shaping their own learning. Various approaches are useful towards that end, including the following:[6]

- **Self-Reflection:** Self-reflection is the foundation of transformative lifelong learning. In self-reflection, you examine situations or inter- actions and gain insights into your behavior that help you shape new approaches to your work. *The Documenting Growth* rubric in the Appendix and other tools and activities in the following section may help guide your self-reflection. Also, in Ada and Campoy's book, *Authors in the Classroom: A Transformative Process,* you will find theories and activities that will deepen your understanding of self-reflection and growth.

- **Setting and Planning Goals and Strategies:** After you reflect on your current work, the next step is to envision your own personal trajec- tory as a teacher or leader and set both short-term and long-range goals. It is important for staff to do this even if they have access to training provided by a set program, dictated by accreditation standards, or delivered by a supervisor. The tools in Appendices 6, 7, and 8 can be adapted for individual and team goal setting, and Appendices 9 and 11–14 can be used to identify program goals, strengths, resources, and strategies.

Commitment to the Development of Others

In Chapter 4, I give a model of cultural ways of learning to help teachers build rela- tionships that enhance the learning process of Latino children. These ideas are also effective for adult learning that is culturally and linguistically responsive to Latino staff. Within the program, teachers' roles include participating as team members, working together with the adults inside and outside the program to extend their responsibilities as teachers and learners. Working with others is one of the main national teaching standards that cuts across content areas. Engaging in active listening and taking initiative in interacting with others are skills listed in this category of competency. These are measures for individual growth. Beyond this, commitment *to* the development of others implies a shared responsibility that is generally ignored in our field's standards, measures, and research. For the director, this may mean creating a climate for people to come together, problem solve, brainstorm, plan, and share best practices.

 Building on Strengths
It Takes All of Us

Yvette Rodriguez—center director—makes professional development a constant activity in the Escuelita Borikén preschool. Every staff member has a responsibility to train others, including the new recruit, volunteers, trained parents, and the teacher assistants. "I make sure each and every one understands as soon as they enter here that it's 50/50," says Rodriguez. "They will get whatever they need, but they are expected to give. I get the help needed for teams to plan together every day so the teacher assistant isn't left outside of the planning. Every lead teacher has a responsibility to come up with a professional development plan and follow through with it, even for our assistants who haven't mastered English. I give them different options. They can fill out a form, write narratives or case studies to illustrate their plans, or report to me verbally on how they will build on their own and their aides' strengths each month. They also let me know what they will do to develop a training presentation for the whole program. One aide, for instance, became interested in finding out about open-ended questioning, so she looked into it, asked other teachers, browsed the web, read books, and practiced with her children. She proudly shared her findings and led a discussion on what she learned, enhancing even our most experienced lead teachers' understanding."

Consider the above description of one approach to professional development. What are your views?

- What are the lessons learned from this director's practice?
- How do you gather information about the strengths—from skills to experiences—that each individual in your program brings?
- Where do you see opportunities for each staff member to take a lead in exploring something new, leading a problem-solving session, or preparing and presenting on a topic or skill of personal interest?
- How can the daily schedule and routines be adapted to give more chances for the classroom team and the program staff to plan together and share best practices?

Commitment to Understand and Incorporate Differences

In a committed learning community, balancing different perspectives and priorities is a given. This means that we need to be aware of how personal beliefs and experiences affect our practice, and that we need to understand and embrace what others bring.

Incorporating differences is a long, rewarding journey of committed action and continuous learning that requires generosity, enthusiasm, and curiosity. It means looking at things from another worldview, or, as the saying goes, walking in another's shoes. It goes far beyond asking staff for translations or including a few multicultural and/or anti-bias activities in your curriculum. The journey has to be shared by all staff and central to the mission and structure of the learning community. The activities and tools in the *"Compromiso in Action"* section can help you begin this journey, as well as Appendix 13.

In seeking to understand differences, it is vital to keep asking questions, keep looking, and assume nothing. For example, I present four values in this book that highlight a particular worldview, and I provide some commonly held beliefs that help shape the every day lives of Latinos. In doing so, I offer some stepping-stones to guide you in exploring differences between mainstream and Latino cultures. However, much more than a shared continent of origin and language affects how each of these four values plays out for different groups of Latinos. So, it is never safe to assume a monolithic profile of Latinos or any other ethnic group.

Every day, children provide teachers with countless "clues" to observe, reflect upon, and interpret. What does it really mean when a child refuses to put on her coat by herself to go out? Do you assume that she won't cooperate? Or that she is too dependent on adults clothing and feeding her? Do you speak to your supervisor and explain that the child may be too immature to be in your classroom of four-year-olds? When you reflect on the child's behavior, shedding your own assumptions, you may find other explanations based in culture, or simply in the realities of a child's family life. The mother may have told the child not to go out, believing that the cold will expose her to the flu. Or, the child may equate having the coat put on her by the adult as an act of protection, a protection much needed because she has recently been separated from her nurturing extended family.

Committing to understanding and incorporating differences can help educators better meet the needs of all of the children they teach and nurture. When we mesh what we know about best practices with what families from other cultures value for their children, we can provide children with the best of both worlds. Sometimes, it is hard to negotiate between conflicting perspectives. Some practices you encounter may cross the line or may not be safe or supportive of the child's well-being, or they may be counter to the policies of your program. Whatever the challenges, however, we must clearly become adept at listening to and learning from those from other cultures and races as well as understanding the assumptions we bring from our own cultures and backgrounds.

 Did You Know?
Latinos and Race

Latinos can be of any race. A peculiarity shared among Latinos in the United States is that they may identify themselves first as Latino or Hispanic, and not necessarily by race. The question of race can be controversial, since blending of races has been going on for hundreds of years. Different regions of Latin America can exhibit different attitudes towards being *mestizo* (mixed European and indigenous peoples) or *prieto* (dark). These may be used as terms of endearment, as in the folk song "*Duerme, duerme, negrito*" (Sleep, sleep little black child) or as statements of pride in a mixed heritage. In some Latin American countries, whole regions may have a majority of Black, Spanish-speaking inhabitants, and others can have exclusively indigenous areas where people still speak their native languages.

 Did You Know?
Circumstances That Affect Values and Practices

- Changing schools, entering and exiting mid-year, and moving from region to region can have detrimental effects on the lives and development of children,[7] especially children living in poverty, and can affect many aspects of their lives, including health and academic and social development. Migration may provide rich experiences and knowledge as well as a capacity to compare and contrast perspectives as individuals make choices. However, forced migration due to political strife and persecution in the homeland also impacts people from other countries.

- In the United States, a disproportionately large number of Latino children live in poverty and in crime-ridden neighborhoods, thus impacting the behavior and discipline their parents impart. Many such factors affect what children, families, and staff from Latino and other backgrounds bring to the program community, how they raise their children, and what they value.

Compromiso in Action

Many everyday professional development practices embody *compromiso*. Your program may already be doing some of what I suggest below. We know that these practices work. For the program, these practices—based on the principles of self and peer development discussed earlier—elicit loyalty to the program, build a feeling of ownership and investment, contribute to staff satisfaction and retention, and benefit each individual's growth. This presumes a willingness to step out of a narrow definition of training to look at the ongoing and long-term creation of a climate for growth for individuals in the context of their learning community.

I describe the following practices in this section:

- Strengthening team relationships
- Honoring multiple communication styles
- Focusing on differences
- Participating as *comprometidos* in planning professional development

Strengthening Team Relationships

Learning is enhanced by interactions, as teachers well know. Opportunities to connect with others, to share ideas, and to problem-solve are enriching for most people. They are also, however, a means to develop the kinds of relationships that foster taking responsibility for the learning of others.

In order to foster such a partnership in a committed learning community, program staff can increase opportunities to connect, communicate, network, and support each other through such approaches as creative scheduling, shared lunchroom space, breakfast "buddies," and collaborative teaching. They can also participate in learning activities such as the *Peer Learning Portfolios* and *Shadowing* activities described below.

 Did You Know?
What's in a Word

The relational model of learning is a thread that runs throughout this book. It is particularly aligned with the Latino values of *la familia, pertenencia, educación,* and *compromiso* that form the *Connections and Commitments* framework. The often-used Spanish words *colega, compañera, compatriota,* and *comadre* all speak to a mutual responsibility with others for a shared focus, be it learning, work, a meal, a country, or the well-being of a child.

Peer Learning Portfolios

In the early childhood field, professional portfolios are often used to prove teaching achievement or attainment of the credits required for the Childhood Development

Associate (CDA) degree. *Process* portfolios can help staff capture their growth and challenges. Try the following Peer Learning Portfolio process to involve teachers and other staff in critical reflection.

Teachers often view portfolios as "albums" or proof of their successful moments or their achievement of standards they submit to supervisors. Using portfolios for reflection, planning, and growth needs to be approached sensitively, as trust is essential for a learner to avoid feeling scrutinized or judged. Directors and lead teachers should, therefore, model and encourage discussing challenges, including samples of lessons learned, gaps, or misjudgments that have helped them improve their practice.

Turning teacher portfolio activities into a peer learning portfolio process can benefit each partner's self-development and build relationships that allows staff to reflect and collaborate on defining a trajectory for their learning. Once trusting and collegial relationships and procedures are established, people will feel safe enough to expose their challenges and weaknesses.

This kind of critical sharing and self-reflection generates rich material for teacher portfolios. The expectation from the beginning in EDC's course *Children's Challenging Behavior: The Ecology of the Classroom*[8] is that teachers reflect on *their own* role and growth, thus fostering a willingness to disclose and let go of what is not working, as this testimonial from a participating teacher shows:

> Understanding the focal child was a most important part of this class! I am so happy that finally *I change,* not him, because I was the one who could not understand his needs and strengths! He was always a great kid, but I wasn't a great teacher. But, it's never too late to learn and try to be better. Keep trying 'til we are satisfied. This is a very open field, without end.
>
> —Wanda Rodriguez

BRINGING IDEAS TO LIFE
Peer Learning Portfolios

Although the idea is **NOT** to prescribe how you construct your portfolios, certain guidelines apply across all styles and types of portfolios.[9] Effective portfolios share these characteristics; they help teachers:

- Have a clear purpose for the use of the portfolio
- Think reflectively about evidence of good teaching
- Engage in peer dialogue
- Avoid a prescriptive approach to format or content

Developing a peer learning portfolio is an ongoing process and should be conceived not as a one-time workshop, but as a means and focus for continued discussion about best practices and as a vehicle for problem solving.

Here is a suggested way to begin this process:

1. Gather and bring to the first session examples of materials, objects, notes, plans, photographs that capture what you feel is:

   - A good teaching moment
   - A challenging moment with a child
   - An opportunity for meaningful teaching
   - Your growth as a professional

2. In teams of two or three, take turns sharing your materials and asking each other questions such as:

   - What did you learn?
   - How did you learn? What prepared you?
   - What are the challenges?
   - How would you do it next time?

3. Plan how you will proceed in future sessions to build a portfolio with your partner.

First discuss:

- Selection and explanation of portfolio pieces
- Analysis criteria and how to extract teaching goals[10]
- Use, revision, and organization

Then establish guidelines and/or a protocol for supporting each other through the portfolio process. For example:

- Witness, not advise
- Ask questions
- Make connections with own ideas

Orientation

Orientation is a chance for program staff to get to know the teacher and make the teacher feel welcome and a part of the program. Often, orientation consists of providing a binder with regulations, schedules, rules, and other important paperwork. Although necessary and helpful for new recruits, this can send the message, "This is the way we do things here." If your program prioritizes building a committed learning community, begin a relationship by conveying that the new staff member's input and growth is valued.

Building a sense of belonging in new staff is just as vital as in children. In order to fully engage staff, they must feel investment and belonging. The following orientation activity, similar to the "*Classroom Guide*" activity in Chapter 2, will foster this sense of *pertenencia*—belonging—to a community in new staff.

BRINGING IDEAS TO LIFE
Shadowing

Directors, supervisors, and lead teachers will find this a useful and welcoming practice in orienting new teachers and teacher assistants. In shadowing, a new teacher accompanies a peer or a supervisor through a routine day, thereby getting an experiential introduction to how a colleague functions and interacts in the environment.

Steps:

1. Begin by preparing some questions that will help you make connections between the new recruit and your staff. Perhaps these questions can also be part of an orientation packet or portfolio that the new teacher keeps to track her growth in the program. Some suggestions:

   - Why did you choose to work in this field?

   - How did you find out about our program?

   - What experiences with children do you bring?

   - What special skills and interests can you share with staff? With children and families?

2. As you go through your day, explain some of your tasks; introduce the recruit to others, perhaps sharing some of the information you learned about the new staff member. Share resources and pertinent background.

3. Review the day by encouraging questions and comments. Ask what other information and resources she would like and make a date for lunch within the next two weeks to touch base.

Providing a supportive learning environment for the adults in the center or school involves developing relationships and connections with the other adults and children.

The teaching team should have ample opportunities for on-going, evolving dialogue across classrooms and collaborative learning as well as more structured planning and professional development within and outside the program.

- Training is tied to goals and assessment, that is, teacher assessment processes include peer collaboration and are adapted individually to accommodate self-defined goals and monitoring.

Figure 5–2 *Professional Development Provides a Chance to Bond*
(Photo © KarlGrobl.com)

- Training includes individual and peer mentoring opportunities in both literacy and practice development (e.g., support and discussion groups to do assignments, observations, portfolio work, etc.).

- Training is based on an inquiry approach, using child observation, listening, classroom and program documentation, and question posing. Developmental theories are used as a point of contrast and discussion, not as a universal standard of development.

- Trainers conduct training with a bilingual peer, a colleague, or an expert from the community to model mutual respect and teamwork as well as provide better access to bilingual staff.

Honoring Multiple Communication Styles

Working on communication strategies and modeling respectful behavior builds a strong foundation for the relationship-based professional development recommended here. This is nothing new. We all know and embrace these best practices. In working to bring *compromiso* to life in a heterogeneous, committed learning community, however, it is especially important to pay attention to staff's diverse modes and styles of communication.

Build group identity and ownership in the program by including multiple entries into the conversation. Strategies that can help Latino staff participate include modeling and providing opportunities for input through informal and formal channels, negotiating roles and responsibilities, resolving conflicts, problem-posing, team building, and, especially, socializing. Program staff whose native language is not English or whose upbringing may discourage initiating dialogue with superiors may feel more comfortable developing bonds and sharing their views in informal, social exchanges.

Making accommodations for a broad range of literacy levels, learning styles, and cultural practices in workshops and training materials is crucial. There should be opportunities for trainees to participate, respond, and do assignments in their language and method of choice, whether verbal or written, in conversations with peers, through one-on-one mentoring, or using any other form that allows participants to feel most comfortable and supported. In this way, participants will be free to express themselves, reflect, and share their relevant experiences.

Small gestures, like the following Points to Consider, are the first step in modeling the basic respect expected in many cultures, as well as expressing interest in what each member of the learning community brings. These tips are particularly important to keep in mind during group discussions and activities.

Key Points
Showing Respect in Small Ways

Although the following suggestions are common courtesy, they are especially important to keep in mind when working with diverse staff.

- Do encourage different, even opposing viewpoints.
- Do encourage people from other cultures to express themselves in their own ways.
- Do cordially greet all colleagues or supervisees one by one every day.
- Do give timely responses to questions.
- Do give credit where credit is due—publicly when appropriate.
- Do not dismiss an individual's input in public.
- Do not single out or compare individuals to criticize one of them.
- Do listen to various sides of an issue.
- Do discourage and dispel gossip.
- Do personally invite participation and input in an equitable manner.
- Do recognize and honor colleagues as professionals, as family members, and as models and leaders in their communities.

To build upon the cornerstone of respect and ensure supportive, clear communication in a learning community, it is vital to be clear and direct in all communication. People of other cultures may not easily grasp the messages and behaviors implicit in American ways of communicating. Without a shared understanding of the meanings and context surrounding a message, subtle miscommunication can occur in intercultural exchanges. Here is an example of a common misunderstanding:

One view:
My assistant is right by my elbow, actually too close, all the time, but she lacks initiative. She doesn't volunteer to help. For instance, I keep trying to get her to clean up, and she just stands there, following me around, talking to the children in Spanish, or she just sits and watches.

Another view:
I try to make myself available all the time to my lead teacher, because she is my boss. But she doesn't give me direction. I don't understand what to do and what not to do. She just says "This needs to be picked up," but she doesn't ask me directly, and I think she doesn't want me to do it, so I try to get the children to pick up, as they should.

Your view:
- Can you think of an occasion when you may have experienced a similar situation, that is, where you may have assumed you were communicating clearly, or thought you had understood what someone said, and later understood the situation differently?
- What helped you see the other person's point of view?
- How would you approach the conversation differently?
- What would you say to the lead teacher in the example above if you were a coworker? To the assistant teacher?
- Use of space and rhythm of movement can vary widely across cultures as well as across personalities. What would be some ways to deal with issues of personal distance and space?

A useful simulation game for adults to explore cultural differences is *Bafa Bafa*, available through Simulation Training Systems at *<www.stsintl.com>* or call (800) 942-2900.

Communication styles and expectations differ across cultures. For example, in many cultures, information given verbally, from a trusted source, is more valued than printed information. American society's heavily print-dependent nature can be confusing and distancing to staff from these cultures. For these staff members, a written assignment may be more effective and accessible when done as a team project in which staff work together to discuss a topic and then use a multimedia recording method they agree upon.

Keep in mind that turn-taking and communication styles can vary markedly between cultures. However, a particular "discourse" pattern dominates educational environments in the United States.[11] This discourse pattern is efficient and linear, with topic sentences, main points, and conclusions. In our programs and other early childhood education settings, professional development and planning often draw on a "meeting" style, where certain kinds of participation are invited and expected.

Some Latino staff, due to their respect for hierarchy and uncertainty regarding a trainer's expectations, may hesitate to voice their opinions during a staff planning or training meeting. On the other hand, because of the priority placed on social interactions and group problem solving, some Latinos may not adhere to the turn-by-turn monologues that many participation structures encourage in order to give equal time to all participants. In some situations, Latinos may tend more towards dialogue, debate, and interruptions in order to deepen their understanding of a topic. They may delve into contrasting opinions, contexts, and make connections that may seem, to some, off-topic.[12]

You can use the Meeting Case Study that follows to generate discussion about inclusive ways to hear and interpret what someone with a different style of participation might contribute, and about how to avoid the misunderstandings that then

Figure 5–3   (Photo © KarlGrobl.com)

affect the building of productive relationships. Once the relationship is established, move into becoming clear as to the boundaries and expectations that form the basis for the more structured, formal interactions that are part of early childhood settings.

Keep in mind that in Latino culture, bringing in the personal is expected even in business meetings, for example asking after family members or scattering personal stories and belief statements. Facilitators and leaders who model this personalization will make participants more comfortable, as well as encourage them to share their own stories and views. One Latino leader I know, María Morales-Loebl, begins each meeting by lighting a candle—a common, and at times daily, custom for some Latinos. Beyond the symbolism that various Latinos attach to lighting candles, María sets a tone of respect and harmony with this simple, although unconventional gesture, as she shared with me: "The ritual of lighting a candle— each light—is an offering, a prayer of gratitude for wholeness and kinship. It is through ritual that we weave *el abrazo* (the embrace) *de conexión* (kinship). Some of us are always doing the weaving, and the weaving rituals are many... mine has always been through lighting of a candle and offering light to each other. We are weavers of community—of kinship, of friendship, of family, of many webs of connections—and wherever we journey it will always be abundance of connection that we carry and can offer to others. In the end there are only two ways to spread light in the world: be the source or reflection of it." *Light every candle* is the motto and message that María carried forward when she led *La Casa Hispana*, The Spanish American Union. This organization brought Latinos together to address the concerns and issues that not only affect their health and well-being, but also their possibilities and potential. Programs initiated and sponsored by *La Casa* include: voter registration, advocating for and supporting five pathways for advancement in early care and education; a Latino Elderly Association that became activist around issues affecting Latino elders; a men's health partnership; and a tobacco-free coalition.

Reaching out to Latino organizations like *La Casa Hispana* is a valuable way to both forge relationships with the community and help your program become more culturally and linguistically responsive. In the following chapter, you will find some models and ideas for building effective partnerships, but now let's move on to an activity idea that may help you look at a situation from different cultural viewpoints.

BRINGING IDEAS TO LIFE
Meeting Case Study

Introduction
Eliana, a middle-aged teacher assistant, has recently been invited to join the program's planning meetings, thanks to a mentoring initiative to advance the career

of Latino assistants. She is late for the second meeting she attends because one of the parents was late picking up his child. She had a heated exchange with the parent, and she is anxious to brainstorm ways to avoid a problem with the parent. When she enters, the other teachers do not greet her nor interrupt their discussion, which is about parent trust activities. When she finds a spot where she can tie her issue to the discussion, Eliana tells the whole story, including the history of the parent's disregard for her time. Mary, a lead teacher who supervises Eliana and who is facilitating the meeting says, "We're not talking about that now, let's get to that later." Eliana's issue is not dealt with during the meeting.

After the meeting, Rena, one of the other teachers, overhears the following conversation between Ruth, a young lead teacher, and Mary, her assistant:

Dialogue

Ruth: Where is Eliana coming from, all riled up, telling us what the priorities are that we should deal with?

Mary: Yes, she always comes in late, then sticks her two cents in without knowing what we're talking about.

Ruth: Well, it's the whole way she steps in that's aggressive and annoying. She got all emotional and defensive when you gave her constructive criticism. She's only seeing things her way. I don't trust her.

Rena is left a little uncomfortable after this exchange. She resolves to do something about the situation, which she feels could fester and make it difficult for all to work together.

Following are two ways to explore alternative solutions that can turn the experience into a cultural learning opportunity.

Alternative 1: Reflection Questions

Use the following questions as a springboard to find a way to improve communication and collegiality at the meeting as well as stop the animosity in its tracks:

1. What would you have done after the meeting if you were Rena?

2. What could the facilitator have done during the meeting to prevent this situation?

3. What are some possible issues that are hidden in concerns expressed by Eliana?

4. How might different views on age, role, and power affect how each teacher feels?

5. What do you think Ruth and Mary assumed about Eliana?

6. How could you engage each one of the teachers to learn from the situation?

Alternative 2: Meeting Role Play

Involve others in exploring an alternative way to handle the situation and extract learnings from the experience. Engage in role play that will bring out some of the issues involved in the case study. Begin by reading aloud the introduction and dialogue above as a whole group, and then improvise and create a scenario together by passing out four role-play cards to four participants to read for themselves. Ask the person with the Rena card to begin the role play. If you have more than four people at the session, you can engage the others in observing and commenting on the dialogue, or you can give four others a chance to act out the scenario.

Rena

You want to help prevent animosity among Ruth, Mary and Eliana, because you work closely with all of them. You heard what Ruth and Mary have to say. You would like to sensitively approach Eliana and hear what she has to say. Maybe you can begin by sharing some of your own challenges during meetings.

Eliana

You feel you were shut down disrespectfully, and this is not the first time during meetings when your comments were disregarded or not dealt with. Your supervisor was leading the meeting, so you don't feel comfortable saying anything to her. You would like to do something about it, and you still have an urgent issue with a parent you need to resolve.

Ruth

You now feel uncomfortable having voiced your criticism of Eliana so strongly to Mary, who is her supervisor. You want to work better as a team, but what can you do to build trust amongst all of you? You feel all should follow the same rules. Take a moment to think about which of the teachers to approach first and about what to say.

Mary

You feel frustrated by the meeting situation. As facilitator, you needed to keep the meeting focused, and yet you recognize that an important issue that needed everyone's input was sidestepped because of the way Eliana brought it up. You also see Eliana is hurt. What can you do now? What can you do at the next meeting?

Figure 5–4 *Meeting Role-Play Cards*

Focusing on Differences

As noted above, professional development needs to work in concert with the teachings of the child's first and lifetime teacher—the family. If professional development activities focus solely on narrow definitions of appropriate practice, they can trivialize and undermine some important family practices and values. In her books and videos for early childhood educators, Janet Gonzalez-Mena has developed scenarios and strategies for dealing with cultural conflict in child-rearing practices, providing a context for practitioners to resolve disagreements in daily routines and practices in many areas and highlighting respectful and nonconfrontational ways to address these differences.[13]

Using the above resources and activities such as those I provide below, committed learning communities can work together to develop skills in negotiating conflicting views on health, gender roles, the difference between play and learning, and other topics that may be sensitive or that people may feel strongly about. The first steps in focusing on differences in an effective way is to hear and understand different viewpoints as deeply as possible. Your own style for reaching this understanding may be different than others. Role play may not be helpful. You may need to read something, or write in your journal, or talk to a best friend. Characteristics that can help in understanding different viewpoints and respecting differences include:

- Being curious and asking questions about what you don't know
- Observing carefully when you enter a new place or a new situation
- Not expecting others to think, feel, and act as you do
- Accepting that rules need to be adjusted in response to different situations, people, and issues
- Being mindful of the reactions of others
- Initiating contact with people you don't know
- Trying new and different approaches
- Tolerating breaks in routines
- Giving others space and time to express themselves
- Being interested in people and how they think
- Being clear and explicit about your beliefs

Discipline

Discipline is another controversial issue that influences professional development and family education efforts. Many programs have workshops for staff, as well as teacher-led workshops for parents, on how to set limits or what to do when a child misbehaves. However, staff and parents come with their own experiences of discipline and the right and wrong ways to ensure that young children are properly socialized. A good way to begin an in-depth discussion with staff and with parents is to open up a dialogue about all the adults' childhood experiences in regard to discipline. Engaging in self-reflection is a good way to reach an understanding and be very clear about what you, as a teacher, value.

Some agencies have developed ongoing training and support groups that introduce newcomers to American laws and practices affecting discipline and are specifically adapted to be culturally and linguistically responsive to Latinos. One example is the training provided for Latino foster parents at the Association House of Chicago Child Welfare Office <*www.associationhouse.org*>.

BRINGING IDEAS TO LIFE
Looking at Your Own Childhood

This exercise is a useful way to begin to make explicit some of the beliefs about childrearing that each of us brings to the table. Once the staff has had a chance to do this, it may also be a good workshop to do with parents. In teams of two or three, think back to your own childhoods and what your parents did when you misbehaved. Reflect and share with your partner:

- What do you think worked in making you aware of your behavior? Why?
- What didn't work? Why?
- What do you do or would you do differently with your own children?
- What in your upbringing is reflected in how you interact with and guide the children in the program?

You may find that even in a teaching team of the same culture, one teacher's perspective and way of handling a situation may be quite different from another's. And yet broaching sensitive subjects and behaviors is absolutely necessary. Once a trusting climate is established, each teacher feels supported in sharing personal views and is willing to engage in discussions that deepen understanding. This, perhaps may cause a change in belief and practice.

Consider that people's upbringings and their social and economic circumstances can impact the way they discipline children very powerfully.

One view:

I went to this workshop at my school on disciplining the children we teach, and they told us we should always keep an even tone, not sound angry, and always give an explanation when a child questions our directions. You know, I'm a mother myself, and I need to know that my child will respond and not question everything I ask her to do. A child needs to hear the urgency in your tone, and you shouldn't have to explain anything if you say, "Come and grab my hand now!" because you see someone with a gun across the street. I think you have to give them a lot of love and tenderness, but from there, you should be able to give them some tough love, too.

Another view:

I can see that many children—when they understand the reasons for *not* doing something—seem to eventually internalize the reasoning and can control their behavior more. When you're telling them just "Don't!" they keep repeating the same behaviors. They don't understand the *why*.

Your view:

As a teacher, trainer, or home visitor, how would you approach the subject of discipline in a way that is respectful and mindful of the two perspectives above? Each situation may call for a different approach. In the early childhood classroom, you may opt for a puppet show, for instance. In a school program, you may want to have a parent/child open house where each family used favorite *dichos*—sayings—to convey what matters to them in terms of social behavior and then work together to make classroom rules based on these sayings.[14] What are some ways your program or school addresses behavior management?

You can use the following activity to help foment the kind of dialogue that encourages multiple perspectives on a situation.

BRINGING IDEAS TO LIFE
Dealing with Differences

Especially when dealing with behavioral problems, teachers may have strong beliefs and diverging approaches. Much training in early childhood and beyond centers around ways to improve children's behavior, from structured reward systems for self-control to community-building circles. However, perhaps the most useful training is a process for self-reflection and discussion that will engage different viewpoints. Beginning with the example below, try brainstorming some different ways to move away from your assumptions and generate some alternative approaches to dealing with behaviors that rub you the wrong way. May sure to consider the possible rationale for the bilingual teacher's approach. In the rows below, build your own examples to work through.

Instructions:

1. In pairs, identify some instances that troubled you recently in your classrooms. This could be a conversation with a parent, a child's demeanor or behavior, interactions between children, and so on.

2. Discuss your immediate reaction or assumptions to the situation, like the example below illustrates.

3. Take turns talking about alternative ways to approach the issue of disciplinary tone.

What you see/hear	What you may assume	What you may need to consider	Alternative approaches to deal with the different beliefs and practices
• A bilingual teacher reverts to the child's native language in order to correct a child's behavior.	• The teacher sounds too directive. • The teacher is using a harsh tone that could hurt the child's self-esteem.	• The teacher is linking with the family's way of disciplining the child. • The teacher is pointing out a serious behavior that could affect other children.	

Culturally responsive professional development opens dialogue, does not prescribe one-sided approaches, and includes the family-teacher partnership as a regular topic for reflection and action. The two activities that follow support early childhood educators in checking their assumptions, looking for alternative explanations, and identifying strategies to use when family practices and developmentally appropriate practices appear to conflict.

BRINGING IDEAS TO LIFE
I Say, You Say, We Agree

Alternative 1

Group: Twelve staff members, divided into groups of two

Time: 5 minutes: Leader read instructions to whole group

             20 minutes: Paired activity

             15 minutes: Whole group sharing and discussion

Instructions

1. In teams of two, choose three of the following issues:
   - Portion control at meals
   - Family priorities versus child absences
   - Gender expectations
   - Discipline
   - Alien status
   - *Santeria* A religious practice in the Caribbean
   - Views on disability
   - Dependence versus independence
   - Social rules
   - Terms of endearment
   - Authority

2. Each pair discuss each topic considering:
   - Their own views on the topics
   - What they see as conflicting views on the topics
   - Different ways these issues could cause problems in interactions and teaching at the center

3. The whole group comes together to present their views and discuss alternative approaches should an issue arise in the center.

BRINGING IDEAS TO LIFE
I Say, You Say, We Agree

Alternative 2[15]

Instructions:

Make ahead of time a series of cards that depict a teacher's perspective of a problem or a sensitive subject and a possible parent's explanation. See the examples below. The workshop facilitator can prepare some ahead of time and have participants brainstorm other possible issues that might arise in the everyday life of the program.

Give a Teacher card to one person and the corresponding Parent card to the other, instructing them not to show each other their cards. Each person looks at their card and prepares a brief script to role play with the other.

Have the pair role play a dialogue and come to a mutually agreeable solution to the problem or the misconception.

Tarjeta 1

Maestra · *Familia*

Problema

Usted está preocupada porque Yahira está llegando tarde todos los días desde hace dos semanas. Además se sienta en su silla y no se mueve de allí. No participa en grupo y cuando usted le habla la niña se queda callada. Antes no era así. ¿Ocurrirá algo en casa?

Problema

Usted y toda su familia están desvelados porque en su casa hay ratones. En la noche hacen mucho ruido y nadie puede dormir. Usted ya le dijo al dueño que haga algo, pero él no hace nada.

Card 1

Teacher · *Parent*

Problem

You are worried because Yahira has been arriving late every day for the past two weeks. She sits most of the day in the reading corner and plays little with other children. When you ask her what is wrong, she doesn't answer. Is something happening at home?

Problem

Your whole family has been having trouble sleeping lately because rats have been coming into your apartment. You have already asked your landlord to do something about it, but he hasn't.

Examples of Other Cards:

Teacher

> **Problem**
>
> Joe came in with a dirty face and dirty clothes yesterday and today. You suspect neglect.

Father

> **Problem**
>
> You are homeless, live in your car, and have told Joe not to share this at the preschool. For the past four days, the gas station bathroom where you usually wash up has been closed.

Teacher

> **Problem**
>
> María comes in every day with a Sunday dress. Her mother scolds her and you when the dress gets dirty.

Mother

> **Problem**
>
> How I dress my child and send her to school shows respect for her teacher and the school. It would embarrass me in front of my neighbors to send my *niña* out to school with casual clothes.

Participating as *Comprometidos* in Planning Professional Development

The community-building work of the *comprometidos*—committed people—in *Villa Victoria* took time, energy, and investment by all. These are also the key ingredients in effective, responsive professional development. Enhancing your program's capacity to improve its cultural and linguistic responsiveness takes a concerted, ongoing effort. The key to doing this successfully is formulating, evaluating, and periodically revising a thoughtful professional development plan. Even if your program can only take one step at a time, the plan and the training *must* be built with a participatory process. Even in programs that have a very defined structure, there is always room for redesign that includes everyone's voice. This section provides some guidance and tools that can be adapted for this purpose.

Taking Stock

Working as a group to gain a sense of individual and program assets and needs and tracking progress towards goals is a way to begin professional development planning. Don't see this as accountability, or measures of your teaching or program quality, but rather as a means to identify gaps and build on strengths. You can use some open-ended questions to generate discussion among your peers about what you each think is important to assess before developing a professional development plan. For a director, keeping staff voices alive in the planning of the training is essential. You can use the *Drawing on Strengths and Struggles Discussion Guide* that follows or one of the other assessment tools such as *Documenting Growth, Goals for My Growth,* or *Our Goals Rubric* in the Appendix as a model to create your own way of documenting personal growth and program growth. The *Training Review Tool* also in the Appendix is for evaluating the training you receive, using the concepts in the *Connections and Commitments* framework as a guide.

 ### Building on Strengths
Discussion Guide: Drawing on Strengths and Struggles

Personal Growth

- What do you struggle with?
- What have you found works for second-language learners?
- How do you inform yourselves about the assets and needs of your students and families?
- What do you need in order to better serve the diverse children and families in your program?
- What opportunities do you have to take leadership in the program?
- What resources do you have at your disposal when you need information or advice?
- How do you each determine your goals for growth? How do you plan and implement these? How do you assess whether you are reaching your goals? What supports do you rely on to help you with your goals and challenges?

Program Growth

- What do you have in place in the program to enrich cultural and linguistic understanding on a daily basis? For instance, how do your plans and activities reflect a focus on cultural competence?[16]
- How can the program's mission statement, brochures, and publicity highlight the value of culture and native language?
- Where can you include familiar words from home languages and family knowledge in your daily routines?
- How can you draw on your diverse staff's strengths?

- Many program and professional standards in early childhood education, whether national, state, or local, may have sections that address culturally sensitivity or competence. How do you address these in your program?

? Did You Know?
Learning from Our Neighbors

Canada has adopted government multicultural policies and programs that encourage equal access and full participation of all citizens. You may want to use the following statement to discuss multiculturalism in your program, "Multiculturalism stands for equal treatment—not special treatment… [These] programs promote quality, fairness, good citizenship, the treatment of people with dignity and respect, conflict resolution, cross-cultural understanding and the building of a community free from discrimination and racism. We all have a cultural heritage. We are all part of a multicultural nation. We all benefit from a society that is productive, prosperous, and united."[17]

Designing the Professional Development Plan

Once you have taken stock of your strengths and challenges, as well as the gaps in your program's capacity to serve Latino children and families, you are poised to begin planning for future professional development. Depending on your setting, your input on the training you get may be limited. Don't let that deter you. You will be better prepared to make a case for comprehensive, needs-based professional development if you have thought out a plan with your team of teachers, a plan that responds to the diverse children and families that you serve, and a plan that supports the advancement of *all* staff. In addition, you will be able to search for the appropriate opportunities when you have identified a focused learning goal.

Using the example in the first row of *Our Goals Rubric* in the Appendix, you can see how the learning goal plays out in action steps for training. When building a plan, you and your co-teachers can reflect on ways to build on the external and internal learning opportunities you identified. If your action steps include connecting with community agencies that serve families, for instance, you may find an agency with an elder social program with which you could collaborate to offer training on working with elders in an intergenerational literacy program. For the internal action step for development, you may identify a college practicum program that can provide mentors to come to your program or school to brainstorm ways to gather information on what "families do, hope, and want for their children," or you can schedule monthly family case studies presented by teachers.

Figure 5–5 *Planning Together* (Photo by Su Theriault)

In addition, as a group, you need to identify how each training piece fits in with a continuum of support or career ladder. Sporadic and disconnected workshops do little to enhance the quality of teaching if they do not lead to a deeper understanding of early childhood development and allow teachers to continuously build on their previous understanding. Working with local community colleges, you may be able to negotiate on-site courses or credit-bearing training that fulfills certification requirements.

In my work as a researcher, I saw some stellar examples of teachers taking over their own learning and going to extremes to continue their development. What made them excited was both what they were learning and how they were learning. A reform initiative gave them a one-week institute to start explorations in a science topic they felt uncomfortable with or wanted to know more about. Various teams of teachers stayed on a rural college campus, and in that week of "playing," as they called it, they grew empowered as learners. They bonded and spurred each other on. On their own, they decided to create a network. This was before the proliferation of learning technologies and interactive online courses. They made a plan to try out new approaches to teach some of the old concepts, and, having realized how valuable the energy of others was to their own growth, they also tried other innovations, such as sharing some classroom activities with a small number of young children with severe handicaps and taking turns with their teacher videotaping the lessons and discussing them together. The network met regularly in different towns across the state to show the videos and discuss their growth, their challenges, and their "mistakes" or oversights. Each of these teachers became leaders in their programs and schools and generated excitement and new directions for the professional development in their communities. Some were whole-heartedly supported by their administrators, others had to struggle to engage colleagues and structure the time for in-depth reflection and dialogue that was teacher-led. Sharing best practices— one of the most successful professional development approaches—grew out of experiences such as this.

Considerations for Formulating a Professional Development Plan

Use this group of questions and the results of your self- and program-assessments to help you—staff and program leaders—work together to develop a plan to support your learning community and help you achieve your goals for children and families.

- **Who benefits from and participates in the training?** Do your training activities include kitchen staff, aides, extended families, bus drivers, and other community caregivers where appropriate?

- **Who gives the training?** Do you reach out to in-house staff— including assistants—community leaders, and outside consultants to provide different expertise and information?

- **What types of training are offered?** Does your program offer different modes: large group, brown bag discussions, teams, or peer observation experiences? Does your program offer training to meet the needs of diverse groups of adult learners, including mentoring, dialogues, audiovisual aides, small group work with mixed literacy levels, journals or other documentation linking practice with concepts?

- **Where does the training take place?** Have you considered a variety of venues, such as in-house, on a field trip, at a college or resource center, at a family's home, or in a community space such as a church?

- **How does the training complement the career advancement of staff?** Does your program offer isolated workshops based on what is readily available or are they part of a continuum of courses? Do the workshops and classes form part of a certification program or steps in a career ladder? Does the program offer scholarships or free training opportunities that fit with the career goals of staff?

Supporting Diverse Staff

The most effective single action in improving the cultural competence of any program is working side by side with people from different cultures.[18] When programs serve diverse populations of children and families for whom English is a second language, as will be increasingly the case, a multilingual and multicultural staff is of the utmost importance. Bilingual/bicultural teachers, assistants, volunteers, extended family, and community liaisons all play vital roles in helping your program build its capacity to support children from Latino or other ethnic backgrounds.

 Building on Strengths[19]
Tap the Resources of Latino Staff

Although the power and responsibility given to teacher assistants varies widely, when these paraprofessionals share the culture and the language of the children, they can potentially contribute to building a climate and support for Latino students by:

- Being respectful and accepting of children in a familial way
- Using *cariño*—caring—and informal interactions to build natural relationships
- Engaging in and encouraging increased conversation among children that is less teacher-directed
- Sharing culture and language, contributing to the children's identity-building
- Incorporating the children's and families' *funds of knowledge* in their teaching
- Accommodating expectations and supports to respond to students' communication and individual needs

---

When possible, staff should be provided with opportunities to participate in professional development using their native language—English, Spanish, or another language. Quality professional development requires reflection and analysis. Because the critical and creative thinking that generates ideas and reflection requires a high level of comfort with language, it is easiest to master reflective practice skills when language is not an obstacle. To address the needs of Latino staff whose native language is Spanish, programs can provide access to Spanish language workshops, coursework, and supports that facilitate access and learning.

Making materials and trainings available in Spanish is especially key for Spanish-dominant teacher assistants, in-home providers, and informal caregivers from the Latino community who have limited access to training opportunities. This growing need has prompted some publishers and professional associations to begin to offer some translated training materials. A resource list of some of these materials is available online at <*www.edc.org/ccf/latinos*>. English as a second language taught with a content-based approach, that is, with early childhood concepts, is also a much-needed approach that allows learners to transfer the knowledge gained in Spanish training. Some efforts are currently underway across the country to provide early childhood training bilingually, such as those of the Urban College of Boston and the California Child Care Resource and Referral Network.

To meet the needs of Latino staff, trainers can co-teach with a bilingual peer or recruit a Spanish-speaking parent or volunteer to participate. Programs can ask Latino social workers, psychologists, entrepreneurs, interpreters, and religious leaders to contribute their expertise about different child-related and family-related topics, as well as in career and program management. Not only can they serve as cultural experts for the non-Latino staff, but also as models and mentors for Latino staff and families.

 Programs That Inspire
That's My Home Town!

Receiving a grant to bring technology to the classrooms of this small, bilingual preschool was a breath of fresh air for the teachers, half of whom were Latinas with little knowledge of computers and no computers at home. The teacher's lunchroom was turned into a computer lab and the administrators asked a local college to recommend a Latino bilingual technology student who could get work-study credit to train her teachers. Pablo came early on the day of the training, turned on all the computers and opened a different web page on each. One was a downloadable teaching unit done in Spanish in the Dominican Republic, complete with photographs and activities about the daily life of a town. Another was a travel web page in English that showed the hills in Puerto Rico. Another was the front page of a newspaper in Guatemala City.

When the teachers came in, they were drawn to the screens immediately. "That's right near my home town! I know that house." "Oh, look how beautiful Puerto Rico is! I didn't know it looked like a jungle in places!" "I can't believe what that hurricane did in my country!" Pablo knew how to hook them immediately because he knew what it felt like; he missed his home in Colombia and he too was hungry for news from home. He gave some brief guidelines in both Spanish and English, then sat by the teachers' elbows while they tried to navigate the computers themselves. Soon, they were expert. Then Pablo asked the teachers to identify some goals for using the computers in their work. All the teachers agreed they wanted to get tips from other teachers and see different activity ideas that they could adapt for their young students. So Pablo wrote a grant with a college professor so he could put computers hooked up to the Internet in three family child care settings where providers spoke Spanish. This time, the preschool teachers taught the introductory lesson to the three providers, and they then established a list serve to exchange ideas, questions, and concerns.

Again, in the spirit of *compromiso*, support for diverse staff can extend out beyond the boundaries of a program to the larger community. You can reach out to share your resources and training for staff with others, including family child care providers. Many programs have a family/community room such as that described in Chapter 2, or forge connections with local family centers or agencies in order to have a place to collect and share materials and development activities in Spanish and other languages that are also accessible to other caregivers outside of the program.

Part of professional development is growing as a leader. Becoming a leader can pose contradictions for people from some Latino cultures, where humility and deference to a hierarchical order may get in the way of developing assertiveness or initiative without appropriate guidance. The word leader in Spanish—*líder*—is adopted from the English, but this concept has not developed in the same way within Latino cultures. For some, *líder* may have a military connotation. A new understanding about leadership, *power with*, instead of *power over* needs to be formulated within diverse communities. When staff see a Latino or Latina at the helm or in a position of power, this sends a message that leadership is not limited by race, culture, or gender. Whether Latino or not, educators who are responsible for a growing population of Latino children will benefit by actively recruiting and supporting Latino and diverse leaders to sit beside them at the table.

? Did You Know?
Qualities Valued in a Latino Leader

- Is responsible for sharing knowledge and opportunities
- Is accountable to others
- Integrates wisdom and knowledge of elders
- Makes direct contact with the people served
- Shows humility
- Shares power
- Has the respect of others
- Provides opportunities that advance others

Summing Up: A Caring Community

As we have explored in this chapter, *compromiso*—commitment—in professional development means participating in a learning community where trust, care, and respect are the foundations for learning and teaching interactions. As *comprometidos*, committed early childhood educators share a vested interest in the growth of peers and the quality of life of the program community.

Being truly committed to your own growth can be disconcerting because it entails pushing beyond your own boundaries—unchartered territory at times. I think expertise is a bit like juggling. Perhaps most people can comfortably juggle two balls, and certainly many try juggling three. This is a bit harder, and surely a ball will drop here and there in the beginning. But *four* balls, that's a challenge! You have to experiment with a new approach, a different rhythm. And most likely, when you miss, all the balls will go tumbling down. Few normal people even attempt this feat. In my view, that's an expert. Being an expert teacher not only takes commitment, it takes courage. For teachers, the fourth ball is going beyond "What's that got to do with me?" and working on making new connections to see the relevance and the possibilities of trying something new, in front of others—the children, your peers— and risking not getting it right. However, in the company of other "jugglers," you may be able to pick up a good technique, and certainly there will be extra hands to pick up that fourth ball when it falls.

Compromiso also means committing to meeting the needs of *all* children and families. As educators, we know we should build on children's previous experiences and knowledge. Yet, when we have children in our programs from a variety of ethnic and linguistic backgrounds, we may not have the strategies and resources to understand the many subtleties of the beliefs and practices with which they were raised. Thus, it is especially important for all of us working with children and families to commit to learning more about the different cultural views on childrearing these families bring, as well as to engage in constant reflection about how our own beliefs and training affect how we teach and learn from others. Taking on a shared responsibility for our own *and* for our team's professional growth keeps this commitment alive.

Reflection and Discussion Questions

Relationship-Based Learning

- What opportunities do staff from across the program have to interact and work together?
- What systems and procedures are in place so staff benefit equally from training and planning activities?

- In what ways do junior and assisting staff lead and initiate planning and training activities?
- What are some venues for sharing best practices in your school or program?
- How is new staff oriented into the program?
- What are the ways that staff can recognize and share strengths and knowledge?
- What are ways you can adjust schedules to allow for team planning?
- Can you take advantage of visits to classrooms in other schools and programs?

Reflection and Analysis

- Do you draw on various ways to process what you do and learn on a regular basis?
- What are the challenges in developing your expertise in areas you wish to develop?
- What resources do you draw on to inspire and motivate your own learning?

Cultural Practices

- What resources at your disposal enable you to deepen your understanding of culturally responsive practices?
- How do you think what you believe about raising children shows in your work with children?
- What are the most sensitive issues that arise between your program and families? How can your program prepare to deal with these issues?
- In what ways could you involve others in constructive dialogues about cultural differences?
- What expectations do you have of children that do not coincide with parents' or colleagues' expectations?
- Where can you find opportunities for informal and social interactions within or outside the building?
- How do the policies in your program encourage equity and attention to issues of diversity?

Related Resources

Relationship-Based learning

Adams, G., and B. Ryan. 1999. "How Do Families Affect Children's Success in School?" *Education Quarterly Review* 6 (1): 30–41.

Rogoff, B., C. Goodman Turkanis, and L. Bartlett (Eds.). 2001. *Learning Together: Children and Adults in a School Community.* New York: Oxford University Press.

Reflection and Analysis

Cronin, S., L. Derman-Sparks, S. Henry, C. Olatunji, and S. York. 1998. *Future Vision Present Work: Learning from the Culturally Relevant Anti-Bias Leadership Project.* St. Paul, MN: Redleaf Press.

Cultural Practices

<www.gse.harvard.edu/hfrp/projects/fine/resources/teaching-case/bilingual.html>
This site has case studies and discussion questions useful for trainers as well as teachers interested in enhancing their understanding of alternative approaches to cultural conflicts.

Klein, M., and D. and D. Chen. 2001. *Working with Children from Culturally Diverse Backgrounds.* Albany, NY: Delmar.

Neuman, S. B., and K. Roskos. 1994. "Bridging Home and School with a Culturally Responsive Approach." *Childhood Education* 70 (4): 210–214.

Barrera, I. 1993. "Effective and Appropriate Instructions for All Children: The Challenge of Cultural/Linguistic Diversity and Young Children with Special Needs." *Topics in Early Childhood Special Education* 13 (4): 461–487.

Lynch, E. W., and M. J. Hanson. 1998. *Developing Cross-Cultural Competence: A Guide for Working with Children and Their Families.* Baltimore, MD: Brooks Publishing.

Project Reach. 1984. *Program Modeling: A Tool for Planning, Management, and Evaluation.* Newton, MA: Educational Development Center.

Williams, L., and Y. DeGaetano. 1985. *Alerta: A Multicultural, Bilingual Approach to Teaching Young Children.* Menlo Park, CA: Addison Wesley.

Dodge, D. Y., Yandian, S. E., and D. Blooms. 1998. *A Trainer's Guide to Creative Curriculum.* Washington, D.C.: Teaching Strategies, Inc.

McCracken, J. B. 1993. *Cultural Links: A Multicultural Resource Guide.* Washington, D. C.: National Association for the Education of Young Children.

Gonzalez-Mena, J. 1992. "Taking a Culturally Sensitive Approach in Infant-Toddler." *Young Children* 47: 2. Washington, D.C.: National Association for the Education of Young Children.

Families and Teachers: Partners for Children. Twenty-one-minute video on multicultural early childhood education in Canada. Westcoast Multicultural & Diversity Services. 210 West Broadway, Vancouver, B.C. V5Y 3W2 Canada.

Teaching Tolerance Project. 1998. Starting Small: Teaching Tolerance in Preschool and the Early Grades. Montgomery, AL: Teaching Tolerance Project.

York, S. 1992. *Roots and Wings: Affirming Culture in Early Childhood Programs.* St. Paul, MN: Red Leaf Press.

Chud, G., and R. Fahlman. 1995. *Honouring Diversity Within Child Care and Early Education.* Vancouver, BC: Ministry of Skills, Training and Labour. This book is an excellent source for materials and activities for working with diverse families and children, and it includes discussion questions for exploring the staff's own childhood and perspectives on the concept of family, a mother's recollection of "parenting in poverty," and children's experiences and thoughts about money and poverty.

Endnotes

1 Eggers-Piérola, C., S. D. Holloway, B. Fuller, and M. F. Rambaud. 1995. "Raising Them Right: Individualism and Collectivism in Low-Income and Immigrant Mothers' Socialization Goals." Paper presented at the Annual Meeting of the Comparative and International Education Society, March, Boston, MA.

2 *Villa Victoria* is a real community that is still alive and well in the middle of downtown Boston, Massachusetts. The description is based on my own observations, relationships, and research on different sectors within the community.

3 "*Learning to be,*" a pillar of lifelong learning according to UNESCO's development framework, is discussed in <*www.unesco.org/delors/ltobe.htm*>.

4 Realizarse: "Sentirse una persona plenamente satisfecha por la consecución de sus aspiraciones." means to realize one's potential, to achieve what one has aspired to. Find out more at <*www.getafedigital.com/traductor.htm*>.

5 Eggers-Piérola et al., "Raising Them Right."

6 Cooperative Community Lifelong Learning Centers. 2003. "Lifelong Learning: A Project of a Coalition for Self-Learning. <*www.creatinglearningcommunities.org/resources/lifelonglearning.htm*>.

7 Novalés Wibert, W. 2000. "Facilitating Post-Secondary Educational Success of First-Generation Migrant College Students." Unpublished paper. East Lansing, MI: Michigan State University. <*www.msucamp.msu.edu/Wilmapaper.doc*>.

8 This course is part of *Excellence in Teaching,* a seven-course package designed for teachers, supervisors, and mentors. For more information go to <*ccf.edc.org/eit.asp*>.

9 Green, J. E., and S. O. Smyser. 1995. *The Teacher Portfolio: A Strategy for Professional Development and Evaluation.* Lancaster, PA: Technology Publishing, 13.

10 In the Appendix are three samples of tools that will aid in this purpose: Appendix 6, Goals for My Growth; Appendix 8, Our Goals Rubric; and Appendix 7, Documenting Growth.

11 Eggers-Piérola, C. 1996. *We Haven't Still Explored That: Science Learning In A Bilingual Classroom.* Doctoral thesis, Harvard University.

12 Ibid.

Eggers-Piérola, C. 1993. "Beyond Inclusion: A Review of Ethnographies of Latino Students." Qualifying Paper, Harvard University.

13 Gonzalez-Mena, J. 1992. "Taking a Culturally Sensitive Approach in Infant-Toddler Programs." *Young Children* 47 (2): 4–9.

Gonzalez-Mena, J. 1996. *Diversity: Contrasting Perspectives.* Video and Manual. Crystal Lake, IL: Magna Systems.

Gonzalez-Mena, J. 1998. *Foundations: Early Childhood Education in a Diverse Society.* New York, NY: McGraw-Hill.

14 This activity is discussed in more detail in Chapter 3.

15 Adapted from Eggers-Piérola, C., and S. Acelas. 2001. *La Escuela de Padres.* Boston, MA: Latino Parent Association, Inc.

16 *Cultural competence* can be defined as respecting, accepting, and integrating cultural differences in our interactions, practice, and thinking. More than a level of achievement, it is a process of ongoing learning and dialogue.

17 Hagen, A. 1993. "Multiculturalism: Myths and Facts." Excerpts from speech in support of Multiculturalism Act 39. Vancouver, BC: Ministry of Education and Ministry Responsible for Multiculturalism and Human Rights.

18 Manoleas, P. 1994. "An Outcome Approach to Assessing the Cultural Competence of MSW Students." *Journal of Multicultural Social Work* 3 (1): 43–57.

19 Research supporting the potential of these strengths is discussed in Center for Research on Education Diversity and Excellence. 2000. *Examining Latino Paraeducators' Interactions with Latino Students.* ERIC Clearinghouse ED447730.

CHAPTER
6

Actúe/Take Action

Supporting and Sustaining Change

Ellen Dodge, Barbara Dulik, and John Kulhanek write eloquently about change as they describe the evolution of an early childhood program and the mission that inspired the change:

> Just as a child is never a finished product, neither is our early childhood program… with the advent of new leadership, new enthusiasm, and new knowledge, we have been able to move rapidly toward our ideal. However, we will never stop looking for ways to improve. We will never stop studying and exploring. We will never give up our ideals. We will always put children first.[1]

Much has been done in the past two decades to ensure equity and opportunity for all. Organizations across the country are actively looking for solutions and blueprints to better reach and serve families and children of Latino backgrounds. At all schooling levels, educators have undertaken to infuse home culture into the curriculum via celebrations, songs, books, games, and other aspects of culture. More and more, training resources are being produced or translated to support the development of Latina paraprofessionals. These are important steps. Latino children, families, and staff need to see themselves and their experiences represented within the mainstream culture. A major challenge, however, is to portray and understand the less palpable aspects of culture, such as those presented here, that have a lasting impact on how Latinos contribute to and become part of American society.

197

As a long-time consultant and researcher for public schools, I began to focus more exclusively on early childhood in the last ten years because I felt that's where I saw the most possibility for responsiveness to the ideas I discuss in this book. The concepts and practices I provide are not meant to represent the blueprint for culturally and linguistically responsive practice. Rather, they suggest some shadings of a complex, evolving, and rich system of beliefs and practices that many Latinos bring to the tapestry of their bicultural development in the United States. In no way do I mean to stereotype or imply what a generic Latino may believe and live by. Neither am I suggesting that we should work towards the preservation of Latino culture. Values and culture are not static, nor generalizable. Latinos, like other long-time or new immigrant populations, are constantly grappling with integrating their most strongly held beliefs with what they need and wish to absorb of the cultures in this country. This, for many, is a conscious choice to blend the best and most useful parts of each culture. In the spirit of this evolving sense of Americanism, which adds, rather than subtracts, value to being a pluralistic nation, our social institutions also need to consider how to reform to best understand and reflect the values and priorities that propel Latinos' choices of child care, schooling, and futures.

Throughout this book, I have been encouraging change in small ways, from how to welcome Latino families and children to every day strategies that build on the best of what young children from diverse backgrounds bring to a learning experience. Understandably, the vision presented here needs to be accompanied by deliberate, incremental program change and advocacy that supports a strong focus on cultural and linguistic responsiveness. The level of commitment implied in the *Connections and Commitments* vision may be a great stretch for many programs and teachers. However, fashioning a conscious agenda for the future is the next step.

Recommendations

Below, I outline a series of recommendations that will help create a climate for change and lead to action, as shaping a mission that truly responds to the future involves change—or evolution—for programs.

Recruit Diverse Families

In Chapter 2, I discuss ways to partner with Latino families in order to better serve Latino children in your program. But what if you don't have a large number of Latinos in your program? Whether you live in Los Angeles, rural Utah, suburban New York, or in the Southeastern shore, you may already have seen an increasing presence of Latinos. They are the fastest growing population of new Americans. They come to work, to have freedom, to build a better future for their children, to become American and vote, and to help others back home. These newcomers are forging our future. If our programs and schools are not diverse, they should change.

And the best way to bring about change in a program that is not diverse is to actively recruit diversity into the program. Furthermore, recruiting diverse families will help support and sustain changes that result in better services for Latino children and families.

What Teachers Can Do

A program's first contact with families, their communities, and the community that physically surrounds your program is instrumental in establishing relationships and support that will broaden the program's cultural and linguistic responsiveness.

As a teacher, the best way to reach out to Latino families effectively is to get the word out whenever you go to communities that Latino families frequent, from church groups to clinics, and from primary schools their older children attend to Spanish-language radio programs. Ask your current Latino families if they know of other families looking for a place for their child. Most Latinos and other newcomers rely on word of mouth as the primary method for choosing an appropriate and comfortable setting for their children. You can also make contact with in-home providers to widen your network and help get the word out.

What Program and School Administrators Can Do

Responding to the needs of families may require innovation and program restructuring. In centers and in-home care settings, flexibility in scheduling and attendance, for example, will aid parents' work and family obligations.

> For us, investing in the future of our children is a give-and-take process. First, we have to listen, and then we have to respond. That's why we have the number of parents we do have, and that's why they are satisfied. We may ask parents to give up a day of work, but we will call the boss if needed, and we will give the parents something they need desperately, on top of time with their children. In a collaboration with Literacy for America, we work with some parents' supervisors so English tutors can go to their work sites—at their lunch hours—and teach them English and skills for real life, from how to navigate their communities to how to pay bills. Paying bills is done very differently in Central America, where people are used to going in person to an office and paying in cash. Families need this. That's why they come. If we just said, "Here, this is what we offer, and if you care about your kids, you'll come," that won't work. We first do a sounding, as well as map out parents' work schedules. What do they need? Parents want early and late coverage for their children, because in the morning they may have an early factory shift and in the afternoon a shift at the mall. We petitioned our program to extend the hours, and now we consciously schedule all our parent activities at varying times so each parent could come to at least a few sessions.[2]

Primary schools also have options to make powerful connections with families. For example, one school I know of participated in a career booth at a Latino cultural festival in the neighborhood of the school. Since the city had a choice program, many of the neighborhood children were bused elsewhere for school. With a community school grant, the principal had earmarked funds for a special before-school program that hired parents to help teachers in their early morning activities with young children. This effort succeeded in bringing new parents to the school, and they in turn brought their children to the school and spread the news about the program.

At the same time, your program can reach beyond boundaries by developing its role as community link. In this role, the program can coordinate efforts with other community leaders, agencies, and business in order to provide appropriate and relevant services and resources in Spanish and English for the whole family. In this way, all the work becomes more efficient and complementary, avoiding duplication and loss of information. The *Community Assets Questionnaire* and *Tool* in the Appendix can help you begin to collect relevant information on the capacities, resources and needs of each of the potential partners.

Strategies That Work for Recruiting Latino Families

- Revise recruitment goals and enrollment policies to increase the percentage of Latino children and develop action steps to reach these goals. For example, if you want to attract five percent more Latino families to the program, contact your local Child Care Resource and Referral (CCR&R) agency to help you recruit. Find out the child care needs of the Latinos in the community and provide the CCR&R information about your program that highlights its cultural responsiveness, such as bilingual staff, lending libraries with books in Spanish for families, or partnership with an agency that provides supports for immigrants.

- Diversify your advertising methods and messages. Use multiple media: announcements on Spanish radio stations, flyers in various languages passed to families, clinics, grade schools, local stores, and community centers. Illustrate flyers and brochures with images that reflect your cultural activities and the children and families you serve.

- Make presentations or enlist community leaders to talk about your program using videos and photos at local libraries, churches, schools, and health clinics.

- Organize some off-site, hands-on activities, such as bilingual storytelling at the local library or a science exploration booth for families and children at a cultural or informational fair.

- Have an orientation policy that matches parents with a Spanish speaking teacher assistant or community volunteer, a co-madre or community mediator who can help them in their communication with teachers, as parents may feel it is inappropriate to question teachers or administrators.

- Draw on college departments or agency staff in different service sectors for translation and outreach.

 ## Challenges for Teachers
A Push to Change

At times, change in a program may not really be sought but rather required. A director of an early childhood program that underwent such a change reflects on the experience:

> Our incentive—no, our mandate—to change came from a program quality review that found us deficient in various areas, most importantly in integration of cultural and linguistic diversity. Of course, we were shaken by this, but we got together with parents and began to plan some changes that we could implement right away, as well as some long-range goals that would help us serve the incoming population of young children, who we knew would be increasingly multicultural. We had to change, and we had to change fast in order to keep our accreditation. Although that was a lot of pressure, the changes—and the planning process—have now made our program stronger and the teachers' work more effective. We reached out to community agencies, really made a grassroots effort to recruit parents, and developed a mission statement and objectives to improve our practices, our communication with parents, and our support of home language.

Bring in Representative Staff

Bringing in representative staff will help support and sustain changes that result in better services for Latino children and families. Many educational programs, from preschool to universities, have affirmative action mandates and policies. Our early care and education field is in desperate need of qualified and diverse staff, especially bilingual, bicultural staff who can help Latino children transition into a center or school program.

What Teachers Can Do

Unfortunately, Latina providers and paraprofessionals (both within and at the margins of regulated programs) lack access to the types of professional development opportunities that are needed to ensure a high-quality educational experience for children in their care. Contributing to the dialogue about how to increase opportunities for development for Latinas and others who are already caring for the young children is essential, as is building the capacity of *all* teachers and programs to work with children and families who come with different backgrounds and languages. Teachers and paraprofessionals can initiate dialogue and sharing of best practices beyond the program. Get your program administrator's support to attend and lead workshops at conferences that attract a bilingual audience. Some regions have Spanish-language or bilingual workshops for teachers and in-home providers. Networking at these venues is a good way to meet potential colleagues and let them know your program is looking for bilingual staff.

What Program and School Administrators Can Do

As an administrator, you recognize the importance of the image of your school or program within the community and within the field. One way to recruit diverse staff is to make your program or school visible. Exhibit the children's work in community centers, city offices, libraries, and storefronts. Be informed about activities and happenings in the neighborhood and throughout your area where children can be taken to participate.

You can encourage and provide resources for staff to engage in activities outside the program and the community. You can also proudly invite visitors to see your program and participate in activities.

Strategies That Work

- Reach out to in-home care providers and kith and kin caregivers. These educators are likely to have the motivation and the experience to further their careers, and also could be key experts that you can draw on for tips on working with Latino families.

- Distribute newsletters, brochures, flyers, position announcements among neighborhood agencies and centers, and create list serves of diverse colleagues to send information to when you are recruiting.

- Try unconventional means to reach new Latino recruits, such as focus groups, videos, and gatherings in homes organized by parents, neighbors, or staff.

- Partner with local Child Care Resource and Referral agencies to provide career information and recruitment.

- Have materials and training in Spanish that are accessible to families and in-home providers. If you do so, also ensure that the material or training is relevant to the home setting and scheduled at a time when in-home caregivers can participate.

Advance the Field

Advocating for changes in training and delivery systems will help support and sustain changes that result in better services for Latino children and families. Both teachers' and administrators' voices are needed in your local community college's planning or advisory boards in order to truly impact the profile of the incoming teachers.

What You Can Do

Although perhaps some teachers and administrators may see this as beyond work in which they can reasonably engage, advancing the field's cultural competence will directly benefit the knowledge and competency of staff members as they strive to get credentials and—in some cases—better pay. For instance, in California, a tobacco tax helps fund increased pay for credits received by early childhood educators. The T.E.A.C.H. program, currently underway in twenty-three states, provides scholarships and bonuses or raises for early childhood teachers taking courses. Advocating for more opportunities for Latinas will also potentially bring in qualified, stable staff who are knowledgeable in working with diverse families and children, thus bringing support and energy where it is most needed.

Training programs in community colleges and teacher preparation programs can design a variety of program enhancements that will help advance the career of non-traditional and diverse early childhood education teachers. Where there is a demand, community colleges can be persuaded to respond to, and—in many cases—welcome significant input from the field. Urban College of Boston, Massachusetts, for example, offers credit-bearing courses in Spanish to help Latinos employed in early childhood education advance in their careers. Many federal and state funds are now specifically targeting non-traditional and diverse early educators. See grant information: <act.dhhs.gov/programs/hsb/programs/>

Strategies That Work

Diversifying the field may include changes in the training and delivery systems, for example, adding an early childhood education career concentration that reflects accreditation requirements. Following are some strategies that you can advocate for in concert with local colleges:

- Develop core course requirements for certification that include separate courses on working with diverse children and families and on supporting second-language learners.

- Create support systems and outreach to work sites to enable para-professional staff to have time and supervision for courses and practicum while securing their employment.
- Enhance partnerships with community agencies and programs.
- Develop multiple pathways for certification.
- Build on existing supports, such as advising and placing early childhood education students.
- Negotiate articulation agreements between community and four-year colleges.
- Create new positions to link programs with professional development sites.
- Establish a process and criteria for granting credits for prior learning.
- Diversify student population by extending opportunities for working adult learners and offering early childhood classes in both evening and daytime hours.

Form Partnerships with the Community

Partnering with various sectors of the community will help support and sustain changes that result in better services for Latino children and families.

Partnerships with the business community, from large corporations to small, minority-owned businesses, will increase support and awareness for the issues and the needs of the ethnically and linguistically diverse populations you serve. In the end, it is in the interest of the business community to support the quality early education of the future workforce.

Partnerships with service agencies, community groups, and institutions can be vehicles for supporting the early childhood program's goals for children. Partnerships also build capacity and streamline efforts to serve the comprehensive needs of the extended family.

What You Can Do

Whenever possible, reach out to Latino agencies, politicians, entrepreneurs, and Latino philanthropists so you can include their voices and support in the shaping of your program change and your partnerships. If you come prepared to a potential partnership, you will be able to have a clear vision of how best to work together. Look at models and best practices, how they were shaped, and how they were funded.

Joining forces with community partners means listening to the needs of the others. As you seek the right partners, ask yourself:

- What do they get out of it?
- Where are the points of intersection?
- What is the common value and vision that can unite you?

Be clear about the needs and resources in your own program and community. You can use the *Pathways to Change Model* in the Appendix as a graphic organizer to shape your program's plan of action. Analyze and prioritize a shared focus for a common long-term vision, as well as short-term needs. You can use the *Programs That Inspire* model as a way to begin, or find community facilitators who can help partners create a common vision. Good examples of visual models and processes are included in *Facilitating Community Change* and in The Grove Consultants International's publications and graphic roadmaps, such as the one below.[3] This Graphic Gameplan template is designed to align a team or organization to what actions need to happen in order to reach a desired goal, outcome, vision, or mission. It visually captures the objectives, who is on the team, the challenges and successes the group can anticipate, and the steps needed to reach the outcomes.

Strategies That Work

- Assess needs, capacities, and resources of each, using tools such as the *Community Assets* tool or the *Evaluate the Compact* chart in the Appendix.
- Identify funding sources and strategies for supporting and sustaining the partnership, including, for instance, foundation, state, and federal funds earmarked for working with diverse communities.

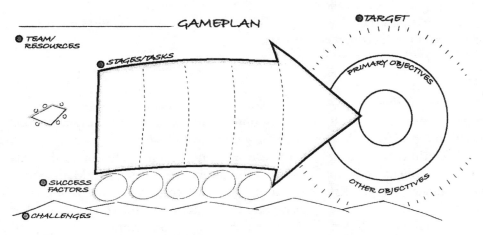

Figure 6–1 *Graphic Gameplan Template*

- Partner with health and other support service providers. Children's quality of life and learning outcomes are positively affected when they do not go to bed hungry, when they have stable housing, when they receive early intervention, when the family has wraparound care for children, and when proper attention is paid to their health.

For instance, many model education programs are now joining forces with community leaders and medical personnel to address gaps in services and to contribute to early detection and prevention of learning difficulties in young children. Refer to the Related Resources Section of this chapter for more information.

 Programs That Inspire
United in a Growing Circle of Care

The AVANCE model, developed more than thirty-one years ago by Dr. Gloria Rodriguez, is a broad-based family intervention program that has grown to encompass many of the comprehensive needs of low-income Latino families in Texas, and now in other states as well. In partnership with other local and state health and welfare agencies, AVANCE has formed a circle of care around the children it serves by focusing on all the aspects that touch the quality of life of the family. Beginning with the child at the center of a series of surrounding circles, each new initiative adds a layer of support around the child and his family. Their services are culturally and linguistically responsive, supporting the entire family through multiple pathways based on prevention, thus supporting an environment that helps the child from birth to three years old transition successfully from the home into early childhood settings and helping them stay in school to college interim and successful completion. As the model in Figure 6–2 shows, services include a parent-child education program, adult literacy, early childhood education, mentoring, career development, fathers' groups, early abuse intervention, housing, and economic development for the family.

Share the Spotlight

An important step towards equalizing opportunities for quality early childhood education is promoting leadership from within the diverse communities.

Oftentimes, well-meaning initiatives and institutions endeavor to diversify their environments and work via ethnically-diverse representatives. Many bodies have mandates that guide them to do so. Others are consciously integrating views and practices that are more inclusive and representative of the communities they serve. In many cases, that might mean extracting knowledge from minority experts and addressing their concerns and ideas in products, projects, and training. As

Family Intervention Model
for Hard-to-Reach Families

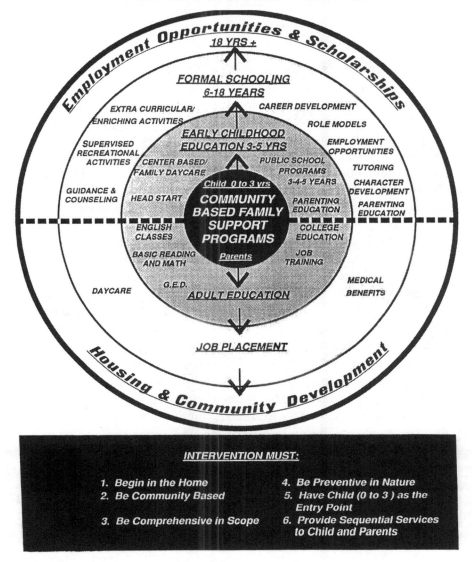

Figure 6-2 *AVANCE Model*

important as these efforts are, they are not sufficient. At times, minority members feel pressured to speak for their group, translate materials, or have their names included in boards and funding proposals. In these cases, the willingness to diversify is superficial at best.

What You Can Do

Taking responsibility entails sharing the spotlight. For instance, curriculum writers can team with Latino experts, giving them first authorship in curricula specifically targeting underrepresented groups. Policymakers, trainers, and project developers can open their ranks to responsive and creative initiatives by actively searching for Latina leaders and giving them a prominent place at the table. We must go beyond giving opportunities to entry and mid-level Latinas, especially given the respect for hierarchy that is present in the culture. We know from our work with many populations, especially those underrepresented in senior and decision-making roles, that models and mentors are needed to encourage the empowerment and advancement of others from diverse groups. And having diverse colleagues at your side sends a clear and powerful message to legislators, funders, business partners, and all who sit at decision-making tables. It says your cause is represented by a broad base and that you are poised to act in an informed way to build on the strengths of these communities.

As a teacher, administrator, trainer, advocate, or policy maker you can take responsibility in small, but significant ways. When asked to sit at these decision-making tables, bring bilingual, bicultural colleagues with you each time and make sure their voices are heard. When doing outreach or publicizing an event or initiative, make sure to enlist cultural experts who are respected by diverse communities. Recruit Latino interns and promote their leadership development.

There is plenty of room at the top for new leaders. In fact, it is imperative that our field have diverse leaders who have a stake, commitment, and a personal vision that reflect the understanding and needs of their constituencies. In this way, our programs will have greater impact on the outcomes for *all* children, and will be more sustainable, as a cadre of new, representative leaders brings forth unheard voices and community investment in our early childhood programs.

Strategies That Work

- Take Latino colleagues to a conference.
- Invite Latino colleagues from your program or school to sit on your advisory boards, but not just as a presence, but as an active decision-maker. Act on their suggestions.
- Make connections with other initiatives that can partner with your program to increase capacity. For instance, the Latino Caucus at the National Association for the Education of Young Children's annual

meetings—which is open to practitioners from any ethnicity—provide a platform for groups to share their best practices and network with others who may have complementary capacities.

- Encourage diversity in early childhood leadership by recognizing excellence in diverse colleagues and supporting them in attaining leadership fellowships now offered by many foundations and programs, for example, the Head Start National Fellowship, the Schott Fellowships in Early Care and Education, and the Children's Defense Fund.

- Target colleges that can send researchers to study the impact of your program on Latino children who co-present at conferences with Latina practitioners and researchers.

- Ask training institutions to offer special leadership classes targeting Spanish-speaking, nontraditional students.

 ## Challenges for Teachers and Administrators
Making Licensing Systems More Responsive

Our field's striving for quality has resulted in a more systematized process for licensing early education settings. Once licensing standards and procedures have been optimized, programs may still face hurdles in licensing. Making licensing systems more responsive will help support and sustain changes that result in better services for Latino children and families. How can you ensure that those who monitor programs for quality and compliance with licensing requirements understand the particular strengths of your program and your teaching?

Training for monitors, licensors, and supervisors needs to include culturally and linguistically responsive criteria. Unfortunately, this is still not adequately addressed in a systematic way. No matter how culturally and linguistically responsive our programs are, if cultural differences are not recognized as such, instead of as developmentally inappropriate, programs can face challenges.

> One year, the evaluator gave us low marks in teacher/child interactions because we used a lot of Spanish in the classroom and because she said our staff used a lot of nicknames like *mis niños*—my children—instead of referring to children by their individual names. Although I'm not Latina, I've learned from my staff how these terms of endearment are so important for the children to feel included, to feel part of the group. If we don't use their native language when we can, how will they know that we value this special skill that they bring? We even use words and songs in other languages so no one feels excluded. Shouldn't the evaluator also have a check box for that?
>
> —An anonymous teacher

Work with Legislators

Civic participation is key for keeping early care and education on the front burner of your state's political agenda. Furthermore, keeping abreast of your own state's progress in early care and education will help you make your case in front of legislators.

What You Can Do

Surprisingly, lawmakers themselves may not have access to day-to-day realities in the field and, in truth, might rely on their constituents to inform them and make them accountable to the needs of their communities. Make sure your message is succinct, clear, and well supported by data so legislators can take your concerns back to their constituents and their colleagues in an articulate way. When you go to the state offices to appeal to legislators, it helps when you are joined by a group that represents different interests but presents a unified voice. Send a message that legislators can relate to: efficiency of procedures and systems, for instance, is of great concern to legislators concerned with trimming budgets.

Those who write policies and make budget decisions may not realize, for instance, that some poor families must fill out up to eight different forms in order to receive subsidized care for their children. In some cases—where families are homeless or transient—they might need to fill out intake forms at each new location because the state database might not keep track of families as they move. Demographics are not routinely disaggregated and taken under consideration when the quality of a program is evaluated, nor are teachers' demographics compared with children's. Some Latino families may not be able to complete forms without guidance in their language, and therefore accurate information may not exist to portray the population you serve. Let legislators know how inefficient this is for intake and for the families.

Strategies That Work

In order for your particular agenda or message to be heard, you have to be well-informed when you go to legislators.

- Find out who the movers and shakers in the education commissions are. Keep abreast of their agendas.
- Contact representatives and early childhood educators' associations to find out what the burning issues in early childhood are at the moment.
- Check the newspaper to see how legislators in your area vote for education programs.

- Help organize the parents and community so they are also informed and active.
- Vote in an informed way, supporting representatives who champion early childhood education and services with their votes and their actions.
- Look for ways to creatively finance what you are advocating for (see resources at the back of this chapter).
- Go to your state house often and lobby for the support of legislators.

Here is a sample written testimony:

Sample Testimony for Advocacy Efforts*

We are here to represent the urgent needs in Early Care and Education and appeal to your support. We are committed to working with communities of color and support the role of public policy in creating educational equity for all.

At this hearing today, we would like to emphasize that efforts to build and improve early education in the State must give particular attention to issues of diversity, while establishing standards for high quality and supporting the cultural and linguistic competence of the early care and education workforce:

- We support policies and initiatives that improve equity in access and opportunity for children, families, and early childhood staff from different racial, ethnic, and linguistic backgrounds.
- We believe that quality and cultural competence in the field are inseparable.
- We believe standards of quality and equity need to be upheld to insure that child care programs reflect the cultural and linguistic diversity of the communities served.
- We believe that training in cultural competency is important for all early childhood providers and support efforts to include in the required core for early childhood certification courses in cultural competence and teaching children with language differences.
- We support the higher education community in efforts to provide multiple pathways to learning, including experiential credit, alternative scheduling, and bilingual courses.

*Based on excerpts from a testimony written by the 2004 cohort of The Schott Fellowship on Early Education and Care <www.schottcenter.org>.

Summing Up: Opening the Gate

Learning to become more responsive to such a quickly evolving population cannot be easily summarized in a checklist or guidelines of appropriate practices to use with Latinos. The values, ideas, and practices laid out here can, however, be used as a springboard for discussion and planning. At the same time, they provide a backdrop from which to formulate new questions in a way that increases our understanding and our capacity to provide the best possible environment for *all* children. Cultural competence should be advanced through an ongoing, open dialogue, not simply as an add-on to an existing structure. Shaping programs and practices to respond to a diverse community is a continuous process of inquiry, reflection, and action that requires many voices.

The *compromiso* I discussed in the previous chapters implies a shared responsibility. While I began with the urgent needs that impel a change in the way we "do business" in early childhood, I want to emphasize that it is in the interest of our field to build on the *strengths* that these newcomers and other Latino populations bring. The previous chapters, and, in fact, the whole *Connections and Commitments* framework, is specifically designed to bring these strengths to the forefront. As they quickly reach a critical mass, Latinos have tremendous power and initiative in this country.

What I've tried to do in this book is present a vision of early childhood education through the viewpoint of a Latina teacher who has gone through the gamut of possible work experiences in this country: political organizing, raking blueberries, researching, clamming, temping, performing in a children's theater, and many other exciting or tedious activities, each time asking questions—many questions—in order to understand the "culture" of the experience. It's taken me a long time to feel truly bicultural, but I got there through my questions and my thirst to know how things were for other people. Understanding the less palpable aspects of culture, such as those touched on in this book, is a challenge that is worth our care and attention.

Liliana Aragón—one of the people to whom this book is dedicated—firmly believed that in the end, those who care for and educate young children are responsible for their place in the society of the future. As her husband—José Luis Perales—shared after Lili passed away:

> *Para ella no era utópico pensar que sólo el amor y la formación recibida en la niñez cambiaría en gran porcentaje los problemas que en estos momentos acarrea la sociedad. Ella se creía capaz de formar parte de ese cambio.*

To her, it wasn't just utopian to believe that only love and the education of the child could change a great percentage of the problems that now assail our society. She believed she was capable of forming part of this change.

Figure 6–3 (Photo by Costanza Eggers)

As our field matures and strives for professional recognition, moving from a child care focus to an early childhood education focus, we mustn't stop "teaching from the heart," keeping the *care*—and the relationships with children and families—at the center of the field. This work and these relationships, now and in the future, require *intercultural* understanding as we reach out across diverse communities to support our common cause: our children.

Children have such possibilities to be windows into the world, and, like my own children and all those I have spent time with, they are apt shapers of the future, as they infuse all that they do with the disarming energy, joy, and openness shown by these young people swinging on the gate above. It's our privilege to help them open the gates that lie ahead.

Related Resources

For information on recruitment, the Head Start program has developed some tips, available at *<www.acf.hhs.gov/programs/core/pubs_reports/hs/hs.html>*.
For model programs and partnerships, see

- The Early Childhood Special Education Project of Columbia County, GA 2004. "Hospital can help parents." Early Childhood Report 15, 5.

- The Step-by-Step Programs: <childrensresources.org/stepbystep.html> For information on promoting credentials, licensing, and quality in kith and kin care, see
- *<www.bankstreet.edu/ICCC/>.* This site of the Institute for a Child Care Continuum is dedicated to supporting all aspects of early education systems, including the involvement of parents, relatives, and friends as well as programs in family and early education centers.
- Partners for Success: <oup.org/pubs/ourentp_2/prov.html>
- Friend of the Family: <friendsofthe family.org/history.html>

You can compare your state's policies and resources to those of other states at *<www.trustforearlyed.org/resources_state.aspx>.*

To find out how federal, state, local, and private funding can be leveraged to serve young children, see examples that can inspire your own state and local legislators and lobbyists at *<www.nccic.org/pubs/ccfinancingmatrix.html#5>.*

Stand for Children's website features the achievements of its chapter members' campaigns and the corresponding dollar amounts these efforts have generated. Consulting these initiatives will give you an idea of what worked, how it was done, and the money involved. Go to *<www.stand.org>.*

For helpful information on advocacy strategies as well as many other downloadable publications in Spanish and English, see *<childcareaware.org/en/tools/pubs/>* and *<naccrra.org/policy/>.*

Endnotes

1 Dodge, E. P., B. N. Dulik, and J. A. Kulhanek. 2001. "Clouds Come from New Hampshire: Confronting the Challenge of Philosophical Change in Early Childhood Programs." Early Childhood Research and Practice. 3, 1. Retrieved June 7, 2004 from *<ecrp.uiuc.edu/v3n1/dulik.html>.*

2 Magdalena Rosales-Alban, Family and Community Partnerships Manager at New Opportunities, Inc. of Waterbury, Connecticut, in interviews June 2004.

3 The Grove Consultants International, 1000 O'Reilly Avenue, San Francisco, CA 94129, USA. *www.grove.com.*

Appendix 1 *Connections and Commitments Cultural Framework*

Values	Implications	Examples in Practice
Family *Familia*	*The teacher and program form alliances with the entire family and community surrounding the child.*	• Involving the extended family and community in the program • Communicating with the extended family in culturally and linguistically responsive ways • Participating in family and community events and forums • Collaborating with families to define goals and programming • Referring to and portraying extended families in daily routines, environments, and activities
Belonging *Pertenencia*	*Programs reflect a powerful sense of group cohesiveness and group identity that gives each child a sense of belonging.*	• Bridging cultural identities • Creating a sense of belonging through daily rituals and routines • Fostering relationships and connections • Using verbal and nonverbal expressions of caring • Building pro-social skills such as respect and responsibility for others • Setting up the learning environment with places where groups can gather
Education *Educación*	*Learning and teaching promote the holistic development of individual children, as well as build capacity through collective learning.*	• Developing the whole child by integrating intellectual, social, creative, and ethical development • Providing informal and formal opportunities for group learning, products, and assessments • Encouraging adults and children of different ages to participate as both mentors and learners • Drawing on everyday experiences of the child, including home language and traditions • Engaging children and adults in many social and verbal ways of learning • Offering context-rich learning opportunities and literacy across the curriculum
Commitment *Compromiso*	*Teachers extend their commitment beyond the classroom. They act as models, mentors, and advocates within the classroom, within the program, within the community, and in the child care field to serve all children and families.*	• Honoring and supporting the roles of teachers as professionals, advocates, models, and members of their families and communities • Focusing on shared commitment to professional growth through relationship-based learning and collaborative planning • Including native language and cultural communication styles in professional activities • Linking families and staff with resources and services • Forming partnerships that build capacity and streamline efforts to serve the whole family • Advocating for and contributing to changing the child care system to improve responsiveness to diversity

Appendix 2 Community Assets Inventory

The purpose of this inventory is to gather the potential points of connection between our child care program's work and the focus of the project we are planning together. Based on the information you provide, we will create a briefing book of each member organization that will facilitate our dialogue and our future collaboration in the implementation phase.

1. What is your organization's mission?

2. Who does your organization serve? *For example, number, types, and regional location of schools, clinics, centers, providers, families.*

3. In your view, what are the most urgent needs of your constituents in terms of early care and education for Latino children and families?

4. Using the chart on the following page, please describe your organization's objectives and strengths in any of the activity areas that relate to our common project focus on _____. Also indicate the resources you currently have or would need in order to further these objectives and build on your strengths.

Appendix 2 Community Assets Inventory *(cont'd)*

		Practices	
		Current What do you do now in each activity area that relates directly to the objectives of this project? Where do you see the work of your organization fitting in with our collaborative project goals?	**Future** What do you plan to do in each activity area that relates directly to the objectives of this project?
Activity Areas	*Direct Service* Technical assistance, advocacy, training, career development		
	Material/Model Development E-learning, video-conferencing, and other learning formats		
	Dissemination Conferences, material distribution, web linkages, outreach		
	Program Development Institutes, CDA programs, workshops, ESL training		
	Partnership Development Collaborations, symposia		

May be copied for classroom use. © 2005 Education Development Center, Inc., by Costanza Eggers-Piérola, from *Connections and Commitments: Reflecting Latino Values in Early Childhood Programs*. Portsmouth, NH: Heinemann.

Appendix 2 217

Appendix 2 Community Assets Inventory *(cont'd)*

		Practices	
		Current What are your resources and supports? Who are the partners you currently have that help you serve your mission, and what do they with/for your organization?	**Future** What do you need in terms of resources, supports, expertise to achieve your objectives in each of the activity areas?
Activity Areas	*Direct Service* Technical assistance, advocacy, training, career development		
	Material/Model Development E-learning, video-conferencing, and other learning formats		
	Dissemination Conferences, material distribution, web linkages, outreach		
	Program Development Institutes, CDA programs, workshops, ESL training		
	Partnership Development Collaborations, symposia		

Appendix 3 Literacy Implementation Observation Tool

Conversation: Teachers engage children in *conversations*				
Conversations During Activity Time	**Conversations While Reading Books**	**Conversations During Writing**	**Conversations During Dramatic Play**	**Conversations During Mealtimes**
• Teacher is available for extended conversations • Teacher encourages one-on-one conversation • Teacher encourages personal narratives • Teacher plans small group activities to encourage children to talk about what they are doing and see • Teacher observes conversations for interests, understanding, and misconceptions • Children engage in conversations among themselves	• Conversations take place during small group book reading to promote comprehension • Book area is arranged to encourage conversations about books	• Teacher records personal narratives • Teacher and children converse around writing • Teacher documents learning process; photos inspire conversations about past events	• Teacher extends conversations during dramatic play	• Teacher plans conversations during mealtimes • Tables are arranged so small groups of children can converse
0 1 2 3 NA	0 1 2 3 NA	0 1 2 3 NA	0 1 2 3 NA	0 1 2 3 NA

Overall Rating for Conversation: 0   1   2   3

*Evidence of teacher interaction that promotes **extended conversations** and child engagement:*

Missed opportunities:

Appendix 4 Science Teaching Observation Rubrics

5. Facilitation of Small and Large Group Science Talks

Evidence	Exemplary (4)	Adequate (3)	Developing (2)	Inadequate (1)
Observation: Teacher-child interaction in small groups and at meeting time as it relates to current science curriculum. **Interview:** You may want to ask questions that give a fuller picture of how this teacher uses group conversations to promote inquiry and science learning.	There is **strong** evidence that the teacher uses small and large group conversations to encourage inquiry and deepen children's science understandings. • Teacher facilitates and sustains conversations in which children share and discuss experiences, data, and ideas. Teacher probes for detailed observations and analysis. Teacher challenges children to contrast differing observations and ideas and refine their theories. • Teacher uses materials and/or documents to stimulate children's memories and thinking. • Teacher encourages careful listening and respect for diverse perspectives by using strategies like modeling, "wait time," and reflective listening. • Teacher expects a high level of participation from children, encouraging child-child communication and scaffolding for children with less verbal skills or limited English.	There is **adequate** evidence that the teacher uses small and or large group conversations to encourage inquiry and deepen children's science understandings. • Teacher facilitates and sustains conversations in which the children connect their work to science by sharing experiences, observations, and data. There may be some analysis. • Teacher uses materials and/or documents to stimulate children's memories and thinking. • Teacher uses strategies for drawing out and respecting diversity in participation. • Conversation flows between children and teacher, and teacher supports some participation by less verbal children or English language learners.	There is **some** evidence that the teacher uses small and or large group conversations to encourage inquiry and deepen children's science understandings. • Teacher facilitates sharing of science-related experiences, but goals for science learning may not be clear or the conversation may just focus on experiences without drawing out data and sharing ideas. • Teacher may use materials and/or documents to remind children of their experiences. • Teacher may guide conversation toward the "right answer." • Teacher facilitates children's turn-taking/reporting. Children's contributions are probably limited with the teacher directing the dialog.	There is **minimal or no** evidence that the teacher uses small and/or large group conversations to encourage inquiry and deepen children's science understandings. • Science may not be talked about. If it is, it may be in the form of a song or finger play related to the "science theme." • Children's participation in conversations about science is minimal or not evident.

Appendix 5 Relationship Observation Protocol (Sample Page)

CENTER:	DATE:	TIME OF DAY:
AGES PRESENT:	RECORDER:	

IV. Cognition: Language

12. Children elaborate and expand on the verbal contribution of others by:

- ☐ talking to them and repeating their sounds/words
- ☐ naming familiar objects
- ☐ discussing routine activities in the child's environment
- ☐ using their home language
- ☐ other: _____
  _____
  _____
  _____

Adults:

- ☐ reinforce
- ☐ encourage
- ☐ support (verbally, physically)
- ☐ model
- ☐ provide opportunities
- ☐ mediate
- ☐ observe at close proximity
- ☐ assist (verbally, physically)
- ☐ other: _____
  _____
  _____
  _____

13. Children spontaneously communicate with each other (verbally/nonverbally):

- ☐ during routines
- ☐ during group times
- ☐ in social cooperative play
- ☐ other: _____
  _____
  _____
  _____

Adults:

- ☐ reinforce
- ☐ encourage
- ☐ support (verbally, physically)
- ☐ model
- ☐ provide opportunities
- ☐ mediate
- ☐ observe at close proximity
- ☐ assist (verbally, physically)
- ☐ other: _____
  _____
  _____
  _____

Appendix 5 Relationship Observation Protocol *(cont'd)*

IV. Cognition: Language

14. Children participate in daily interactions with others regardless of race, culture, gender, and/or language by:

- ☐ watching
- ☐ imitating
- ☐ dialoguing
- ☐ asking questions
- ☐ using their home language
- ☐ making complex statements
- ☐ labeling
- ☐ other: _____

_____
_____
_____

Adults:

- ☐ reinforce
- ☐ encourage
- ☐ support (verbally, physically)
- ☐ model
- ☐ provide opportunities
- ☐ mediate
- ☐ observe at close proximity
- ☐ assist (verbally, physically)
- ☐ other: _____

_____
_____
_____

15. The oldest children verbally respond to younger children to:

- ☐ gain their attention
- ☐ redirect their behavior/action
- ☐ engage in interactions with them
- ☐ provide information to them
- ☐ greet them
- ☐ return their verbal initiative
- ☐ other: _____

_____
_____
_____

Adults:

- ☐ reinforce
- ☐ encourage
- ☐ support (verbally, physically)
- ☐ model
- ☐ provide opportunities
- ☐ mediate
- ☐ observe at close proximity
- ☐ assist (verbally, physically)
- ☐ other: _____

_____
_____
_____

Appendix 6 Goals for My Growth

	IN MY CLASSROOM	IN MY PROGRAM	IN MY WORK WITH FAMILIES	IN THE COMMUNITY
WHAT I NEED TO KNOW				
WHAT I NEED TO SUPPORT ME				
WHAT I NEED TO DO				

Adapted from Eggers-Piérola, Costanza, and Stella Acelas. © 2001. *La Escuela de Padres.* Boston, MA: Latino Parent Association, Inc.
May be copied for classroom use. Citation: Costanza Eggers-Piérola (2005) *Connections and Commitments: Reflecting Latino Values in Early Childhood Programs.* Portsmouth, NH: Heinemann.

Appendix 6 Goals for My Growth *(Spanish)*

	EN MI AULA	EN LA ESCUELA	EN MI TRABAJO CON FAMILIAS	EN LA COMMUNIDAD
ENTERARME Lo que tengo que aprender				
PREPARARME Los recursos que necesito				
ACTUAR Lo que propongo hacer				

Appendix 7 Documenting Growth

Phase of Understanding[1]	Novice[2]	Apprentice	Practitioner	Expert
1. Explanation Making sense of things with supportive evidence				
2. Interpretation Organizing information in a disciplined way				
3. Application Using knowledge in new situations and diverse contexts				
4. Perspective Making assumptions explicit				
5. Empathy Ability to get inside another person's feelings and worldview				
6. Self-Knowledge Awareness of what one knows and does not know and how one's thought and action affect understanding and prejudice				

[1] Adapted from Wiggins & McTighe (1998)
[2] Adapted from Froc, Rog, Loftsgard (1999), <*www3.sk.sympatico.ca/fiss/rubric.htm*>

Appendix 8 Our Goals Rubric

Instructions:

1. In teams of two or three teachers, identify learning goals important to your development.
2. Individually, describe or summarize what each goal means to you.
3. Together, brainstorm some steps you can take to achieve each goal, be it a theme for a team-led workshop or selecting teacher/parent partners to lead a focus group.
4. What will happen or what will you see when you have achieved this goal? Place a photo, collage, or description of what you expect to see in the EVIDENCE box.
5. Later, you can use the same box to document the activities or interactions that you see as evidence of working on your goal. (See below for an example.)

Learning Goal	Meanings	Action Steps for Training	Evidence
Improving knowledge about how to partner with families	• Getting to know who lives in the household and what role each plays in raising the children	• Connect with community agencies that serve families • Look, listen, and document what families do, hope, and want for their children	• Families communicate more with teachers and director • Photos of families are in every room • Families bring in special toys, books, and objects from home • Families lead activities • Parent groups are formed to plan, problem-solve

Appendix 9 Training Review Tool

Title of Training

Trainer/trainers/facilitators

Type of material used
Please check all that apply

- ☐ Training manual
- ☐ Training textbook
- ☐ Video tape
- ☐ Audio tape
- ☐ CD-ROM
- ☐ Other (describe):
- ☐ Other (describe):

- ☐ Activity sheets/cards
- ☐ Article
- ☐ Journal
- ☐ Software program
- ☐ Website

Publishing/Purchasing Information

This training can be used to work with:

- • Families
- • Family child care providers
- • Center-based care providers
- • Directors or supervisors

	without adaptations	with adaptations
Families	☐	☐
Family child care providers	☐	☐
Center-based care providers	☐	☐
Directors or supervisors	☐	☐

Cost

Language

Spanish   English   Spanish & English

Overall Content Areas Covered:

- ☐ Safety
- ☐ Health
- ☐ Learning Environment
- ☐ Physical Development
- ☐ Cognitive Development
- ☐ Communication
- ☐ Creative Development
- ☐ Self and Self-Development
- ☐ Guidance
- ☐ Families
- ☐ Program Management
- ☐ Professional Development

Do you know if the training lead to any certification?

Appendix 9 Training Review Tool *(cont'd)*

Familia ★ Family

Value: *The whole network of family and friends is involved in the upbringing of the children.*

Implication: *The caregiver forms alliances with the extended family.*

Circle the number that best applies for each area and comment or describe below:

The training encourages:	1 Training in this area is minimal	2 Training in this area provides some examples of theory and practice	3 Training includes various activities, instructions, or tasks	4 Training is extensive in this area and forms part of an ongoing plan
★ Knowing the extended family	1	2	3	4
★ Interacting with the extended family	1	2	3	4
★ Going to the family and community	1	2	3	4
★ Bringing in the extended family	1	2	3	4
★ Showing and referring to extended families in daily routines, environment, and activities	1	2	3	4
★ Other:	1	2	3	4

Appendix 9 Training Review Tool *(cont'd)*

Pertenencia ★ Belonging

Value: Children find their own identity in relationships.

Implication: Programs reflect a powerful sense of group cohesiveness and group identity that give each child a sense of belonging.

Circle the number that best applies for each area and comment or describe below:

The training encourages:	1 Training in this area is minimal	2 Training in this area provides some examples of theory and practice	3 Training includes various activities, instructions, or tasks	4 Training is extensive in this area and forms part of an ongoing plan
★ Bridging cultural identities	1	2	3	4
★ Creating a sense of belonging through daily rituals, rules, and routines	1	2	3	4
★ Fostering relationships and connections	1	2	3	4
★ Using verbal and nonverbal expressions of caring	1	2	3	4
★ Building pro-social skills	1	2	3	4
★ Setting up the learning environment with places where groups can gather	1	2	3	4

Appendix 9 Training Review Tool *(cont'd)*

Educación ★ Education

Value: Children are guided to reach their potential and give to their communities.

Implication: Learning and teaching focus on holistic and collective development.

	1 Training in this area is minimal	2 Training in this area provides some examples of theory and practice	3 Training includes various activities, instructions, or tasks	4 Training is extensive in this area and forms part of an ongoing plan
	Circle the number that best applies for each area and comment or describe below:			
★ Integrating intellectual, social, creative, and ethical developments	1	2	3	4
★ Providing informal and formal ways for children to learn together	1	2	3	4
★ Encouraging mentor and learner roles in children and adults	1	2	3	4
The training encourages: ★ Building on everyday and home knowledge	1	2	3	4
★ Encouraging context-rich and inquiry-based learning	1	2	3	4
★ Other:	1	2	3	4

Appendix 9 Training Review Tool *(cont'd)*

Compromiso ★ Commitment

Value: *Committed adults have a duty to go beyond own interests and contribute to others' well-being.*

Implication: *Teachers are models, mentors, and advocates for the children and the program.*

	1 Training in this area is minimal	2 Training in this area provides some examples of theory and practice	3 Training includes various activities, instructions, or tasks	4 Training is extensive in this area and forms part of an ongoing plan
	Circle the number that best applies for each area and comment or describe below:			
★ Supporting teachers in expanding their roles in the program and in their community	1	2	3	4
★ Designing professional development as a shared commitment among teachers	1	2	3	4
★ Understanding and including differences	1	2	3	4
The training encourages: ★ Strengthening team relationships	1	2	3	4
★ Other:	1	2	3	4

Overall Quality Criteria

On a scale of 1 to 5, with 5 being the highest, please rate the overall quality of the training and/or training material by circling the number:

CONTENT:

★ Clarity	1	2	3	4	5
★ Reflective of best practice	1	2	3	4	5
★ Easily applied to practice	1	2	3	4	5

PRESENTATION:

★ Organization	1	2	3	4	5
★ Visuals	1	2	3	4	5

Other: *(please explain)*

★ _____	1	2	3	4	5
★ _____	1	2	3	4	5
★ _____	1	2	3	4	5

Appendix 10 Evaluate the Compact[1]

Directions:

1. Identify three or four major categories of responsibility. See chart below for an example.
2. Under each category of shared responsibility, identify the key areas of responsibility. The examples shown are relevant to kindergarten and upwards.
3. The next step is to develop a set of questions that you would like to pursue within each area.
4. Next, put a number to what you want to see as indicator that you have reached a goal in that area. This can be a percentage, a number, or a specific score. Having something concrete to strive for and to measure up to will aid you in evaluating whether your collaboration goals are realistic.
5. Re-evaluate your areas of shared responsibility, questions, and indicators to identify trends and places the partners are falling short. Perhaps new questions need to be formulated or indicators should be divided by language and background of families.

Early Learning Programs	Families	Partnering Organization
Shared Responsibility for Supporting Learning		
Area 1: Knowledge of pre-literacy milestones ____% of families report that programs show them examples of children's work	____% of families and ____% of teachers report their expectations for children's pre-literacy milestones match	____# of families receiving support services for their children report counselors have high expectations of the children that are in line with school milestones
Area 2:		
Area 3:		

[1] Adaptation of Activity Sheet A: Evaluating the Quality of the Compact Process: 38–39
From Russo, Mary; Topolovac, Ellie; Kosman, Gary; Ginsburg, Alan; Thompson-Hoffman, Susan, and Pederson, Julie. 1999. "A Compact for Reading Guide: A Reading Partnership Action Kit." U.S. Department of Education. May be copied for classroom use. ©2005 by Costanza Eggers-Piérola, from *Connections and Commitments: Reflecting Latino Values in Early Childhood Programs*. Portsmouth, NH: Heinemann.

Early Learning Programs	Families	Partnering Organization
Shared Responsibility for Communicating		
Area 1:		
Area 2:		
Area 3:		
Shared Responsibility for Building Capacity		
Area 1:		
Area 2:		
Area 3:		

May be copied for classroom use. © 2005 by Costanza Eggers-Piérola, from *Connections and Commitments: Reflecting Latino Values in Early Childhood Programs.* Portsmouth, NH: Heinemann.

Appendix 11 Feedback Loop for Program Change

The feedback loop is a process tool used as a debriefing and planning tool to assess a reform during a trial period. The purpose is for the stakeholders — including staff and families, as well as board members, partners, and advisors — to react to the incremental steps taken during critical stages of the change process.

When: Feedback loops are scheduled several times between project milestones, such as before specific events or before and after formative assessments.

Procedures:
1. First, stakeholders look for evidence of reaching results, which can be part of bigger objectives.
2. Define effectiveness: What worked well?
3. Identify gaps: What needs improvement?
4. Plan supports needed for the next step.
5. Revisit trajectory and plan:

During this critical exploratory period, the stakeholders should be prepared to go back to the starting point to redefine the objectives and trajectory if they see no indication of change. Revisiting the cause that propelled the change may be necessary. Perhaps the needs were inadequately framed, or perhaps a critical piece of the puzzle is missing because families were not involved in the design.

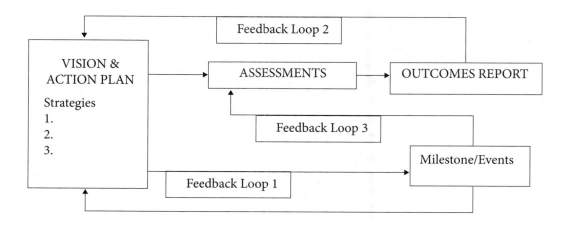

Appendix 12 Paths to Change Model

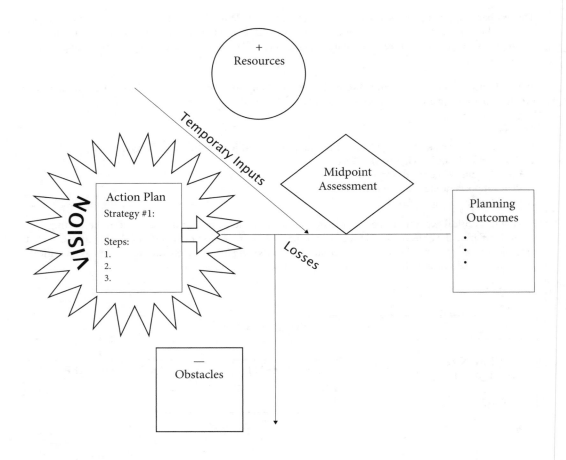

Appendix 13 Diversity Action Plan
Early Childhood Multicultural Services

	next week	1 month	2 months	3 months	6 months	1 year
Program/ Curriculum Outcomes						
Person/ People						
Community Resources						
Materials						
Money						
Other (Field Trips, etc.)						

Reprinted by permission from Activity 7.11, Cloud, Gyda, and Ruth Fahlman. 1995. *Honoring Diversity Within Child Care and Early Education.* Vancouver, Canada: Ministry of Skills, Training and Labor. May be copied for classroom use. Citation: Costanza Eggers-Piérola (2005) *Connections and Commitments: Reflecting Latino Values in Early Childhood Programs.* Portsmouth, NH: Heinemann.

Appendix 14 Diversity Action Plan Model
Early Childhood Multicultural Services

	next week	1 month	2 months	3 months	6 months	1 year
Program/ Curriculum Outcomes			Purchase multi-racial puzzles.	Introduce first people's cultural content into language arts program.	Expand celebration of winter festivals to include Hanukkah and Chinese New Year.	
Person/ People	Talk to family and ask for assistance.		Ask family for input on materials. Ask your parents for program suggestions.	Involve family in planning introduction of materials and activities.		
Community Resources	Approach first people's organizations and request assistance, resources	Ask children's librarian to do a search for children's books – then write away for catalogs, ordering, and source info.	Write or call ECMS for resources, ordering info.		Contract cultural organizations in your community.	
Materials		Review materials and shortlist items for purchase. Review catalogs, choose puzzles to buy.	Finalize materials list.	Display posters, read stories, etc., linking topic content to children's own experience.	Develop/make materials, duplicate resources.	
Money	Approach your funding body with a tentative budget for – Puzzles – Language Arts – Festivals	Compare local and mail order prices and purchase/order puzzles.	Place orders.		Place orders for materials.	
Other (Field Trips, etc.)				Invite native elders to tell stories. Encourage children to develop and tell their own stories.	Read/learn about festivals.	

Reprinted by permission from Activity 7.11, Cloud, Gyda, and Ruth Fahlman. 1995. *Honoring Diversity Within Child Care and Early Education.* Vancouver, Canada: Ministry of Skills, Training and Labor. May be copied for classroom use. Citation: Costanza Eggers-Piérola (2005) *Connections and Commitments: Reflecting Latino Values in Early Childhood Programs.* Portsmouth, NH: Heinemann.

INDEX